COHERENCE OF THE EUROPEAN UNION TRADE POLICY WITH ITS NON-TRADE OBJECTIVES

Bringing together leading experts in trade law and policy, this volume investigates the coherence between the European Union's trade policy and its non-trade objectives. Adopting an interdisciplinary approach, it highlights previously unaddressed dimensions of EU policy objectives and outcomes. With a range of illustrative case studies, the contributions offer in-depth analysis while making key issues and policy conclusions accessible to readers without specialist training. Pushing the frontiers of research on trade, investment, and non-trade issues, the volume advances debates concerning the reform of the international trade regime and the EU's adoption of a new trade policy. Bolstered by a diverse range of contributors and perspectives, this expansive collection recognises the achievements of the current EU trade policy, assesses its limits, and puts forth actionable recommendations for how it may be improved.

MIRIAM MANCHIN is Associate Professor at Politecnico di Milano, Italy, and Senior Researcher at the World Trade Institute in Bern, Switzerland. Her current research and past publications focus on economic integration, trade agreements, cross-border production chains, business groups, multinational firms, trade and development, and migration.

LAURA PUCCIO is part-time Professor at Université Libre de Bruxelles, Belgium. She was previously Research Fellow at the Global Governance Programme of the Robert Schuman Center for Advanced Studies, working for the RESPECT project on EU external relations and trade law and policy.

AYDIN B. YILDIRIM is a postdoctoral researcher in the Department of Humanities, Social and Political Sciences of the Swiss Federal Institute of Technology (ETH Zurich). He previously served as Marie Curie Fellow at the World Trade Institute and Max Weber Fellow at the European University Institute, Florence, Italy. His research focuses on international relations, international political economy, and the politics of trade policy.

COHERENCE OF THE EUROPEAN UNION TRADE POLICY WITH ITS NON-TRADE OBJECTIVES

World Trade Forum

Edited by

MIRIAM MANCHIN

Politecnico di Milano

LAURA PUCCIO

Université Libre de Bruxelles

AYDIN B. YILDIRIM

ETH Zurich

CAMBRIDGE
UNIVERSITY PRESS

CAMBRIDGE
UNIVERSITY PRESS

Shaftesbury Road, Cambridge CB2 8EA, United Kingdom

One Liberty Plaza, 20th Floor, New York, NY 10006, USA

477 Williamstown Road, Port Melbourne, VIC 3207, Australia

314–321, 3rd Floor, Plot 3, Splendor Forum, Jasola District Centre, New Delhi – 110025, India

103 Penang Road, #05–06/07, Visioncrest Commercial, Singapore 238467

Cambridge University Press is part of Cambridge University Press & Assessment, a department of the University of Cambridge.

We share the University's mission to contribute to society through the pursuit of education, learning and research at the highest international levels of excellence.

www.cambridge.org
Information on this title: www.cambridge.org/9781009308151

DOI: 10.1017/9781009308137

First published 2024

A catalogue record for this publication is available from the British Library.

Library of Congress Cataloging-in-Publication Data
Names: Puccio, Laura, editor. | Manchin, Miriam, editor. | Yildirim, Aydin Baris, editor.
Title: Coherence of the European Union Trade Policy with Its Non-Trade Objectives / edited by Laura Puccio, Université Libre de Bruxelles; Miriam Manchin, Politecnico di Milano; Aydin B. Yildirim, ETH Zurich.
Description: Cambridge, United Kingdom ; New York, NY : Cambridge University Press, 2023. | "World Trade Forum" | Includes bibliographical references and index.
Identifiers: LCCN 2023006685 (print) | LCCN 2023006686 (ebook) | ISBN 9781009308151 (hardback) | ISBN 9781009308144 (paperback) | ISBN 9781009308137 (epub)
Subjects: LCSH: European Union countries–Foreign relations. | European Union countries–Foreign economic relations.
Classification: LCC KJE5105 .C64 2023 (print) | LCC KJE5105 (ebook) | DDC 341.242/2–dc23/eng/20230728
LC record available at https://lccn.loc.gov/2023006685
LC ebook record available at https://lccn.loc.gov/2023006686

ISBN 978-1-009-30815-1 Hardback

CONTENTS

CONTRIBUTORS

LÁSZLÓ BRUSZT is Professor of Sociology at the Central European University (CEU) and Co-director of the CEU Democracy Institute, Budapest, Hungary.

KAMALA DAWAR is Lecturer in International Commercial Law at the Sussex University Law School, United Kingdom.

ALESSANDRO FERRARI is Assistant Professor at the Department of Economics of the University of Zurich, Switzerland.

MATTEO FIORINI is Research Fellow at the Robert Schuman Centre for Advanced Studies at the European University Institute (EUI), Florence, Italy.

JOSEPH FRANCOIS is Managing Director and Professor of Economics at the World Trade Institute, Bern, Switzerland.

BERNARD HOEKMAN is Professor and Director, Global Economics, Robert Schuman Centre for Advanced Studies, European University Institute, Florence, Italy.

PETER HOLMES is Fellow of the UK Trade Policy Observatory, University of Sussex, United Kingdom.

LISA LECHNER is Assistant Professor for Methods and Methodology in Political Science at the University of Innsbruck, Austria.

FRANKLIN MADUKO is Lecturer in the Department of Accounting, Finance, and Economics at Ulster University Belfast, Northern Ireland, United Kingdom.

JULIA MAGNTORN GARRETT is a former Research Officer at the UK Trade Policy Observatory, University of Sussex, United Kingdom.

MIRIAM MANCHIN is Associate Professor at Politecnico di Milano, Italy, and Senior Researcher at the World Trade Institute in Bern, Switzerland.

TIMEA PÁL is a researcher affiliated with the Center for International Studies (CEI) at the University Institute of Lisbon (ISCTE-IUL), Portugal.

JACQUES PELKMANS is Associate Senior Fellow at CEPS, visiting professor in the Economics Department of the College of Europe and Visiting Professor in the Economics Department of Goethe University Frankfurt, Germany.

HUGO ROJAS-ROMAGOSA is a Research Economist at the World Bank, Washington, DC, United States.

JIM ROLLO is Fellow of the UK Trade Policy Observatory, University of Sussex, United Kingdom.

FILIPPO SANTI is a post-doctoral research fellow at the Faculty of Business Administration and Economics at the University of Bielefeld, Germany.

WOLFGANG WEIß holds the Chair in Public Law, Public International and European Law at the German University of Administrative Sciences in Speyer, Germany.

RORDEN WILKINSON is Pro-Vice-Chancellor for Education and the Student Experience and Professor of International Political Economy at the University of New South Wales, Sydney, Australia.

AYDIN B. YILDIRIM is a postdoctoral researcher in the Department of Humanities, Social and Political Sciences of the Swiss Federal Institute of Technology (ETH Zurich), Switzerland.

Introduction

MIRIAM MANCHIN, LAURA PUCCIO, AND AYDIN YILDIRIM

The European Union's trade policy has seen a dramatic increase in attention over the past few years. In face of the challenges facing the global trade regime, ranging from trade conflicts between the EU and major world powers to the maintenance of a rules-based trade order under the auspices of the World Trade Organization (WTO), policy-makers, experts, and the public have converged in highlighting the importance of trade policy making. The attention paid to trade policy has increased disproportionately in the wake of Covid-19, which led to political pressure to re-shore global value chains and enhance "strategic autonomy", and reinforced the need to use trade as a tool to pursue non-trade policy objectives (NTPOs) – such as human rights, labour rights, and environmental commitments – in third countries.

The dynamics underlying the EU's ability to pursue NTPOs is at the heart of recent developments and debates surrounding the EU Trade and Common Commercial policy. From the debates surrounding the now-suspended Transatlantic Trade and Investment Partnership (TTIP) and recently concluded Comprehensive Economic and Trade Agreement (CETA), to the reforms of the state–investor dispute settlement system, to the more recent necessity of implementing the Green Deal in every aspect of EU external policy and the strategy for an open, sustainable, and assertive EU trade policy, the theme of the coherence of EU trade policy with NTPOs has become central to the new developments in EU trade policy. The recent trade strategy communicated by the EU that aims to promote the "strategic values and interests" of the EU is further testament to the importance of the EU's pursuit of NTPOs, and of the

Some of the authors and editors of this volume acknowledge funding from the European Union's Horizon 2020 research and innovation programme under grant agreement No 770680 (RESPECT). Responsibility for the information and views set out in the contributions to this book lie entirely with the authors. The information and views expressed in the book do not necessarily reflect the views of the European Commission.

analysis of the conditions under which the EU can pursue such objectives while remaining consistent with its trade objectives.

This book proposes a multidisciplinary approach to reflect on the coherence of the EU's trade policy with its non-trade objectives. Merging different disciplinary approaches allows for critical analysis of the coherence of EU trade policy with NTPOs and the instruments used to achieve it. We look at the issue of coherence from political science, legal, and economic perspectives, aiming also to evaluate the impact and effectiveness of EU action in this field. In addition to looking at provisions in trade agreements, various chapters also discuss soft power instruments and how they can help foster the promotion of NTPOs.

Several political science and legal authors have been interested in the definition of coherence in EU external relations law (we recall here particularly den Hertog and Simon Stroß, 2013; Cremona, 2011; Hillion 2008; Portela and Raube 2012). The legal literature on vertical coherence has extensively analysed the disputes brought before the Court of Justice to clarify implementation of the duty of sincere cooperation (see for example Neframi, 2010; Klamert 2014; Hillion, 2009; Blockmans and Wessel, 2012; Koutrakos, 2019; De Baere, 2011; Konstadinides, 2015). The political science literature has also analysed vertical coherence in the context of the unity of representation of the European Union in international organizations (IOs) and its capacity to speak with one voice on certain topics (see for example Conceição-Heldt and Meunier, 2014; Macaj and Nicolaïdis, 2014; Meunier, 2014; Moschella and Quaglia, 2016; Rommerskirchen, 2013). Several books look at various examples of the EU's participation in IOs and how these different types of participation will have an impact on its capacity to establish its external identity and its influence in international organizations, and to promote its values (de Waele and Kuipers, 2013; Jørgensen, 2009; Kaddous, 2015; Orsini, 2016).

The legal and political science literature on horizontal coherence focuses mainly on some specific "trade and . . ." debates, such as looking at the connection between trade and human rights and the use of essential clauses in trade agreements (see for example Bartels, 2013; Hachez, 2015; Cremona, 2021; Conconi and Perroni, 2002; Meissner and McKenzie, 2019: Donno and Neureiter, 2018; and Sicurelli, 2017), trade, social, and labour rights (see for example Van den Putte and Orbie, 2015; Bronkers and Gruni, 2019, 2021; Raess et al., 2018), the EU's approach to the trade and environment debate (see for example Durán and Morgera, 2012; Krämer-Hoppe, 2019), and the coherence of EU trade policy with its climate change and renewable energy objectives (see for example Leal-Arcas and Alvarez Armas, 2018; Marhold, 2019; Espa and Durán, 2020). Scholars have also examined the conditions under which NTPO–trade linkages are more likely to be successful – highlighting the support of domestic organized interests as key to successfully pursuing NTPOs through trade policy (Meunier and Nicolaidis, 2006; Young and Peterson, 2014; Poletti and Sicurelli, 2018; Dür et al., 2019). Studies have shown that integrating the preferences of business and other stakeholders into EU trade policy making increases the EU's bargaining power vis-à-vis third countries and further strengthens legitimacy (Elsig and Dupont, 2007; Woll 2009; Van den Hoven 2006; Bouwen 2002). Other studies have looked at whether using hard law could help enforce compliance, showing that binding rules are more effective than soft power (Mitchel and Hensel, 2007; Hafner-Burton, 2009; Spilker and Böhmelt, 2013).

The economics literature has also long contributed to the debate on the pursuit of NTPOs via trade instruments. First of all, the political economy literature has addressed how trade agreements could be instrumental in promoting non-trade objectives by creating negotiation linkages (such as when trade and non-trade provisions (NTPs) are negotiated jointly in the context of a single bargain, as opposed to separate bargains) or participation linkages (if, for example, the incentives of a country to enter a trade agreement are used to also encourage participation in cooperation on non-trade objectives). Conconi (2019) reviews part of this political economy literature (including Ederington, 2001; Conconi and Perroni, 2002; Copeland, 2000; Limão, 2005, 2007; Maggi, 2016; Poast, 2012).

The empirical evidence on the effects of NTPs is still rather scarce and tends to be limited in scope. Most of the literature adopts a cross-Preferential Trade Agreement approach and focuses on a specific NTPO of interest, seeking to identify causal relationships. Examples include Baghdadi et al. (2013) and Abman et al. (2021) on environmental and air quality, Van den Putte and Orbie (2015) and Aissi et al. (2018) on labour and workers' rights, and Zerk (2019) on civil and human rights. Another stream of literature focuses on specific PTAs, and includes case studies of those PTAs and the provisions and conditionalities included there, or is country-specific (see for instance Hafner-Burton, 2009; Kim, 2012; Spilker and Böhmelt, 2013; Postnikov, 2014). Hafner-Burton (2009) argues that binding human rights clauses in trade agreements are more likely to induce compliance. This finding has been qualified by Spilker and Böhmelt (2013), who show that the positive effect decreases if one accounts for the selection process of human rights clauses in PTAs. The extant econometric evidence suggests that, despite the great efforts of the EU, United States, and other high-income countries to include NTPs in PTAs, most provisions fall short of delivering substantial change with respect to the policy outcome they target. Most empirical studies fail to identify a causal relationship between PTAs and NTPOs, or to find a significant impact of NTPs on policy outcomes of interest (a recent exception is Abman et al., 2021, which explores the causal impact of environmental provisions in PTAs, specifically looking at the impact of environmental protection obligations on forest coverage loss).

The Legal Duty of Coherence in EU Law

As the EU is a multi-governance structure, the issue of coherence has been analysed following two dimensions: the horizontal dimension (i.e., coherence between two different policies) and the vertical dimension (i.e., coherence between different polity levels acting in the same policy field). The idea of coherence was developed in EU law to cover at least two different dimensions: consistency (requiring absence of contradictions) and the broader concept of coherence, which encompasses the need for cooperation on NTPOs and the use of trade to promote bilateral, regional, and multilateral cooperation in NTPOs.

While the main obligation of vertical coherence (as expressed in the duty of sincere cooperation) was already enshrined in the Treaty of Rome of 1957 (Article 5 Treaty establishing the European Economic Community), references to horizontal coherence in EU external relations date back to the 1970s when European Political Cooperation laid the foundations of the EU's foreign policy. Horizontal coherence in external relations was first enshrined in Treaty law in the Single European Act, which referred only to "consistency" between foreign policy objectives and the external policy of the European Community.[1] A general consistency provision was introduced in the Treaty on the European Union of 1992 (Article C of Title 1 on Common Provisions). The Lisbon Treaty further develops that obligation of horizontal coherence. The principle of consistency finds its expression first in Article 7 of the Treaty on the Functioning of the EU (TFEU), which requires the Union to ensure

[1] Paragraph 5 of Article 30 of the SEA refers to "The external policies of the European Community and the policies agreed in European Political Co-operation must be consistent".

consistency between its policies and activities, taking into account all of its objectives, and in accordance with the principle of conferral. This is reinforced in Article 21 of the Treaty on the EU (TEU), which stresses that the Union shall ensure consistency between the different areas of its external action and between external actions and its other policies. Article 21 TEU also requires the EU to respect its founding principles, values, and objectives, such as democracy, rule of law, human rights, fostering sustainable development (economic, social, and environmental), preserving peace and international security, and promoting multilateral cooperation. This is echoed in Article 3 TEU, which codifies the values and objectives of the EU. Under Article 3(5) TEU, in its wider relation with the world, the Union "should uphold and promote its values and interests. It shall contribute to peace, security, the sustainable development of the Earth, solidarity and mutual respect among peoples, free and fair trade, eradication of poverty and the protection of human rights".

The legal framework for vertical coherence includes the duty to comply with obligations under EU law (stemming from the EU but also from international agreements concluded by the EU). That entails a duty of consistency of EU Member States' external actions with EU law. The so-called principle of sincere cooperation under Article 4 TEU further imposes a duty to refrain from taking actions which could jeopardize the attainment of EU objectives. From the very early case law, the principle of sincere cooperation was not limited to competences conferred on the EU and where only the EU is entitled to act at the international level. The principle of sincere cooperation more generally applies to all areas of EU competences, including those where the EU shares competences with the Member States (such as energy or environment) as well as those areas where the EU acts in parallel (such as development cooperation and aid), or where the EU supports and complements Member States' actions (such as in the area of health or education). The duty to refrain from actions that could jeopardize the attainment of EU objectives covers both the need to comply with EU external competences (in the areas covered by the two paragraphs of Article 3 TFEU where there is exclusive EU competence)[2], but also a broader duty of cooperation applicable in all competences. The latter includes a duty to inform and to consult but also a reciprocal duty of assistance in carrying out the tasks under the Treaty.

[2] Exclusive competence implies that the Member States cannot act unilaterally, only the EU can conclude agreements in these areas.

A specific duty of cooperation also exists in the context of international organizations under Article 211 TFEU. Finally, a duty of cooperation between Member States' actions was enshrined in the chapter on the Common Foreign and Security Policy (CFSP), which covers all areas of foreign policy (so in principle also energy diplomacy). In that context, Article 24(3) TEU requires the Member States to support the Union's foreign and security policy

> actively and unreservedly in a spirit of loyalty and mutual solidarity and shall comply with the Union's action in this area. The Member States shall work together to enhance and develop their mutual political solidarity. They shall refrain from any action which is contrary to the interests of the Union or is likely to impair its effectiveness as a cohesive force in international relations.

Coherence and Trade Policy

EU trade policy is one of the most well-developed external policies of the EU. An exclusive competence since the founding Treaty of Rome, the Common Commercial Policy has over the years expanded the scope of its competence to extend beyond trade in goods to include also services, intellectual property, and foreign direct investments. Trade agreements have also developed to cover matters that go even beyond the strict scope of the Common Commercial Policy, such as regulatory cooperation, provisions related to public procurement, competition, and energy.

EU trade policy has two main goals: (1) regulating competition from non-EU products and producers; and (2) reducing market access restrictions confronting EU products and producers in foreign markets. The first objective is pursued through trade barriers and regulatory measures enforced at the EU border to protect EU producers from foreign competition, including instances in which such competition reflects behaviour by firms or foreign governments that is deemed to distort competition ("unfair trade"), and to ensure that EU regulatory requirements for products and producers are met. The second goal is pursued through the negotiation and implementation of international trade agreements, both multilateral (the WTO) and preferential (bilateral and regional), including economic diplomacy and development assistance undertaken by the EU and the Member States, working together (e.g., the Market Access Partnership) and independently (trade promotion, export credit agencies).

The EU has long been a champion of introducing NTPOs in its trade agreements. The Commission issued the Trade for All strategy of 2015 (European Commission, 2015), whereby EU trade policy must follow four main objectives. The first is the conclusion of balanced trade agreements – i.e., agreements that should reach a reciprocal and balanced market access, while also being consistent with and promoting NTPOs, such as respect for human rights, labour, environmental, health and safety protection regulations. Second, the strategy called for more effective implementation of EU trade agreements (including NTPO provisions) via reinforced monitoring. The third objective focused on unfair trade practices; while the fourth focused specifically on NTPOs and on promoting a sustainable approach to trade. In a 2017 Report on the Implementation of the Trade for All strategy, the Commission noted that there was rising public debate concerning the purpose, legitimacy, and effects of the EU trade negotiations (European Commission, 2017). A clear politization of the negotiation of certain trade agreements (see De Bièvre and Poletti, 2020) was signalled inter alia by the negative outcome of the Dutch advisory referendum on the agreement with Ukraine in 2016, or the mass protests against the EU trade negotiations with the United States (the TTIP agreement that was never concluded) or during the conclusion of the EU agreement with Canada (CETA). In that context, the Commission confirmed the need to reaffirm the fundamentals of the Trade for All strategy guiding the EU's approach: to deliver openness combined with ensuring a level playing field, high standards of labour, and environmental, consumer, and social protection (European Commission, 2017). Trade and trade agreements were identified as a key instrument for achieving the objectives of the European Green Deal in the Commission Communication (European Commission, 2019) aimed at making Europe the first climate-neutral continent. The Russian war in Ukraine only accelerated the need to implement the Green Deal and emphasized the importance of an external energy strategy for achieving those objectives, inter alia via provisions in trade agreements and bilateral engagement with third countries (Joint Communication of the Commission and the High Representative on an EU External Energy Engagement in a Changing World, of June 2022). That Communication not only highlights the importance of trade agreements but also of non-binding instruments such as Memoranda of Understanding or dialogues. Further following this line, the Commission published a Communication on the power of trade partnerships as tools to foster green and just economic growth. The Communication reveals a plan by the Commission to reinforce the implementation and enforcement of trade and sustainable development chapters in trade agreements and thus enhance the contribution of trade agreements to NTPOs such as climate, the environment, and labour rights.

In light of these political objectives, ensuring horizontal coherence is a fundamental priority of EU trade policy. This book will essentially focus on horizontal coherence of trade policy with NTPOs (with the only exception of one contribution looking at development aid and trade-related aid, an area where the EU and its Member States acts simultaneously, also known as parallel competence).

In the framework of horizontal coherence, it is proposed to review how the codification of the duty of coherence has translated into the practice and instruments of EU trade policy, and how the EU has reconciled its normative ambitions of promoting and achieving NTPOs (including development goals) with the objectives of EU trade policy. Moreover, our knowledge remains limited as to what results have been achieved so far by the instruments currently used or planned by the EU to achieve coherence of its trade policy with NTPOs. These challenges and research questions are fundamental in the current political context, as shown for example by the Commission's Communication of June 2022.

Chapter Overview

The first contribution in the book provides an overview of the state of the art in the trade–NTPO linkage. **Lechner and Yildirim** start by reviewing the existing data and literature on the EU's use of trade policies to pursue NTPOs such as labour rights and environmental commitments. The authors examine the political economy of the EU's pursuit of objectives beyond trade, and review novel data on EU stakeholder preferences over NTPOs. They propose that researchers focus on the monitoring and implementation of NTPOs, exploring how (and to what extent) stakeholders affect the pathways that link implementation of non-trade policies to trade policies and the extent to which compliance with NTPOs in the past influences stakeholders' political mobilization in future trade agreements and policies.

Following this overview, the first part of the book focuses on various trade and trade-related policies that the EU has employed in its pursuit of non-trade policy objectives. **Holmes, Magntorn Garrett, and Rollo** look at the relationship between the values embodied in trade and development aid and examine the extent to which EU Member States and the EU institutions align their strategies. The authors show that the EU and its

Member States are to some extent pulling in the same direction, but that the degree of coherence with the EU institutions varies across the key Member States – namely, while France and Germany largely align their aid allocations, the Netherlands and (a recently exited member) the United Kingdom do not. They conclude that the EU and its Member States have been complementing rather than either replicating or contradicting each other's actions. Moving on from development aid to export financing instruments, in Chapter 3 **Kamala Dawar** explores the challenges and controversies in public export financing in the EU. She highlights the inadequacy of the international rule book in regulating Export Credit Agencies (ECAs) with a specific focus on non-transparency. The chapter then sets out what is known about the operation of ECAs internationally and in the EU. Lastly, shifting the debate towards the linkage between NTPOs and investment, **Hugo Rojas-Romagosa** empirically tests the specific relation between non-trade provisions contained in preferential trade agreements (PTAs) and bilateral Foreign Direct Investment (FDI). He finds that non-trade provisions have, if any, a positive relation with bilateral FDI. The civil and political rights index has a positive, significant, and robust correlation with bilateral FDI. However, economic and social rights, and environmental protection, usually have positive coefficient signs, but they are not robust to different specifications.

The second part of the book focuses on the EU's relationship with key trade partners and its actions. In particular, two contributions look at three very different but major trading partners such as China, the countries that are part of the European Neighbourhood Policy (the foreign policy framework aiming at bringing the EU and its eastern and southern neighbours closer, including inter alia Moldova and Morocco), and the United Kingdom after its exit from the EU. All these are important EU trade partners either because of their vicinity or because of their importance in the world economy. However, the EU enjoys different levels of economic and trade integration with these countries and therefore has used very different approaches to cooperate on NTPOs (ranging from dialogues with China to regulatory alignment with Moldova). The contributions analyse the impact of those cooperation and dialogue efforts as well as their potential limitations. In particular, Chapter 5 by **Jacques Pelkmans** sheds light on the process of convergence, as captured by environment and climate indicators, between the EU and China and further focuses on the sustained and wide-ranging EU effort to stimulate China to go "green". The author proposes that a slow process of convergence seems to have solidified by 2020. Moreover, given reasonable expectations, the EU stimulus has been well-received – occasionally even requested (e.g., carbon-trading; sustainable forestry, etc.). As a result, the author shows that cooperative EU trade policy for purposes of value promotion might be beneficial. Taking a more comparative approach, in Chapter 6 **Franklin Maduko, Timea Pál, and László Bruszt** examine how economic and political factors in developing economies influence the ability of key stakeholders – governments, businesses, and labour organizations – to undermine or reinforce EU governance efforts in different countries. The authors show that improvements in labour standards are closely associated with standards in key export markets and the freedom of civil society organizations (CSOs) – among others. They further shed light on the potentials and limitations of EU governance efforts through divergent pathways of improvements in labour standards, using examples from Moldova and Morocco.

The third and final section of the book analyses the effectiveness of some key institutional and legal instruments that have been or could be further used to achieve better coherence. Chapter 7 is a quantitative analysis by **Ferrari et al.** that asks whether the inclusion of NTPs in EU PTAs has had a systematic effect on non-trade outcomes in partner countries. The authors move beyond simple correlation, and use synthetic control methods to look at the causal relationship between NTPs in EU PTAs and the performance of EU partner countries on the corresponding non-trade outcome variables. They do not find any conclusive evidence on the significant impact of NTPs on outcomes. Chapter 8, by **Bernard Hoekman and Rorden Wilkinson**, concerns a different kind of instrument used to achieve stronger promotion of NTPOs, the so-called *soft power*, privileging forums, discussion groups, and non-binding agreements such as Memoranda of Understanding, with the aim of promoting discussion and cooperation. Chapter 8 convincingly shows, from a multilateral perspective, the importance of the Group of Twenty (G20) as a platform to gather a critical mass for the EU to pursue its policy objectives. The authors highlight the difficulties surrounding the maintenance of a rules-based international trade regime and how the EU can take more of a global leadership role by addressing current challenges through a mix of opportunities within international organizations such as the WTO and the G20. The EU has a much better chance to effectively pursue its policy objectives, including NTPOs, by involving key players from the G20 and creating a critical mass. Moreover, beyond the constitutional obligations of coherence between trade and NTPOs, enshrined in the EU Treaties, other drivers work for the inclusion of NTPO objectives in trade policy. The promotion of NTPOs, such as rules on the environment, labour, or consumer safety and rights, are very close to the general citizen's interests and naturally led to the recent politization of the conclusion of major trade agreements and their potential impact on NTPOs (such as in the case of CETA or TTIP). The orientation of contemporary trade politics towards the behind-the-border issues of national regulation has caused trade policy to become closely intertwined with domestic regulatory policy. Therefore, the actors primarily responsible for legislation – i.e., parliaments – have become important advocates for their extended participation in determining trade policy for reasons of transparency, scrutiny, and political inclusiveness. The European Parliament has also become a champion of stronger NTPOs in trade agreements using the consent vote acquired in the Lisbon Treaty to press for stronger negotiations on these issues. **Chapter 9** by **Wolfgang Weiß** describes this process of involvement of the European Parliament in promoting NTPOs. The author considers that an institutional design of policy formulation cycles and decision making in an EU trade policy that strives for better coherence of trade concerns with NTPOs must focus on strengthening the influence of the EP, and improve its participatory rights in decision making and its control and monitoring mechanisms. Consequently, he proposes ways to improve the European Parliament's monitoring mechanisms for the benefit of NTPOs in trade policy from an analysis of weaknesses in the negotiation and implementation stages of trade policy.

References

Abman, R., Lundberg, C., & Ruta, M. (2021). *The Effectiveness of Environmental Provisions in Regional Trade Agreements*. Washington, DC: World Bank.

Aissi, J., Peels, R., & Samaan, D. (2018). Evaluating the Effectiveness of Labour Provisions in Trade Agreements: An Analytical and Methodological Framework. *International Labour Review*, 157, 671–698.

Baghdadi, L., Martinez-Zarzoso, I., & Zitouna, H. (2013). Are RTA Agreements with Environmental Provisions Reducing Emissions? *Journal of International Economics*, 90(2), 378–390.

Bartels, L. (2013). Human Rights and Sustainable Development Obligations in EU Free Trade Agreements. *Legal Issues of Economic Integration*, 40(4), 297–313.

Blockmans, S., & Wessel, R. A. (2012). Principles and Practices of EU External Representation. CLEER Working Papers 2012/5.

Bouwen, P. (2002). Corporate Lobbying in the European Union: The Logic of Access. *Journal of European Public Policy*, 9(3): 365–390.

Bronckers, M., & Gruni, G. (2019). Taking the Enforcement of Labour Standards in the EU's Free Trade Agreements Seriously. *Common Market Law Review*, 56 (6), 1591–1622.

Bronckers, M., & Gruni, G. (2021). Retooling the Sustainability Standards in EU Free Trade Agreements. *Journal of International Economic Law*, 24(1) 25–51.

Conceicao-Heldt, E. D., & Meunier, S. (2014). Speaking with a Single Voice: Internal Cohesiveness and External Effectiveness of the EU in Global Governance. *Journal of European Public Policy*, 21(7), 961–979.

Conconi, P. (2019). Linking Trade Policy to Non-Trade Issues: Selected Survey of the Literature. Unpublished manuscript. https://respect.eui.eu/wp-content/uploads/sites/6/2020/01/D2.1-Issue-Linkage.pdf

Conconi, P., & Perroni, C. (2002). Issue Linkage and Issue Tie-in in Multilateral Negotiations. *Journal of International Economics*, 57, 423–447.

Copeland, B. R. (2000). Trade and Environment: Policy Linkages. *Environment and Development Economics*, 5, 405–432.

Cremona, M. (2011). Coherence in European Union Foreign Relations Law. In P. Koutrakos (Ed.), *European Foreign Policy: Legal and Political Perspectives* (pp. 55–91). Cheltenham: Edward Elgar.

Cremona, M. (2021). Human Rights as a Value of EU Trade Policy. In M. Balboni & C. Danisi (Eds.), *Human Rights as a Horizontal Issue in EU External Policy: Les droits de l'homme comme domaine horizontal de la politique extérieure de l'Union européenne* (pp. 161–194). Napoli: Editoriale scientifica.

De Baere, G. (2011). 'O, Where Is Faith?' Some Thoughts on the Duty of Loyal Cooperation and the Union's External Environmental Competences in the Light of the PFOS Case. *European Law Review*, 36(3), 405–419.

De Bièvre, D., & Poletti, A. (2020). Towards Explaining Varying Degrees of Politicization of EU Trade Agreement Negotiations. *Politics and Governance*, 8(1), 243–253.

de Waele, H., & Kuipers, J. J. (Eds.). (2013). The Emergence of the Union's International Identity: Views from the Global Arena. Leiden: Martinus Nijhoff Publishers.

den Hertog, L., & Simon Stroß, S. (2013). Coherence in EU External Relations: Concepts and Legal Rooting of an Ambiguous Term" *European Foreign Affairs Review*, 18(3), 373–388.

Donno, D., & Neureiter, M. (2018). Can Human Rights Conditionality Reduce Repression? Examining the European Union's Economic Agreements. *Review of International Organizations*, 13(3), 335–357.

Dür, A., Eckhardt, J. and Poletti, A. (2019). Global Value Chains, the Anti-globalization Backlash, and EU Trade Policy: A Research Agenda. *Journal of European Public Policy*, 2(6), 944–956.

Durán, G. M., & Morgera, E. (2012). Dedication. In *Environmental Integration in the EU's External Relations: Beyond Multilateral Dimensions* (pp. v–vi). London: Hart Publishing.

Ederington, J. (2001). International Coordination of Trade and Domestic Policies. *American Economic Review*, 91, 1580–1593.

Elsig, M. and Dupont, C. (2007) European Union Meets South Korea: Bureaucratic Interests, Exporter Discrimination and the Negotiations of Trade Agreements. *Journal of Common Market Studies*, 50(3), 492–507.

Espa, I., & Durán, G. M. (2020). Promoting Green Energy through EU Preferential Trade Agreements: Potential and Limitations. *Legal Issues of Economic Integration*, 47(2), 115–150.

European Commission (2015). Directorate-General for Trade, Trade for All – Towards a More Responsible Trade and Investment Policy, Publications Office. https://ec.europa.eu/commission/presscorner/detail/en/IP_15_5806

European Commission (2017). Report on the Implementation of the Trade Policy Strategy Trade for All Delivering a Progressive Trade Policy to Harness Globalisation, COM/2017/0491 final.

European Commission (2019). Communication to the European Parliament, the Council, the European Economic and Social Committee and the Committee of the Regions. The European Green Deal, COM/2019/640 final.

Hachez, N. (2015). 'Essential Elements' Clauses in EU Trade Agreements: Making Trade Work in a Way That Helps Human Rights? KU Leuven Working Paper 158.

Hafner-Burton, E. M. (2009). *Forced to Be Good: Why Trade Agreements Boost Human Rights*. Ithaca, NY: Cornell University Press.

Hillion, C. (2008). Tous pour un, un pour tous! Coherence in the External Relations of the European Union. In Marise Cremona (Ed.), *Developments in EU External Relations Law, Collected Courses of the Academy of European Law*. Oxford: Oxford University Press (online ed., Oxford Academic, 2009, https://doi.org/10.1093/acprof:oso/9780199552894.003.0002).

Hillion, C. (2009). Mixity and Coherence in EU External Relations: The Significance of the Duty of Cooperation. CLEER Working Papers 2009/2.

Jørgensen, K. E. (Ed.). (2009). *The European Union and International Organisations*. London: Routledge.

Kaddous, C. (Ed.). (2015). *The European Union in International Organisations: Recent Developments*. London: Hart Publishing.

Kim, M. (2012). Ex Ante Due Diligence: Formation of PTAs and Protection of Labor Rights. *International Studies Quarterly*, 56(4), 704–719.

Klamert, M. (2014). *The Principle of Loyalty in EU Law*. Oxford: Oxford University Press.

Konstadinides, T. (2015). In the Union of Wine: Loose Ends in the Relationship between the European Union and the Member States in the Field of External

Representation – Case C-399/12 *Germany* v. *Council*, Judgment of the Court of Justice of 7 October 2014. *European Public Law*, 21(4), 679–689.

Koutrakos, P. (2019). Institutional Balance and Sincere Cooperation in Treaty-Making under EU Law. *International and Comparative Law Quarterly*, 68(1), 1–33.

Krämer-Hoppe, R. (2019). *Positive Integration – EU and WTO Approaches towards the 'Trade and' Debate*. Special issue of the European Yearbook of International Economic Law. Cham Springer.

Leal-Arcas, R., & Alvarez Armas, E. (2018). The Climate–Energy–Trade Nexus in EU External Relations. In S. Minas & V. Nitousas (Eds.), *EU Climate Diplomacy: Politics, Law and Negotiations* (pp. 153–169). London: Routledge.

Limão, N. (2005). Trade Policy, Cross-Border Externalities and Lobbies: Do Linked Agreements Enforce More Cooperative Outcomes? *Journal of International Economics*, 67, 175–199.

Limão, N. (2007). Are Preferential Trade Agreements with Non-Trade Objectives a Stumbling Block for Multilateral Liberalization? *Review of Economic Studies*, 74, 821–855.

Macaj, G., & Nicolaïdis, K. (2014). Beyond 'One Voice'? Global Europe's Engagement with Its Own Diversity. *Journal of European Public Policy*, 21(7), 1067–1083.

Maggi, G. (2016). Issue Linkage. In K. Bagwell & R. Staiger (Eds.), *Handbook of Commercial Policy* (pp. 513–564). Amsterdam: Elsevier.

Marhold, A. (2019). Externalising Europe's Energy Policy in EU Free Trade Agreements: A Cognitive Dissonance between Promoting Sustainable Development and Ensuring Security of Supply? *Europe and the World: A Law Review*, 3(1), 1–18.

Meissner, K. L., & McKenzie, L. (2019). The Paradox of Human Rights Conditionality in EU Trade Policy: When Strategic Interests Drive Policy Outcomes. *Journal of European Public Policy*, 26(9), 1273–1291.

Meunier, S. (2014). Divide and Conquer? China and the Cacophony of Foreign Investment Rules in the EU. *Journal of European Public Policy*, 21(7), 996–1016.

Meunier, S., and Nicolaidis, K. 2006. The European Union as a Conflicted Trade Power. *Journal of European Public Policy*, 13(6): 906–925.

Mitchell, S. M., & Hensel, P. R. (2007). International Institutions and Compliance with Agreements. *American Journal of Political Science*, 51(4), 721–737.

Moschella, M., & Quaglia, L. (2016). To Agree or Not to Agree? Explaining the Cohesiveness of the European Union in the Group of Twenty. *Journal of European Public Policy*, 23(6), 906–924.

Neframi, E. (2010). The Duty of Loyalty: Rethinking its Scope through Its Application in the Field of EU External Relations. *Common Market Law Review*, 47(2), 323–359.

Orsini, A. (Ed.). (2016). *The European Union with(in) International Organisations: Commitment, Consistency and Effects across Time*. London: Routledge.

Poast, P. (2012). Does Issue Linkage Work? Evidence from European Alliance Negotiations, 1860 to 1945. *International Organization*, 66, 277–310.

Poletti, A., and Sicurelli, D. (2018). *The Political Economy of Normative Trade Power Europe*. London: Palgrave.

Portela, C., & Raube, K. (2012). The EU Polity and EU Foreign Policy Coherence. *Journal of European Contemporary Research*, 8(1), 3–20.

Postnikov, E. (2014). The Design of Social Standards in EU and US Preferential Trade Agreements. In D. A. Deese (Ed.), *Handbook of the International Political Economy of Trade* (pp. 531–549). Cheltenham: Edward Elgar Publishing.

Raess, D., Dür, A., & Sari, D. (2018). Protecting Labor Rights in Preferential Trade Agreements: The Role of Trade Unions, Left Governments, and Skilled Labor. *Review of International Organizations*, 13(2), 143–162.

Rommerskirchen, C. (2013). Keeping the Agents Leashed: The EU's External Economic Governance in the G20. *Journal of European Integration*, 35(3), 347–360.

Sicurelli, D. (2017). The Conditions for Effectiveness of EU Human Rights Promotion in Non-democratic States: A Case Study of Vietnam. *Journal of European Integration*, 39(6), 739–753.

Spilker, G., & Böhmelt, T. (2013). The Impact of Preferential Trade Agreements on Governmental Repression Revisited. *Review of International Organizations*, 8(3), 343–361.

Van den Hoven, A. (2006). European Union Regulatory Capitalism and Multilateral Trade Negotiations. In S. Lucarelli and I. Manners (eds.), *Values and Principles in European Foreign Policy*. London: Routledge.

Van den Putte, L., & Orbie, J. (2015). EU Bilateral Trade Agreements and the Surprising Rise of Labour Provisions. *International Journal of Comparative Labour Law and Industrial Relations*, 31(3), 263–283.

Woll, C. (2009). Who Captures Whom? Trade Policy Lobbying in the European Union. In D. Coen and J. Richardson (Eds.), Lobbying in the European Union. Oxford: Oxford University Press.

Young, A., & Peterson, J. 2014. *Parochial Global Europe: 21st Century Trade Politics*. Oxford: Oxford University Press.

Zerk, J. (2019). Human Rights Impact Assessment of Trade Agreements. Chatham House Research Paper, London: Royal Institute of International Affairs. https://www.chathamhouse.org/2019/02/human-rights-impact-assessment-trade-agreements

1

European Union Trade Policy and Non-Trade Issues

What Do We Know and Where Do We Go from Here?

LISA LECHNER AND AYDIN B. YILDIRIM

Introduction

The European Union is commonly portrayed as utilizing trade policies to pursue additional objectives vis-à-vis its trade partners. As the growing literature in this line of research has demonstrated, the EU has been noted to use preferential trade agreements (PTAs), foreign aid, and market access to achieve results on non-trade issues (NTIs) that include civil, political, social, environmental, and security standards – such as the promotion of human rights or environmental protection – in third countries (Hirsch 2017; Lechner 2019; Poletti and Sicurelli 2018; Raess et al. 2018).

As the EU's use of trade policies to induce change in other policy areas has increased, those trade policies have become more salient in the public arena (e.g., Young 2015). Domestic contestation of EU trade policies, growing popular discontent with the global economic order in the wake of COVID-19, and the politicization of international cooperation thus demand a fresh analysis of what we actually know and how we can improve our understanding of EU trade policy as a tool to achieve non-trade policy objectives. In this chapter, we conduct that analysis and review the existing data and literature on economic and political determinants of the EU's use of trade policy to pursue NTIs and suggest avenues for further research. More specifically, we highlight the need for additional research that focuses on the *implementation* of measures covering non-trade issues linked to trade policies. We argue that researchers would benefit from exploring how (and to what extent) stakeholders effect the pathways that link implementation of NTIs to

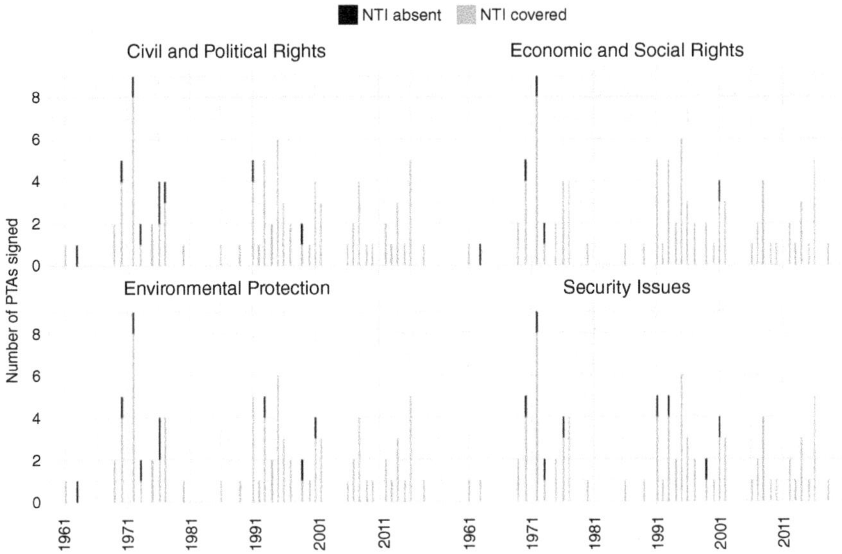

Figure 1.1 Non-trade issues covered in EU agreements over time

trade policies and the extent to which compliance with non-trade policies in the past influences stakeholders' political mobilization over NTIs in future trade agreements and policies.[1]

In the following, we first review the institutional design choices of the EU, then we take a deeper look into the determinants of these design choices, before we discuss research gaps in the current literature and new avenues for future research.

Design of EU PTAs: Wide, but Not So Deep, Coverage of NTIs

The EU is one of the leading actors in linking NTIs to its trade policies (Barbu et al. 2018; Bastiaens and Postnikov 2017; Lechner 2019; Postnikov 2019; Van den Putte 2015). Figure 1.1 shows how many PTAs signed per year cover at least one aspect of civil and political rights, economic and social rights, environmental protection, or security issues.[2] Overall, the figure illustrates that there are few cases in which the

[1] Cezar (2020) argues in a qualitative case study on the North American Free Trade Agreement (NAFTA) that the implementation of past agreements matters for future designs.

[2] Data used for figures derives from Lechner (2016, 2018, 2019).

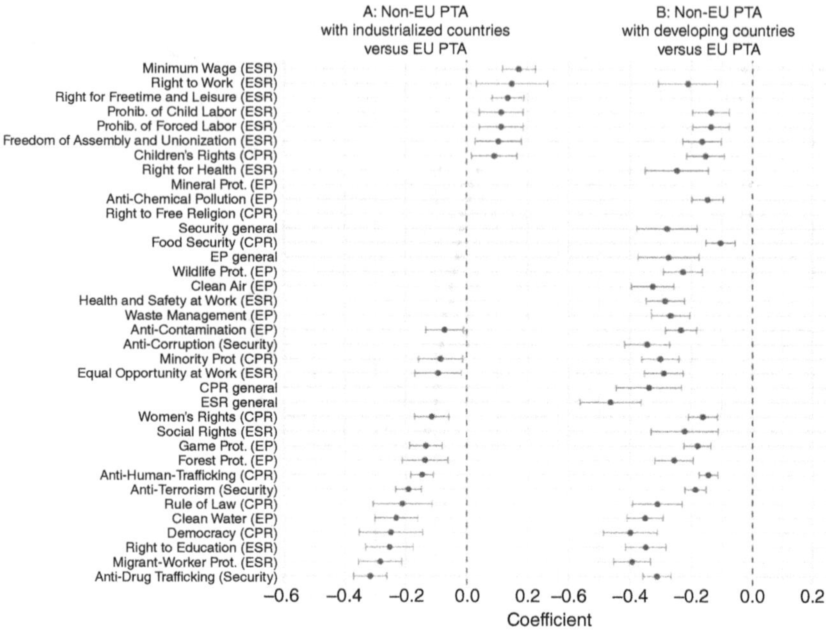

Figure 1.2 Non-trade issues in non-EU PTAs versus EU PTAs

respective non-trade issues are completely absent; this is especially rare for economic and social rights.

Next, using multivariate regressions, we assess whether the EU covers particular issues to a greater extent than other industrialized countries or other developing countries in their PTAs. Figure 1.2 summarizes these findings, where the left-hand panel shows the comparison of EU versus non-EU PTAs with industrialized countries and the right-hand panel the comparison of EU versus non-EU PTAs with developing countries. Unsurprisingly, the EU leads with respect to most NTIs in PTAs over developing countries. Also, in many areas, the EU sets higher standards than other industrialized countries. However, other industrialized countries seem to be more zealous in covering the basic principles of the International Labor Organization (minimum wage, right to free time and leisure, prohibition of child labor, prohibition of forced labor, and freedom of assembly and unionization). Also, the EU covers children's rights in PTAs less frequently than other industrialized countries.

Despite the lead in terms of NTI coverage, there has been criticism that the clauses on NTIs, particularly those on the environment and labor

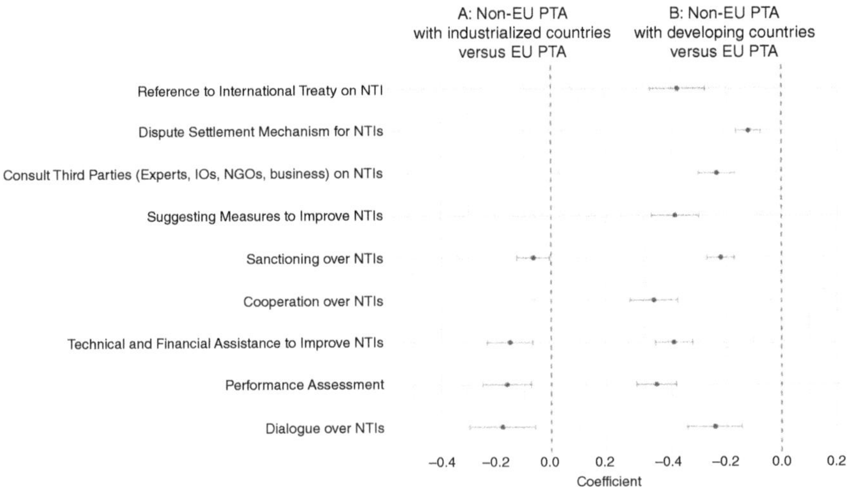

Figure 1.3 Mechanisms to regulate NTIs in non-EU PTAs versus EU PTAs

rights, should have more teeth (Rose 2020). Figure 1.3 shows how the EU's approach to regulating NTIs compares to the approach used by other political systems, with the EU preferring dialogue and cooperation on NTIs as well as technical and financial assistance more than the others. Yet the figure also shows that the EU more frequently uses relatively "harder" conditionality clauses on NTIs. In this regard it is, however, important to note that conditionality provisions are rare in general, with only 39 out of 663 PTAs covering such a provision. The numbers tentatively suggest that dispute settlement mechanisms are less often used in EU PTAs than in PTAs signed by other industrialized countries. It is also interesting that while EU PTAs tend to refer less often to international treaties than other agreements, they are not significantly less strict in regulating NTIs. In this respect, it can be noted that clauses on NTIs are limited in their enforceability; this applies for both EU and non-EU PTAs.

In Figure 1.4 we add the time dimension and compare the development of NTI commitments by the EU and by non-EU countries – both developing and industrialized countries – over time. The commitment scores summarize a multitude of data points for each dimension. As an aggregation method, the authors applied latent trait analysis (Lechner 2016; Rasch 1980). The data suggests that the EU has maintained a slightly higher average commitment level than many of its other trade

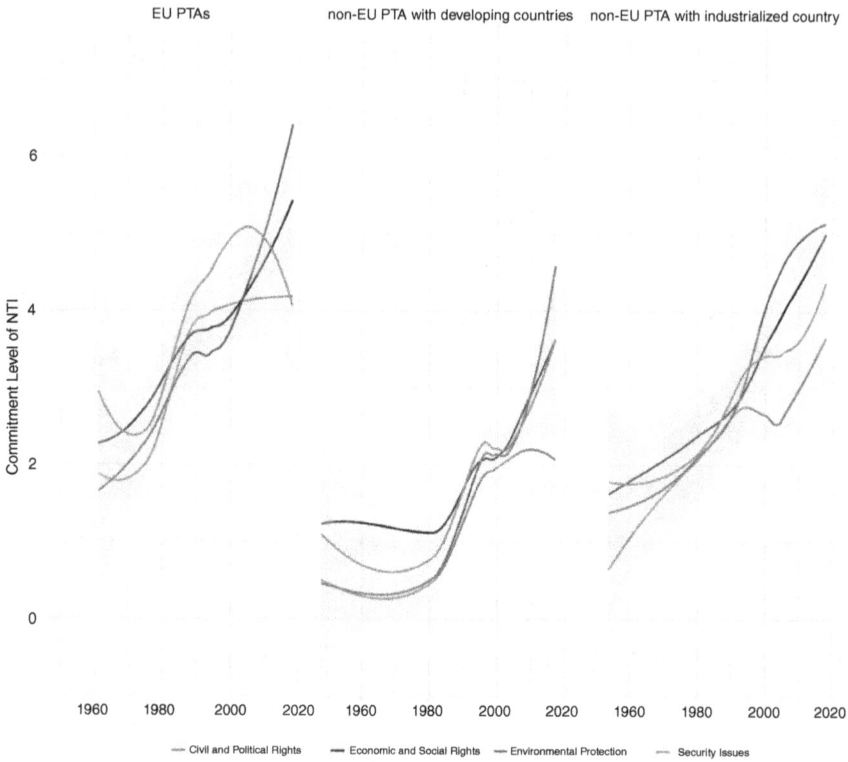

Figure 1.4 NTI commitment level over time (EU versus other countries)

partners, and this applies from the early years in the dataset. Overall, Figure 1.4 shows that modern treaties are stricter than older ones. Especially after 2009, when the Korea EU PTA was signed, the EU has tried to add more teeth to its NTIs in PTAs.

In terms of variation across issue areas, the EU, among others, seems especially eager to promote environmental protection and labor rights issues in its modern treaties. For EU PTAs, civil and political rights as well as security issues decrease in importance.

In summary, we can surmise that the EU signs agreements covering a wide range of NTIs. These aspects are, however, not much deeper in EU PTAs than in non-EU PTAs. Even though detailed datasets[3] help us

[3] Figures 1.1–1.3 build on Lechner (2016). Other valuable datasets on NTIs have been published (Morin et al. 2018; Raess and Sari 2016).

grasp the varying institutional design choices on NTIs in PTAs, we know little about their consequences. Inclusion of different policy instruments notwithstanding, our understanding of how – and to what extent – these measures are implemented on the ground in third countries is virtually nonexistent. For future research, it would be important to take a closer look at the implementation of NTI provisions. Which designs are most likely to lead to domestic policy changes and which are mere window-dressing clauses? This should also matter for the political economy of non-trade objectives in trade agreements, which we address in the following section.

Political Economy of EU Trade Policy and Non-Trade Policy Objectives

The literature on EU trade policy has long noted that the EU's ability to pursue NTIs through its trade policy hinges on garnering support from domestic organized interests, including businesses and civil society organizations (CSOs) (Lechner 2016; Meunier and Nicolaidis 2006; Yildirim et al. 2020; Young and Peterson 2014). Civil society organizations are often portrayed as the main promoters of non-trade issues to be linked to EU trade policy (Dür and De Bièvre 2007; Poletti et al. 2020; Young, 2016). These groups are said to favor linking strong labor, environmental, and human rights commitments to trade, as CSOs are sensitive to such goals (FIDH 2013; Fritz 2010).

Business preferences, on the other hand, seem more diverse. Scholars have suggested that import-competing firms and sectors are likely to be in favor of exporting labor and environmental standards because of their potential to impose additional costs on foreign competitors (DeSombre 2000; Raess et al. 2018; Vogel 1995). In contrast, the literature has suggested that import-dependent firms and sectors should mobilize against NTIs (Lechner 2016, 2019). Since the average importer has a strong interest in accessing cheap imports (Eckhardt 2015; Yildirim 2017), they can be expected to oppose costly regulations imposed on EU trade partners – regardless of relying on final products or intermediate goods. The same logic applies to vertically integrated multinationals that rely on their supply chain partners in different countries – which are expected to oppose the inclusion of NTIs that increase their costs of doing business (Lechner 2016). On the other hand, horizontally integrated multinationals supposedly remain silent on (or are in favor of) non-trade objectives as they are arguably less sensitive to the changes in supply chain operations and fear incurring reputational costs. Lastly, on the policymakers' side, EU officials are often assumed to be highly in favor of pursuing NTIs, while developing trade partners of the EU are portrayed as being against such measures, which curb their comparative advantage (Poletti and Sicurelli 2016, 2018).

This divergence in stakeholders' views is said to reflect EU policymakers' close alignment to business interests (Woll 2009). The logic underlying EU policymakers' inclusion of business preferences arguably follows the European Commission's strategy of integrating firms and sectors into trade policymaking, which increases its bargaining power vis-à-vis third countries, strengthens its technical expertise, and increases its legitimacy (Bouwen 2002; Van den Hoven 2006; Woll 2009). Therefore, CSOs' input is often put forward as epiphenomenal to business interests.

Taking into consideration the growing politicization and public salience of trade policy, however, these conventional views on the political dynamics and coalitions underlying EU trade policy have recently been questioned (De Ville and Siles-Brügge 2017). Indeed, recent scholarship has demonstrated that CSOs bear significant influence on EU trade policymaking (Eliasson and Garcia-Duran 2018; Pollack and Shaffer 2009) and that EU policymakers take into account the views of CSOs in the formulation of trade policy and NTIs. The literature on the so-called normative power Europe highlights the EU's pursuit of sustainable development goals in a "new generation" of trade agreements, with civil society supporting the foundations of a value-based discourse in trade policy (Poletti and Sicurelli 2018; Van den Hoven 2006; Van den Putte and Orbie 2015; Young and Peterson 2014).

The evidence on *when* EU policymakers' preferences align with those of CSOs and other stakeholders is sparse. While we know EU trade policy officials often agree with the views of nonbusiness stakeholders, when are they more (or less) likely to do so? When do the preferences of CSOs overlap with those of EU policymakers? Do actors' support of and opposition to the inclusion of NTIs also depend on the policy instruments employed?

In this section we rely on a novel survey instrument to shed light on these questions. First outlined in Yildirim et al. (2020), the survey instrument covers a wide range of stakeholders and their views on EU trade policymaking – including practitioners in EU institutions, governments (EU and non-EU), businesses and associations, civil society organizations working on trade, and academics in and outside the EU. The data presented in the survey complements existing surveys that tend to target public opinion more generally, such as Eurobarometer polls, Pew Research Centre global surveys, the Bertelsmann Foundation's recent survey on economic globalization (Bluth 2018), and the EU Commission's public consultations.[4] The specific perspective taken in this survey instrument adds value to the body of existing evidence regarding views on the connection between trade policy and non-trade policies.[5]

Who Supports the Inclusion of NTIs?

In order to demonstrate stakeholders' and EU policymakers' preference alignment over non-trade issues, we observe two sets of evidence. First, a general overview can be seen with regard to actors' views on supporting NTIs and the strategy of linking trade policy to achieve such objectives. Civil society organizations and EU policymakers jointly agree on pursuing non-trade issues via trade policies. Yet stakeholders' views over the efficacy of this linkage strategy varies significantly as CSOs do not actually think it is a useful strategy. Secondly, to further delineate these divisions over actor preferences on NTIs, we take a closer look at the data and provide more details on what particular policy instruments actors actually prefer. The patterns of preference alignment here suggest that CSO agreement to pursue non-trade goals is contingent upon using targeted assistance measures and expert dialogue, rather than the trade agreements favored by EU policymakers. In short, we show in this section that EU policymakers and organized interests involved in trade policymaking do not disagree on the strategy itself, but rather the ways in which objectives beyond trade can actually be achieved. Their agreement on pursuing goals beyond trade is thus contingent upon particular policy strategies.

To understand various stakeholders' positions on supporting NTIs via trade policy and whether or not they think such a strategy is productive, we focus on three statements presented to participants from the survey

[4] A description of different types of Eurobarometer editions and polls can be accessed from the web portal of DG Communication: http://ec.europa.eu/COMMFrontOffice/publicopinion/index.cfm. The list and reports of the EC Public Consultations can be found at https://ec.europa.eu/info/consultations_en. The Pew Global Survey list can be found via www.pewglobal.org/category/publications.

[5] See Fiorini et al. (2019) for a detailed description of the survey design and implementation, as well as responses to all questions.

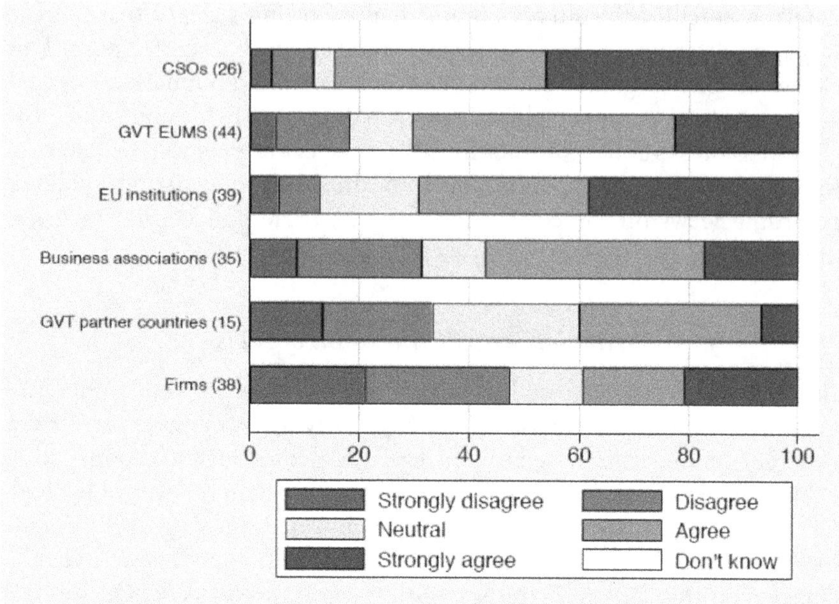

Figure 1.5 The EU should make access to its markets by other countries conditional on non-trade outcomes (such as human rights, labor, environmental protection, and anti-corruption)

Note: Categories are sorted according to the percentage of strongly agree plus agree responses (from highest to lowest). Total number of respondents for each category is reported in parentheses.

instrument, outlined in Figures 1.5, 1.6, and 1.7. The results point to expected differences in stakeholder preferences over NTIs. With regard to conditional access to the EU market, presented in Figure 1.5, CSOs and EU institutions show the greatest agreement to make access conditional upon non-trade policy outcomes. We see the opposite reaction from business groups and EU trade partners, which are the strongest opponents of linking market access to non-trade policy objectives.

Figure 1.7 shows stakeholder responses on whether or not they think EU trade policy is "less effective with NTIs". Mirroring the results shown in Figure 1.2, we see that businesses and EU trade partners all think trade policy becomes less effective when it is utilized to pursue goals beyond trade. On the other hand, CSOs overwhelmingly disagree. While a significant number of CSOs do not think the strategy pays off (as shown in Figure 1.2), they do not think it prevents trade objectives being

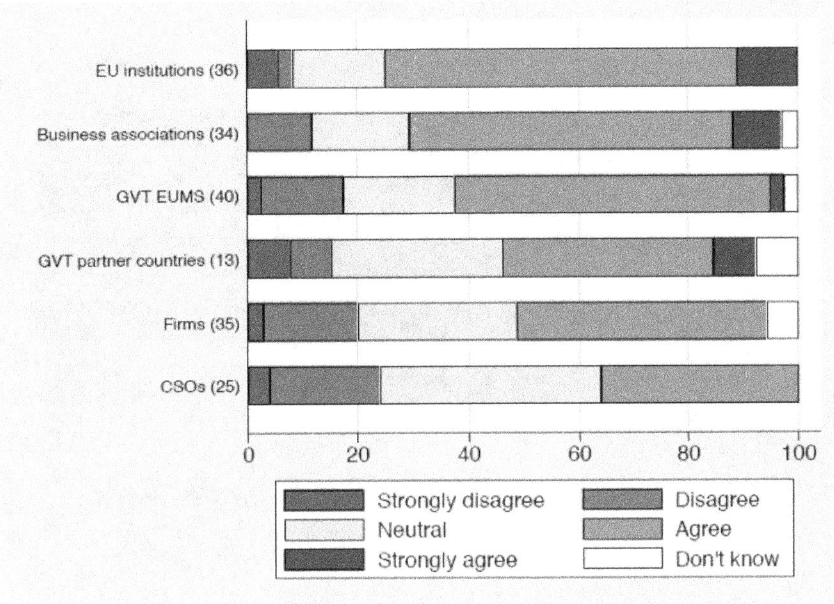

Figure 1.6 EU trade policy supports the realization of EU non-trade objectives (such as human rights, labor, environmental protection, and anti-corruption)
Note: Categories are sorted according to the percentage of strongly agree plus agree responses (from highest to lowest). Total number of respondents for each category is reported in parentheses.

achieved. In other words, it seems that CSOs think trade policy *can* be used to induce change in non-trade-related areas, such as human rights and environmental protection.

These results give support to the growing literature highlighting EU trade policies' inclusion of non-trade issues on the one hand, and civil society's (part) influence on trade policy on the other. Indeed, we find that the EU prefers to link trade policy to NTIs, mirroring the preferences of CSOs and in contrast to businesses. Moreover, we expect the lowest support for non-trade objectives from EU trade partners, whose competitive advantage is curbed by costly regulations (Harrison et al. 2019), and businesses, whose costs might increase due to burdensome regulations imposed by the EU on trade partners. While we would have liked to know the views of importers and exporters separately, unfortunately current empirical evidence – including the survey we use here – does not differentiate types of firm and the anonymized nature of the

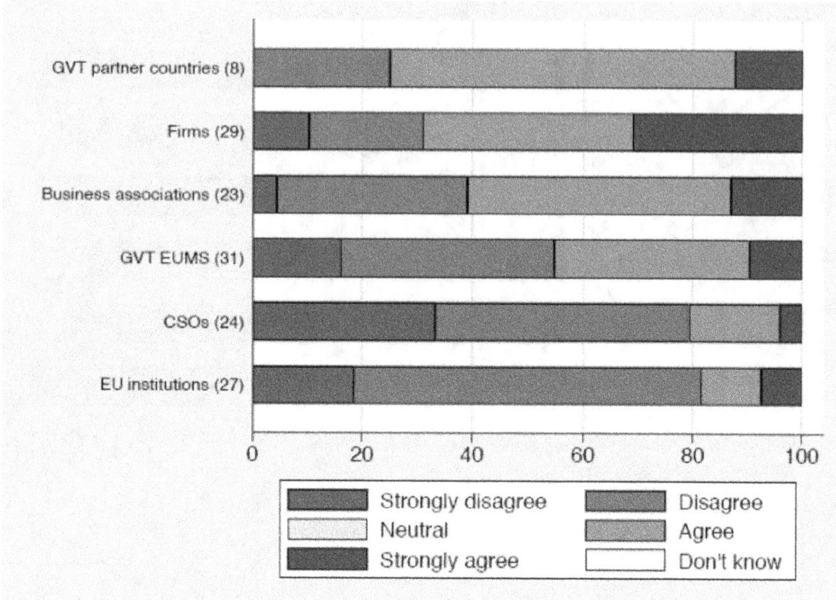

Figure 1.7 The inclusion of non-trade objectives reduces the effectiveness of EU trade policy
Note: Categories are sorted according to the percentage of strongly agree plus agree responses (from highest to lowest). Total number of respondents for each category is reported in parentheses.

data makes it difficult to categorize the firms. Generally speaking, however, the data we observe does support these expectations; third-country officials and firms are the strongest opponents of conditional access to EU markets while business associations are close behind.

Do Actors Think Pursuing NTIs through Trade Policy Actually Works?

Complementing stakeholders' views on pursuing non-trade objectives via trade policies, we also look at their views on the efficacy of such a strategy. From Figure 1.6 we can observe that EU institutions and businesses think using trade policy to realize non-trade objectives pays off, while CSOs do not think the strategy works. In other words, while CSOs are in favor of this strategy, they are not entirely convinced of its efficacy. On the other hand, EU policymakers are quite happy with the state of play.

Which Policy Instruments Are Preferred?

So far, we have shown EU policymakers' and stakeholders' broad views over pursuing non-trade objectives. We note that the survey's CSO participants do indeed agree with the linkage strategy in principle, but they seem to think that it is not a productive one. What, then, do CSOs prefer? What do other stakeholders favor using as a policy instrument to achieve results on NTIs? In order to explore these questions, we move on from stakeholder positions on supporting NTIs and provide information about various actors' views on using particular trade policies such as trade agreements, technical assistance, and development assistance, as presented in Table 1.1.

Overall, we see quite a divergence of preferences between EU policymakers, CSOs, and businesses. For instance, the highest share of respondents that favor using trade agreements to pursue issues beyond trade are EU officials. Only EU and Member State officials tend to prefer using trade agreements. In line with this, we are able to observe that CSOs seem to prefer targeted assistance and expert dialogues, while businesses also prefer such instruments. In this sense, CSO and business preferences converge; both tend to favor using targeted and technical assistance – avoiding trade agreements to pursue non-trade policies. This finding indicates that businesses often avoid including NTIs in PTAs and instead support using other instruments to pursue such goals.

In sum, the survey reveals interesting variation in policy preferences. What is missing, however, is a full understanding of the cost–benefit calculations of these actors. How costly or beneficial are these NTIs to the various stakeholders? The answer to this question ultimately depends on the de facto implementation of NTIs provisions. We expand on this research gap in the next section.

Challenges and Ways Forward

Taking stock of our observations, we turn to two broad challenges facing research on NTIs. First, while we gather more data on the design of trade policies and the views of various stakeholders over NTIs, we still lack knowledge on the consequences of NTI–trade policy linkage. The literature has clearly shown that a wide array of issues beyond trade are included in trade agreements, linked to other trade policies, and are becoming increasingly visible over time. Evidence also suggests that stakeholders hold contrasting views on pursuing objectives beyond trade,

Table 1.1 *Instruments for the realization of non-trade issues, percentage share by professional category*

Professional category	Expert dialogues between EU and partner country stakeholders	Technical assistance	Trade agreements	Targeted assistance for NGOs/ unions/ regulatory bodies	Development assistance for infrastructure improvement	Direct investment by European multinational firms	Total number of respondents by professional category	Total number of responses by professional category
EU institutions	20	11	16	20	4	5	33	96
GVT EUMS	15	12	7	20	3	3	39	143
GVT partner countries	15	15	0	18	8	10	13	39
Firms	19	12	8	17	3	7	33	95
Business associations	18	14	8	16	4	6	33	106
Civil society	14	10	9	23	3	5	25	92
Total number of respondents	96	69	50	108	22	32		

See Yildirim et al. (2020) for additional details on the table.

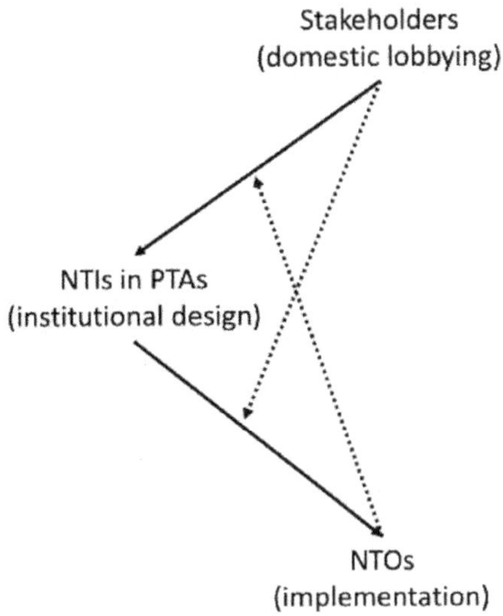

Figure 1.8 Implementation-focused research agenda (solid line represents direct effect and dotted line mediating effect)

as well as which policy instruments should be utilized to pursue them. Yet, we still lack understanding of how policies are implemented in third countries – e.g., whether domestic policy changes have taken place – and what influence stakeholders have on policy design and implementation.

Shedding light on implementation of non-trade policies in third countries is critical to understanding the EU's ability to exercise its soft power and produce change in areas beyond trade. Theorizing about the EU's soft power is only credible if we know what changes are actually taking place – and if not, what can be done to remedy non-compliance. In this context, we raise three research questions. First, which institutional design of NTIs in PTAs fosters domestic policy change? Second, and strongly linked to the first question, how and under what conditions do domestic stakeholders influence the effect of NTIs in PTAs on NTOs – e.g., the implementation of NTIs? Third, to what degree does the domestic implementation or non-implementation of NTIs in PTAs affect stakeholder lobbying on the institutional design of NTIs in PTAs? Figure 1.8 summarizes these interconnected questions for the purpose of an expanded research agenda.

The first (and relatively naïve) question points to the fact that only a few studies actually discuss the effect of NTIs on NTOs. The reason for this is twofold: (a) data on NTOs is difficult to match to the requirements posed by NTIs in PTAs and (b) the pathway from treaty to implementation is complex. Careful consideration is necessary to find measures that truly capture the implementation of NTIs and not general trends. What we mean by this is that the effect of a provision on equal opportunities at work can only be understood by knowing the de facto domestic changes in equal opportunities at work. Often, however, very specific clauses (such as equal opportunities at work) are matched with general trends such as performance in labor rights.

The second question points to the complexity from treaty to implementation, where we emphasize that domestic stakeholders moderate this effect. We should observe different political mobilization strategies as well as different preferences of stakeholders over the implementation of NTIs. For instance, we could expect more skeptical stakeholders – e.g. importers – to be in favor of less stringent implementation requirements for NTIs. These actors might mobilize in favor of particular policy instruments such as bilateral dialogues or push for vague implementation requirements in trade agreements. It might be in the interest of other actors, however, to downplay the severity of domestic NTI violations. To better understand the implementation of non-trade objectives, we suggest that future research focus on the political mobilization of stakeholders and the conditions under which they can influence policy outcomes.

Related to the third question, Cezar (2020) has shown – in a qualitative study on NAFTA – that it is reasonable to expect stakeholders to adapt their lobbying behavior based on implementation of existing policies. In other words, certain organized interests might find it best to avoid making their political activity public if they believe past trade agreements have yielded little actual change in their trade partners. If stakeholders are convinced of window-dressing policies and prefer the status quo, they are likely to redirect their political activities to other areas.

In conclusion, we want to highlight that theory-driven empirical research on NTIs is limited to what it can offer without additional data. The political dynamics of NTI inclusion and implementation requires researchers to gather additional data on stakeholder preferences and political activity. In order to shed light on the impact of stakeholders on the design of policy instruments, and the effect of such policies on the political mobilization of organized interests, we need to undertake extremely difficult, but necessary, data-gathering exercises. Stakeholder preferences should be matched with lobbying data that can help us understand the extent to which actors' expressed preferences are in line with their behavior. Such data on political activity would be particularly useful if we can gather additional data on implementation of non-trade policies in third countries. Doing so would reveal stakeholder behavior regarding implementation – and the extent to which they mobilize over implementation – ultimately helping us better understand the dynamics of trade and non-trade linkages.

References

Barbu, M., Campling, L., Smith, A., Harrison, J., and Richardson, B. 2018. The Trade–Labour Nexus: Global Value Chains and Labour Provisions in European Union Free Trade Agreements. *Global Labour Journal*, 9(3): 258–280. https://doi.org/10.15173/glj.v9i3.3354

Bastiaens, I., and Postnikov, E. 2017. Greening Up: The Effects of Environmental Standards in EU and US Trade Agreements. *Environmental Politics*, 26(5): 847–869. https://doi.org/10.1080/09644016.2017.1338213

Bluth, C. 2018. A Safety Net to Foster Support for Trade and Globalisation. Global Economic Dynamics, Bertelsmann Stiftung. www.bertelsmann-stiftung.de/de/publikationen/publikation/did/a-safety-net-to-foster-support-for-trade-and-globalisation/

Bouwen, P. 2002. Corporate Lobbying in the European Union: The Logic of Access. *Journal of European Public Policy*, 9(3): 365–390.

Cezar, R. F. 2020. Change and Continuity from NAFTA to NAFTA: Policy Feedbacks and the Design of Labor Provisions in Preferential Trade Agreements. Seminar Paper at PEIO. www.peio.me/wp-content/uploads/2021/papers/PEIOo21_paper_52.pdf

De Ville, F., and Siles-Brügge, G. 2017. Why TTIP Is a Game-Changer and Its Critics Have a Point. *Journal of European Public Policy*, 24(10): 1491–1505.

DeSombre, E. 2000. *Domestic Sources of International Environmental Policy*. Cambridge, MA: MIT Press.

Dür, A., and De Bièvre, D. 2007. Inclusion without Influence? NGOs in European Trade Policy. *Journal of Public Policy*, 27(1): 79–101.

Eckhardt, J. 2015. *Business Lobbying and Trade Governance: The Case of EU–China Relations*. Basingstoke: Palgrave Macmillan.

Eliasson, L. J., and Garcia-Duran, P. 2018. TTIP Negotiations: Interest Groups, Anti-TTIP Civil Society Campaigns and Public Opinion. *Journal of Transatlantic Studies*, 16(2): 101–116.

FIDH. 2013. Open Letter. Vietnam and Free Trade Agreement Negotiations: NGOs Urge the EU to Carry Out a Human Rights Impact Assessment. Press Release. www.fidh.org/en/asia/vietnam/open-letter-vietnam-and-free-trade-agreement-negotiationsngos-urge-the-eu-13221

Fiorini, M., Hoekman, B., Ralaison, N., and Yildirim, A. 2019. The RESPECT Survey Instrument. EUI Working Paper RSCAS 2019/59. http://respect.eui.eu/publications/

Fritz, T. 2010. *The Second Conquest: The EU Free Trade Agreement with Colombia and Peru*. Amsterdam: Transnational Institute.

Harrison, J., Barbu, M., Campling, L., Richardson, B., and Smith, A. 2019. Governing Labour Standards through Free Trade Agreements: Limits of the European Union's Trade and Sustainable Development Chapters. *Journal of Common Market Studies*, 57(2): 260–277. https://doi.org/10.1111/jcms.12715.

Hirsch, M. 2017. Identity Matters: The Enforcement of Global Human Rights Treaties by European Union's Trade Instruments. In *International Economic Law and Human Rights*, ed. L. Biukovic and P. Potter. Cheltenham: Edward Elgar.

Lechner, L. 2016. The Domestic Battle over the Design of Non-Trade Issues in Preferential Trade Agreements. *Review of International Political Economy*, 23 (5): 840–871.

Lechner, L. 2018. Good for Some, Bad for Others: US Investors and Non-Trade Issues in Preferential Trade Agreements. *Review of International Organizations*, 13(2): 162–187.

Lechner, L. 2019. The Trend to More and Stricter Non-Trade Issues in Preferential Trade Agreements. In *The Shifting Landscape of Global Trade Governance*, ed. M. Elsig, M. Hahn, and G. Spilker. Cambridge: Cambridge University Press.

Meunier, S., and Nicolaidis, K. 2006. The European Union as a Conflicted Trade Power. *Journal of European Public Policy*, 13(6): 906–925.

Morin, J.-F., Dür, A., and Lechner, L. 2018. Mapping the Trade and Environment Nexus: Insights from a New Data Set. *Global Environmental Politics*, 18(1): 122–139. https://doi.org/10.1162/GLEP_a_00447

Poletti, A., and Sicurelli, D. 2016. The European Union, Preferential Trade Agreements, and the International Regulation of Sustainable Biofuels. *Journal of Common Market Studies*, 54(2): 249–266.

Poletti, A., and Sicurelli, D. 2018. *The Political Economy of Normative Trade Power Europe*. London: Palgrave Macmillan.

Poletti, A., Sicurelli, D., and Yildirim, A. 2020. Promoting Sustainable Development through Trade? EU Trade Agreements and Global Value Chains. *Italian Political Science Review*, 51, 339–354.

Pollack, M. A., and Shaffer, G. C. 2009. *When Cooperation Fails: The International Law and Politics of Genetically Modified Foods*. New York: Oxford University Press.

Postnikov, E. 2019. Unravelling the Puzzle of Social Standards' Design in EU and US Trade Agreements. *New Political Economy*, 24(2): 181–196.

Raess, D., and Sari, D. 2016. *LABPTA: Labour Provisions in Trade Agreements (LABPTA): Introducing a New Dataset*. Working Paper. https://snis.ch/wp-content/uploads/2020/01/2014_Raess_Working-Paper.pdf. https://snis.ch/projects/a-social-clause-through-the-back-door-labor-provisions-in-preferential-trade-agreements/

Raess, D., Dür, A., and Sari, D. 2018. Protecting Labor Rights in Preferential Trade Agreements: The Role of Trade Unions, Left Governments and Skilled Labor. *Review of International Organizations*, 13: 143–162.

Rasch, G. (1980). *Probabilistic Models for Some Intelligence and Attainment Tests.* Chicago: University of Chicago Press.

Rose, M. 2020, May 10. French, Dutch Join Forces to Urge EU to Show Teeth on Trade. *Reuters.* www.reuters.com/article/us-eu-trade-france-netherlands/french-dutch-join-forces-to-urge-eu-to-show-teeth-on-trade-idUSKBN22M0CH

Van den Hoven, A. 2006. European Union Regulatory Capitalism and Multilateral Trade Negotiations. In *Values and Principles in European Foreign Policy*, ed. S. Lucarelli and I. Manners. London: Routledge.

Van den Putte, L. 2015. EU Bilateral Trade Agreements and the Surprising Rise of Labour Provisions. *International Journal of Comparative Labour Law and Industrial Relations*, 31(3): 263–283. www.kluwerlawonline.com/api/Product/CitationPDFURL?file=Journals%5CIJCL%5CIJCL2015015.pdf

Van den Putte, L., and Orbie, J. 2015. EU Bilateral Trade Agreements and the Surprising Rise of Labour Provisions. *International Journal of Comparative Labour Law and Industrial Relations*, 31(3): 263–283.

Vogel, D. 1995. *Trading Up: Consumer and Environmental Regulation in the Global Economy.* Cambridge, MA: Harvard University Press.

Woll, C. 2009. Who Captures Whom? Trade Policy Lobbying in the European Union. In *Lobbying in the European Union*, ed. D. Coen and J. Richardson. Oxford: Oxford University Press.

Yildirim, A. 2017. Firms' Integration into Value Chains and Compliance with Adverse WTO Panel Rulings. *World Trade Review*, 17(1): 1–31.

Yildirim, A., Fiorini, M., Hoekman, B., and Basedow, R. 2020. Non-Trade Objectives and EU Trade Policy: Looking beyond Trade Agreements., *Journal of Common Market Studies*, 59(3): 556–568. https://doi.org/10.1111/jcms.13100.

Young, A. 2015. Liberalizing Trade, not Exporting Rules: The Limits to Regulatory Co-ordination in the EU's "New Generation" Preferential Trade Agreements. *Journal of European Public Policy*, 22(9): 1253–1275.

Young, A. 2016. Not Your Parents' Trade Politics: The Transatlantic Trade and Investment Partnership Negotiations. *Review of International Political Economy*, 23(3): 345–378.

Young, A., and Peterson, J. 2014. *Parochial Global Europe: 21st Century Trade Politics.* Oxford: Oxford University Press.

2

The European Union

Soft and Smart Power in Aid and Trade?

PETER HOLMES, JULIA MAGNTORN GARRETT, AND JIM ROLLO

Introduction

This chapter explores the ability of the EU to act coherently through its institutions and its Member States to influence attitudes and non-trade policies across the world through soft power and trade-related policies, notably through aid policies. The questions we aim to address include:

- What is "soft power"?
- How is it related to trade and aid policies?
- Do the EU institutions and the Member States project the same values and strive towards the same objectives via trade-related policies? And are these more coherent within the EU than with an outside country such as the United States?

The first section of this chapter explores the notion of "soft power". On close examination, it emerges that the term soft power as originally used by J. Nye has an extremely narrow meaning: "Soft power is the ability to obtain preferred outcomes by attraction rather than coercion or payment" (Nye, 2017:2). In its original meaning, soft power is not an instrument that can be used, but rather it is a kind of gravitational or reputational force exuded by a country or region whose polity and culture creates admiration and goodwill, and inspires a wish by other

This is based on part of a longer joint study undertaken in partnership with ECDPM as part of the H2020 RESPECT project (see Apiko et al., 2019). The authors are extremely grateful to RESPECT colleagues Bernard Hoekman, San Bilal, Kathleen van Hove, Kamala Dawar, Dan Liu, and Jacques Pelkmans for advice; and to Sewek Gasiorek and Anna Szamely for excellent research assistance; to Dr. Hammed Roohani for surveying the IR literature on soft and smart power; and to Charlotte Humma for editorial support.

countries to imitate.[1] Soft power is therefore not so much exercised as experienced, and, in Nye's view, it emanates from civil society even more than from government. It is necessary here to point out that soft power in the strictest sense of the term differs sharply from the notion of "soft law" as discussed in the seminal article by Abbott and Snidal (2000). Soft law creates obligations that are somewhat imprecise, with unclear enforcement mechanisms, but with obligations nonetheless. Soft power may well be conducive to the signing of agreements but pure soft power creates a wish on the side of one party to follow the approach of the other.

The most striking example of EU soft power occurred in the early 1990s when there was a rush by Central and Eastern European countries (CEECs) to join the EU after the collapse of communism, although not in any way led by the EU itself. Soft power manifested itself in the wish of countries such as Poland to copy the EU regulatory model. The Commission of the European Communities (CEC, 1995) White Paper gave the EU's view on the link between trade and regulation and spelt out conditions for market access. Nye later acknowledged the limits of the concept of soft power. For Nye, *any* use of coercion or incentives are forms of hard power and any combination of carrots and sticks in a context where there is soft power in place qualifies as *smart power*.[2] Smart power is a package in which soft power supports the use of harder power tools. There is a perception, especially in the United States, that the EU is trying to export its regulatory integration model by demonstrating that integration and regulatory harmonisation are consistent with improved economic welfare. To the extent that other countries spontaneously copy the EU, this is pure soft power, but where the EU gives incentives in the form of trade and aid policies this is better described as "smart power". The very process of collective action by the EU, as illustrated by the evolution of the EU system, may generate soft power, though utilising this needs "smart power" as well.

Our study is therefore about the interrelationship of soft power and smart power with each other and with trade and aid policy. In the second section of this chapter, we look at the extent to which the EU is able to diffuse its values in a way that might eventually lead to the adoption of similar regulatory norms. We seek to identify the role of "soft power" in trade and trade-related policies and to assess how far there is coherence between the EU institutions and the Member States. Clearly, individual

[1] Soft power as a cultural force is extensively dealt with in Chitty et al. (2016).

[2] Interestingly, Nye developed his ideas further in evidence he gave to the UK House of Lords' study of the United Kingdom's soft power influence (Nye, 2013).

Member States do not have separate national trade policies, but they do have their own *trade-related policies*. One of the most important of such related policies is development aid. The ability to use aid to influence domestic regulatory policy depends on the initial predisposition for or against such alignment – that is, the existence of soft power. Recipients are more willing to accept aid with conditions from countries with which they feel an affinity. This often includes relations with ex-colonies. During a study we took part in (Gu et al., 2017) comparing UK–China relations with countries in Africa, we found that there was more suspicion of China's aid interventions than the United Kingdom's on the part of African partners, which was clearly related to the nature of soft links associated with the colonial past.

In our review of the soft power literature, we found a number of references to aid and trade policies as soft power, an issue we discuss in the next section, before moving on to our empirical work. Here, we explore the degree of similarity in the values projected through the EU's trade-focused aid (notably Aid for Trade) and the interrelationship between the non-trade objectives embodied in the EU's trade policy and aid programmes of the EU Institutions and the Member States. When we undertook this study, the United Kingdom was part of the EU. We found the United Kingdom's orientation was a little less aligned to that of the EU institutions than France or Germany but no less so than the Netherlands.

Conceptual Considerations: Soft and Smart Power

Definition and Definitional Issues

It is hard to define soft power, and it is even harder to explicitly delineate its dimensions and the conditions under which it manifests itself (see, for instance, Dunn, 2009:41; Commuri, 2012:43). Even though the concept is frequently used in academic as well as policy circles, as noted by Commuri (2012:43), it is a term that defies generalisation. Soft power is a hybrid concept which may shape agendas in ways akin to Mann's (2012) concept of ideological power.

Soft power as a concept was introduced – in fact reintroduced, as the idea had been around for a long time – in the 1990s by Joseph Nye in a series of studies, and Nye has remained the main reference for the concept ever since. The basic idea is that, rather than coercing, soft power co-opts; the thesis is that once a country is admired for its values, or for its general success, other countries will want to follow it and such a desire has a meaningful effect on the outcomes. To Nye, soft power is the "power of attraction", the influence of example, as opposed to the influence derived from harder forms of power that include coercion or inducement (such as military force, economic sanctions and even economic aid). That is, soft power is the power to seduce others to follow you because of the magnetism exerted by your culture, political values or foreign policies (Nye, 2004:11). Nye (2008b) states: "Soft power is the ability to affect others to obtain the outcomes one wants through attraction rather than coercion or payment. A country's soft power rests on its resources of culture, values, and policies". This is the core definition that we find most helpful, though we acknowledge we may find ourselves using the term more loosely.

Nye argues that both hard power and soft power are important – for instance in the war on terrorism – but attraction is much cheaper than coercion, and an asset that needs to be nourished (Nye, 2004). However, as Lawson (2015:105) has noted, Nye warned that arrogance can turn attraction to repulsion, the consequences of which are significant for a country's influence and security.

Measuring Soft Power

Scholars are puzzled by the processes through which soft power unfolds and its impact on bringing about desired policy change. Intuitively we understand that soft power must exist and does exist, and yet attempts to grasp it give only limited clarity. Many political scientists believe that soft power, like other demonstrations of power, are abstract concepts that cannot be measured objectively and precisely. Power – in general – is a contested concept in political science (Badie et al., 2011).

For the same reason, one cannot readily measure the extent to which the soft power exercised (or possessed) by the individual EU Member States contradicts or enhances the EU's soft power as a solidarity unit. The annual Softpower30 reports[3] are an attempt to quantify soft power by worldwide polling and the use of digital indicators of influence. The report ranks countries of the world based on six components: digital, cultural, enterprise, engagement, education, government. This index includes factors such as the reputation of universities, tourist attractions, internet connectivity and attitude surveys. In all years since 2015, three out of the top five countries have been EU Member States (the United Kingdom, France and Germany). In 2019, four out of the top five were EU countries, as Sweden was scored at number four.

[3] https://softpower30.com/blog/

Studies have identified a number of factors that may decrease or increase a country's soft power. The use of hard power may, for example, diminish an actor's soft power. Indeed, the EU has hoped to be able to benefit from its "non-threatening" attitude towards its neighbours to induce them to adopt its norms even if it is hesitant about accepting them as members.[4]

Some studies also suggest that the rise of soft power of one actor may decrease the soft power of another. In a *Wall Street Journal* Commentary, Nye (2005) highlights that China pursues its interests through dialogue and cooperation based on accepted norms of culture, political values and diplomacy, rather than through unilateral action. China's increasing adherence to soft power has increased its regional dominance at the expense of the United States and Japan. By engaging in a variety of multilateral settings, China claims its own status as a great power. It participates in multilateral forums such as "ASEAN+1", where Beijing is capable of playing a leadership role and garnering "soft power" through the provision of collective goods such as market access, development funding and common security through secure frontiers and common opposition to separatism (Kavalski, 2009:54). China would gain soft power in this context by making unilateral concessions to others and generating goodwill.

Having strong scientific institutions such as top universities also boosts soft power. According to Archibugi and Filippetti (2015:64), there has been a proliferation of academic rankings of world universities in recent years, but their importance has gone beyond the interests of students and university administrators and has caught the attention of policymakers. Having top universities will secure global "soft power" in the sense of "knowledge is power". The attraction and retention of international talent by its top universities feeds into a country's knowledge system by boosting its innovation capacity.

The concept of soft power has been applied in many areas, political, economic and social; it appears in conjunction with terms such as culture, communication and international cooperation.

[4] https://europe.unc.edu/iron-curtain/power-and-politics-the-prisoners-dilemma/the-eu-and-soft-power/. Monocle, https://monocle.com/film/affairs/soft-power-survey-2016-17/, carried out its survey in late 2016 and had the United States at the top of the table, while surely correctly anticipating that the election of President Trump was likely to change that (Brown, 2019:132).

Soft Power Shaping the International System

Power is addressed in different guises; hard power, soft power, smart power, structural power, sticky power and so on. The relationship between these types of power is complicated and multidimensional.

As far as hard power and soft power are concerned, the main question is whether they are substitutes or complementary. The answer is affirmative to both questions. As expressed earlier, the two can be substitutes because the more an actor exercises its hard power the less its soft power will be. It is unlikely that the United States gained soft power in the Trump era and uncertain if the United Kingdom's passion for sovereignty post-Brexit will create more influence.

The concept of smart power captures the complementarity between soft and hard power. According to Nye (2009), *smart power* involves an intelligent combination of the two, to advance an actor's strategic purposes. Bjola and Kornprobst (2018:192) similarly state that smart power brings together hard and soft power via the strategic and simultaneous use of coercion and co-option. In other words, smart power is the capacity of an actor to combine elements of hard power with the impact of soft power in ways that are mutually reinforcing, such that the actor's purposes are advanced effectively and efficiently (Wilson, 2008:110).

This represents not a repudiation of realist premises but, rather, a combination of realist and liberal perspectives in what its proponents see as a more efficacious way forward for actors' foreign policy in the contemporary period (Lawson, 2015:106). This conceptualisation is driven by the Liberal approach that observes the international scene, in which the logic of confrontation does not disappear to the benefit of the logic of influence, but is integrated into a continuum which deeply renews diplomatic action. On this matter, Bjola and Kornprobst (2018) explain that the reasoning behind smart power is that, by combining hard and soft power, the limitations of each could be offset by the strengths of the other. The way to achieve this is by making sure that the elements of hard power (military intervention, legal sanctions, economic conditionality) and soft power (for example public diplomacy, educational exchange) of a diplomatic strategy reinforce rather than undermine each other.

Smart power is very much used in conjunction with diplomacy, both inter-state and public diplomacy. As noted by Ruffini (2017:13–14), smart power as a concept in the field of diplomacy or foreign and security policy was defended by US former Secretary of State Hillary Clinton in the Senate's Foreign Relations Committee: "We must use what has been called 'smart power', the full range of tools at our disposal – diplomatic, economic, military, political, legal, and cultural – picking the right tool, or combination of tools, for each situation."[5] This approach is also central to the foreign policy of emerging countries such as Brazil, China and India (Foucher, 2013:10; see also Ruffini, 2017).

For many, smart power is less an issue of catalysing diplomatic transformations in various regions of strategic interest, but rather one of pragmatically building alliances by investing in the production and delivery of global public goods. As pointed out by Nye and Armitage in their report on smart power, "states and non-state actors who improve their ability to draw in allies will gain competitive advantages in today's environment. Those who alienate potential friends will stand at greater risk" (Armitage and Nye, 2007:10). The upshot of this argument is that, similar to soft power, smart power requires a broader time horizon to yield results, but like hard power, it requires significant material resources to create, deliver and sustain global public goods.

Trade and Trade-Focused Aid: Moving from Soft to Smart Power

Soft and Smart Power in the European Union

The theoretical review in the previous section has interesting implications for EU trade and aid policy. In a country over which the EU has soft power – that is, a country which has goodwill towards the EU – the amount of suasion that is needed by the EU to achieve a certain outcome is lessened. In an extreme case, the partner will have internalised EU norms so much that it voluntarily does what the EU would wish it to do in a spirit of emulation. For example, during the cold war era many countries wished to copy the US example; this was followed in the 1990s by an era in which the neighbours of the EU sought to adopt the EU's social and economic model and values in their entirety. A small example would be Kosovo's introduction of a public smoking ban.[6] More remotely, during participation in a study on the impact of the EU's Generalised Scheme of Preferences Plus (GSP+) conditionality in Pakistan the point was repeatedly made in consultation meetings in Islamabad that many (if not all) actors in Pakistan positively welcomed

[5] https://2009-2017.state.gov/secretary/20092013clinton/rm/index.htm
[6] https://balkaninsight.com/2013/04/05/kosovo-bans-smoking-in-public-areas/

the incentives to respect labour rights embodied in GSP+ conditionality. These were aspirations embodied in the constitution which it was sometimes hard to fulfil (see Development Solutions, 2017).

The lesson from our reading is that trade and trade-related policies, such as trade-focused aid, while not coercive, embody incentives and carry implicit penalties, and as such these policies do not by themselves constitute soft power, but they may create it if the EU action is welcomed by the other party/parties.

For simplicity, we will sometimes write as if there is a single package incorporating soft and smart power, though the reader should be aware of the underlying distinction. In the next section, we seek to explore the way that the EU collectively, and as individual Member States, tries to achieve what could, very loosely, be described as soft power objectives, by which we mean the values it aims to instil in other countries. We do not have a precise index of soft power or a way to measure its link with policies. Therefore, our analysis is necessarily indirect, and we infer the soft power objectives of the EU institutions and the Member States by looking at the values that are promoted through trade and trade-related policies. More precisely, we aim to explore whether the institutions of the EU, and the Member States, appear to support the same goals and project the same values.

Since trade policy is uniform across Member States, we focus on an area where Member States have autonomy over their own policies. Trade-focused aid (such as Aid for Trade) is particularly interesting in this light, since it "blurs the distinction between the European Union (EU)-member state shared competence of development with the EU single competence of trade" (Brazys and Lightfoot, 2016:120).

Data and Methodology

We set out to map the way that the EU Institutions and Member States[7] deploy their potential smart power by looking at data on development aid, and the link between this and EU trade policy. We hope that by looking at the coherence of the EU's approach we may gain an insight into the way that the EU can potentially create soft power, by inducing countries to adopt its values. A higher degree of coherence in

[7] The United Kingdom was a member of the European Union during the years covered by our analysis and is therefore referred to here as a Member State of the EU.

the values it is projecting may give a higher chance of partners signing up to common principles.

We use development finance data from the OECD's Development Assistance Committee (DAC) Creditor Reporting System (CRS), and construct a dataset containing bilateral Official Development Assistance (ODA) commitments by EU Member State donors, as well as by EU institutions over the period 1997–2017. This dataset covers 206 individual aid sectors/purposes and around 200 different aid recipients. We only include aid given to developing countries and thus exclude any aid given to multilateral organisations. Further, since we are interested in the link between aid allocations and strategic objectives in a given year, we choose to look at aid commitments rather than aid disbursements. The former measures new undertakings by each donor in a relevant year, and thus gives a sense of the donors' intentions in a given year. In contrast, aid disbursements measure the actual payments made by a donor in a given year, and, as there are sometimes lags between a commitment and a payment, disbursements can reflect commitments made several years in the past.

We wish to establish the level of coherence (similarity) between EU institutions' aid allocations and those of individual Member States. To do this we use a Finger–Kreinin Index (Finger and Kreinin, 1979). The Finger–Kreinin Index (FKI) provides a way of measuring the similarity of two sets of numbers. In the equation below, i_1 and i_2 are two donor countries, x^k refers to the aid flow by functional category k, and X refers to total aid across all categories. Thus, $x^k{}_{i1}/X_{i1}$ is the share of country i_1's total aid that is allocated to category k. $x^k{}_{i2}/X_{i2}$ is the corresponding share of category k in the comparator country (i_2)'s total aid. The FKI essentially measures the minimum overlap between these two shares, and sums across all categories to obtain a figure for the overall overlap/similarity between country i_1 and i_2's aid allocation by aid category. The same formula applies when measuring the similarity across k aid recipients rather than aid categories.

$$FKI_{i_1 i_2} = \sum_k \min\left[\left(\frac{x^k_{i_1}}{X_{i_1}}\right), \left(\frac{x^k_{i_2}}{X_{i_2}}\right)\right]$$

The FKI varies between 0 and 1, where an FKI equal to 1 means that a pair of countries have identical proportions of aid spending across all relevant categories or recipients. When the indicator is equal to zero, this means that there is no aid spending in common. A key advantage of using the FKI, compared to a simple measure of correlation, is that FKIs are, by design, well equipped to handle data where observations are restricted to taking values between 0 and 1. In contrast, correlation coefficients are known to be reduced when the range of one or both variables are truncated (Im et al., 2017). This is important since we are predominantly working with proportions of aid commitments, whether by functional category or by recipient, which by its nature are restricted to the (0,1) range.

Aid for Trade: Coherence between Member States and EU Institutions

Aid for Trade: An Overview

In 2005 the WTO launched the Aid for Trade (AfT) initiative. Aid for Trade aims to help developing countries take advantage of trade as an engine for growth, by assisting them in tackling domestic obstacles which act as internal barriers to trade. Overall, the AfT programme is focused on four key areas:[8]

1. **Technical assistance for trade policy and regulations**: includes help to develop trade strategies, negotiate and implement trade agreements.
2. **Economic infrastructure**: help to build roads and ports in order to better connect domestic regions with markets abroad, as well as improvements to telecommunications networks.
3. **Productive capacity building**: includes aid aimed at supporting the private sector to diversify exports and make the most of their comparative advantages.
4. **Trade-related adjustment assistance**: helps developing countries with the costs arising from trade liberalisation.

Since the AfT programme was designed to cover a wide range of potential barriers to trade, it is classified in relatively broad terms. The categories defined under Aid for Trade cover around 37 per cent of EU Institutions' total bilateral ODA commitments by value, 30 per cent for France and 22 per cent, 19 per cent and 16 per cent for Germany, the Netherlands and the United Kingdom respectively. The broad classification of AfT has raised concerns as to whether some of the projects

[8] There is a further AfT category, "Other trade-related needs". However, no data is collected by OECD for this category and as such we do not consider this category when analysing Aid for Trade commitments. For more information, see www.oecd.org/dac/aft/aid-fortradestatisticalqueries.htm

classified as AfT may in reality have limited trade focus (Brazys and Lightfoot, 2016). Nevertheless, Aid for Trade is an adopted definition widely used in the context of trade and development, and we therefore use this definition in most of our analysis.

The EU adopted an Aid for Trade Strategy in 2007, which was subsequently updated in 2017. The 2007 strategy identified five key objectives:

(1) "Increasing the collective volumes of EU AfT within the ambitious development commitments to raise overall EU aid gradually";
(2) "Enhancing the pro-poor focus and quality of EU AfT";
(3) "Increasing EU-wide and Member States' donors capacity in line with globally agreed aid effectiveness principles";
(4) "Building upon, fostering and supporting ACP regional integration processes with an ACP-specific angle of the Joint EU AfT Strategy"; and
(5) "Supporting effective AfT monitoring and reporting" (Council of the European Union, 2007).

The subsequent 2017 strategy emphasised the need to address the fragmentation of EU AfT, and "improve the coordination and coherence of their [the EU institutions and the Member States] AfT with other forms of assistance", as well as the need to enhance the coherence of AfT with EU trade policy, and increase AfT for Least Developed Countries (LDCs) (Council of the European Union, 2017).

Development assistance is given directly by the individual Member States, and each Member State has autonomy over how to allocate its bilateral aid. In addition, there is aid administered centrally at the EU, by EU institutions such as the Directorate-General for International Cooperation and Development (DG DEVCO) at the European Commission. Even at the central EU level (EU Institutions), EU Member States can influence the aid spending. At the European Development Fund (EDF), for example, new projects must be approved by at least thirteen Member States, whose voting weights are in part determined by the amount of money the Member States contribute to the EDF (Concord, 2012).

While the EU's Aid for Trade strategy aims to establish a collective EU strategy, development policy in the European Union is an area of "soft law" (Orbie and Carbone, 2016). Indeed, while trade policy is an exclusive competence of the European Commission, aid policy is not. This is also recognised in the 2007 AfT strategy which states that "'the EU will' should be understood as referring to Member States and the Commission acting on a voluntary and flexible basis, fully respecting existing competences".

Since development policy is an area of soft law, Member States are able to allocate aid to purposes, and to recipient countries, according to their own strategic interests and priorities. Due to the lack of *de jure* obligations in this area, if the Member States and EU institutions allocate their aid to similar purposes or countries, this can be viewed as a manifestation of the Member States and the EU Institutions voluntarily (or coincidentally) projecting similar values (Brazys and Lightfoot, 2016).

Of course, although Member States ultimately decide over their own aid spending, this does not necessarily mean that they do so in isolation. Indeed, the European Commission's Code of Conduct on Division of Labour in Development Policy (CEC, 2007) presents a set of concrete measures that aim to enhance the complementarity and coordination of aid spending by EU donors. The communication states that "complementarity starts with co-ordination, but goes much further: it implies that each actor is focusing its assistance on areas where it can add most value, given what others are doing". Thus, the communication encourages EU donors to divide aid spending between themselves to let each donor focus on its areas of comparative advantage. It also aims to avoid certain areas, whether within countries or across countries, being saturated while others are under-funded.

If such coordination between EU institutions and the Member States is widespread, it could result in very little overlap (similarity) across aid allocations, as each Member State focuses on its particular area of responsibility while relying on other donors to cover other areas. Since we are looking at the similarity (overlap) of aid commitments between EU Institutions and EU Member States, this could pose a problem for our methodology.

However, we do not believe this to be a significant threat to our analysis for two main reasons: First, even the Code of Conduct acknowledges that, since development aid is part of donor countries' foreign policy, donors may be reluctant to give up aid cooperation in a given sector or country, as it may lead to reduced visibility for their actions. In addition, as development policy often involves a considerable amount of money, "EU member states continue to jealously guard their national prerogatives in this area" and there still exist strong national identities in development policy (Orbie and Carbone, 2016). Previous work looking at EU Member States' Aid for Trade Strategies has found considerable variation between Member States in their degree of "Europeanisation" (Brazys and Lightfoot, 2016).

Second, the correlation between EU Member States and EU Institutions' total aid allocations, by aid category or by recipient, are almost all positive, indicating that the EU and its Member States are to some extent pulling in the same direction.[9] If there was widespread division of labour within EU aid policy, we would expect a higher degree of negative correlations. With this in mind, we believe that the level of coordination between EU Member States is unlikely to seriously undermine our analysis, although it should still be kept in mind.

Similarity of Aid for Trade Commitments by Aid Category

Among the four key areas of AfT, "Productive capacity building" and "Economic infrastructure" are by far the biggest two in value terms, for both the EU Institutions and its Member States. Looking at a slightly more disaggregated level (across eleven different categories),[10] Energy Generation, Transport and Storage, Banking and Financial Services and Agriculture have accounted for over 80 per cent of EU Institutions' total Aid for Trade in all years from 2012 onwards, and similarly also for many Member States.

At the most detailed level, 104 different functional aid categories are defined as Aid for Trade in the Organisation for Economic Co-operation and Development (OECD) data. This covers around half of all functional categories to which aid can be allocated. Table 2.1 shows the similarity between some of the key EU Member States' and EU Institutions' aid allocations across these functional categories. We start from the year 2007, as this was the year when the EU's AfT strategy was introduced. If the share of a Member State's AfT is distributed identically to that of the EU Institutions, this would give a similarity index of 1 in that year. If, on the other hand, no aid allocations are common, this would give a score of 0.

It can be seen that both Germany and France have become gradually more aligned with EU Institutions in their allocation of Aid for Trade across aid categories. In fact, out of all the Member States reported in OECD's dataset, they have consistently been the most similar to EU Institutions in the most recent years of data. Further, complementary analysis assessing the similarity of aid allocations to those of the United States shows that both are considerably more similar to the EU than they are to the United States.

[9] This largely holds also when looking only at AfT allocations, although negative correlations are somewhat more prevalent in this case, particularly when looking at AfT by recipient country.

[10] These categories are Banking and Financial Services, Business and other services, Energy generation, distribution and efficiency, Fishing, Forestry, Industry, Mineral resources and mining, Tourism, Trade policy and regulations, Trade-related adjustment, and Transport and storage.

Table 2.1 *Similarity of total Aid for Trade commitments by functional category, with EU as base*

Year	US	FRA	DEU	NLD	GBR
2007	0.51	0.10	0.27	0.31	0.21
2008	0.40	0.14	0.18	0.35	0.29
2009	0.39	0.27	0.18	0.20	0.39
2010	0.59	0.25	0.25	0.20	0.37
2011	0.36	0.35	0.37	0.17	0.26
2012	0.26	0.32	0.48	0.42	0.39
2013	0.34	0.34	0.51	0.24	0.55
2014	0.17	0.28	0.54	0.11	0.60
2015	0.32	0.42	0.63	0.30	0.29
2016	0.41	0.63	0.56	0.17	0.40
2017	0.42	0.46	0.61	0.31	0.36
Average	***0.38***	***0.32***	***0.42***	***0.25***	***0.37***

Data on total Aid for Trade commitments across 104 sectors, from the OECD's Creditor Reporting System (CRS), bulk download 22 July 2019. The Finger–Kreinin Index is based on the share of each sector in total AfT commitments by donor and gives an index for the similarity of Member States' AfT spending and that of the EU Institutions.

The United Kingdom displayed a high degree of similarity with EU Institutions in 2013–2014, in part driven by spending a relatively large share of AfT on formal-sector financial intermediaries in those years, but less so in more recent years. However, the United Kingdom still shows a higher degree of similarity with the EU than with the United States. In contrast, the Netherlands does not appear to have become more aligned with the EU over the time period. In fact, the Netherlands appears to be somewhat more similar to the United States than to the EU.

Similarity of Aid for Trade Commitments by Aid Recipient

Table 2.2 gives total AfT commitments across twelve recipient groups in 2017. The recipient groups are defined according to their trade relationship with the EU in 2017. The table gives the share of each donor's AfT that is allocated to each region and also the respective AfT per capita given to each region.

The largest share (21.7 per cent) of EU Institutions' Aid for Trade is allocated to the Customs Union (CU) group, which reflects the aid given

Table 2.2 *Total AfT commitments to developing countries, by recipient category in 2017*

Trade relation with the EU	EU institutions		US		Germany		France		United Kingdom		Netherlands	
	Share of total AfT (%)	Total AfT per capita	Share of total AfT (%)	Total AfT per capita	Share of total AfT (%)	Total AfT per capita	Share of total AfT (%)	Total AfT per capita	Share of total AfT (%)	Total AfT per capita	Share of total AfT (%)	Total A4T per capita
AA	17.8	4.65	9.0	0.68	6.5	1.19	23.8	2.65	0.9	0.03	1.0	0.27
CU	21.7	22.35	0.0	0.01	0.3	0.22	1.4	0.56	0.1	0.01	0.0	0.00
EBA	10.6	0.98	36.0	0.97	10.9	0.70	15.0	0.58	11.3	0.17	20.5	0.27
EPA	6.3	2.53	6.0	0.74	5.2	1.44	6.2	1.04	0.5	0.03	6.2	0.47
FTA	2.4	0.89	3.2	0.34	3.6	0.92	9.2	1.33	0.5	0.03	0.0	0.00
GSP	7.7	0.32	4.9	0.06	26.6	0.76	15.6	0.26	3.8	0.02	1.4	0.03
GSP+	1.4	0.33	9.0	0.61	1.6	0.25	5.0	0.45	3.5	0.11	0.0	0.00
SAA	7.7	36.25	2.9	3.92	6.3	20.10	0.0	0.00	0.0	0.01	0.0	0.00
British OCT	0.0	0.00	0.0	0.00	0.0	0.00	0.0	0.00	0.5	612.52	0.0	0.00
French OCT	0.0	0.00	0.0	0.00	0.0	0.00	0.1	318.67	0.0	0.00	0.0	0.00
No pref.	5.9	0.24	5.0	0.06	7.8	0.22	5.9	0.10	4.9	0.03	4.1	0.26
Unspecified*	18.5	–	23.9	–	31.2	-	17.8	–	74.0	–	66.8	–

* The group "Unspecified" relates to aid allocated to wider regions, such as "Africa, regional" or "Central Asia, regional". As it is not possible to distinguish the individual aid recipients of such groups, we are unable to estimate the ODA per capita for this category.
Source: Data on total AfT commitments across all individual recipients from the OECD's Creditor Reporting System (CRS), bulk download 22 July 2019. Includes recipients unspecified by region. Population data for 2017 from the World Bank Development Indicators, supplemented with data from World Population Review.

Table 2.3 *Similarity of total Aid for Trade commitments by bilateral recipient, with EU as base*

Year	US	FRA	DEU	GBR	NLD
2007	0.16	0.21	0.27	0.12	0.23
2008	0.26	0.28	0.28	0.14	0.22
2009	0.23	0.18	0.23	0.24	0.18
2010	0.21	0.25	0.27	0.17	0.09
2011	0.18	0.09	0.24	0.13	0.05
2012	0.22	0.25	0.33	0.16	0.06
2013	0.23	0.17	0.37	0.18	0.07
2014	0.16	0.15	0.34	0.10	0.04
2015	0.22	0.36	0.50	0.24	0.10
2016	0.25	0.35	0.36	0.20	0.07
2017	0.27	0.31	0.39	0.19	0.09
Average	***0.22***	***0.24***	***0.33***	***0.17***	***0.11***

Data on total Aid for Trade commitments across aid recipients, from the OECD's Creditor Reporting System (CRS), bulk download 22 July 2019. The Finger–Kreinin Index is based on the share of each recipient in total AfT commitments by donor and gives an index for the similarity of Member States' AfT spending and that of the EU Institutions. Any recipients not identified by country (e.g. regional groupings or unspecified recipients) have been excluded.

to Turkey. Further, the countries with an Association Agreement (AA) with the EU also received a large share (17.8 per cent) of EU Institutions' AfT, followed by countries under the EU's Everything But Arms (EBA) programme (10.6 per cent). Only 5.9 per cent of EU Institutions' AfT in 2017 was allocated to countries with no preferential trade relationship with the EU.

These patterns are not matched in the key Member States. Barely any of Germany's Aid for Trade went to Turkey (the CU group). Instead, 26.6 per cent of Germany's total Aid for Trade was allocated to countries under the Generalised System of Preferences (GSP), and 10.9 per cent to Everything But Arms countries. In France, the AA countries received 23.8 per cent of total AfT, GSP countries received 15.6 per cent and the EBA group 15 per cent. The Netherlands and the UK allocated 20.5 and 11.3 per cent respectively of their total AfT to the EBA group.

Table 2.3 gives the similarity between EU Member States' AfT allocations across individual recipients compared to EU Institutions. Overall, there are around 170 individual aid recipients, excluding any regional groupings or recipients unspecified by country.

It is clear that there is less similarity across recipients than there was across aid categories (Table 2.1), although this could partly be driven by the fact that there are more recipients (170) than there were functional categories (104). It could also be driven by Member States and the EU coordinating better with respect to aid recipients than for aid categories (thereby reducing the overlap in aid spending), or it could be a reflection, as Table 2.2 alluded to, of domestic priorities playing a greater role when Member States identify their target countries compared to their target categories.

Similar to Table 2.1, Germany and France appear more similar to the EU overall than to the United States, and have grown increasingly so over the time period. In contrast, the United Kingdom and the Netherlands both appear more similar to the United States than to the EU, with an average similarity with the EU of 0.17 and 0.11 respectively, compared to 0.30 and 0.25 with the United States. The United Kingdom, in particular, has grown more similar to the United States over the time period, driven by, for example, both countries giving a considerably larger share of AfT to Pakistan than the EU institutions do.

Aid and Non-Trade Provisions in the EU's Trade Agreements

Having established that there is a varying degree of commonality in the EU's aid for trade policies, we now move away from Aid for Trade and look at the underlying objectives of the EU institutions' and the Member States' development aid, and explore whether there is any evident correlation between the inclusion of non-trade provisions in the EU's trade agreements and the underlying policy objectives of the donors' development aid.

Aid by Underlying Policy Objective

While aid by functional category (such as aid allocated to "Basic health care" or "Early childhood education") can give an indication of the type of activities which a donor prioritises and the values which a donor wishes to promote, it is an imperfect measure of the donor's underlying policy objectives. Even if two donors make aid commitments under the same aid category, the underlying objectives motivating such commitments may differ. Equally, if two donors make commitments in two separate functional categories, they may serve to support the same underlying objective.

To identify the policy objectives that drive donors' aid commitments, we make use of the OECD's policy objective markers. The policy marker system is a useful complement to the data on aid by category, as it identifies activities targeted to certain policy objectives. The markers, which are designed to cover the key aims of the Sustainable Development Goals (SDGs), cover four policy areas: Gender Equality; Aid to Environment; Participatory Development/Good Governance (PDGG); and Trade Development.[11] Each marker gives information about how crucial a policy objective was in motivating an aid commitment (ether "principal", "significant" or "not targeted"). The scores are supplied by the donors, based on their intentions at the design stage of aid commitments. The four policy objectives (gender, environment, PDGG and trade) are not mutually exclusive, meaning that the same aid commitment could have more than one principal or significant policy objective. Further, not all aid commitments have been screened against policy objectives and, as a result, policy objective markers are sometimes missing.[12]

Table 2.4 focuses on the four key Member States, as well as EU Institutions, and gives the share of screened aid that is marked as significantly or principally motivated by the relevant policy objective. Typically, and perhaps as can be expected, the "principal" marker covers a smaller share of ODA than the "significant" marker.

Overall, a larger share of EU Institutions' ODA is motivated, either to a significant or principal extent, by the gender equality objective compared to the four Member States. On Aid to Environment there are quite large discrepancies, with 71 per cent of all screened ODA having a significant or principal score in France compared to around 28 per cent in EU Institutions, and only around 6 per cent in the Netherlands. Similarly, there are differences with respect to the PDGG objective, with 87 per cent of French aid focused (either principally or significantly) on

[11] The full definitions can be found here: www.oecd.org/officialdocuments/publicdisplaydocumentpdf/?cote=DCD/DAC/STAT(2018)9/ADD2&docLanguage=En

[12] For the EU Institutions, the Netherlands, and the United Kingdom, all aid in 2017 was screened, whereas 30.9 per cent of Germany's aid and 18.4 per cent of France's aid in 2017 was not screened against the objectives.

Table 2.4 *Share of aid commitments marked as either "significant" or "principal" in 2017 (%)*

	Gender		Environment		PDGG	
	Significant	Principal	Significant	Principal	Significant	Principal
EU Institutions	45.0	2.4	17.1	10.8	22.1	33.1
DEU	37.4	1.1	24.5	15.5	27.8	16.1
FRA	31.0	3.2	56.7	14.3	61.5	25.5
GBR	40.1	2.5	14.2	8.0	0.8	24.3
NLD	34.2	7.0	4.2	1.5	8.2	13.3

NB: The shares are calculated by excluding any values that had not been screened in 2017.

this objective, compared to only 21.5 per cent and 25.1 per cent of the Netherlands' and the United Kingdom's total aid.[13]

Aid Objectives and Non-Trade Provisions

Many of the EU's trade agreements contain so-called non-trade policy objectives, aimed at promoting sustainable development by conditioning access to the EU market on partner countries making certain commitment in areas such as environmental protection, human rights and labour rights. One such example is the EU's GSP+ programme. This scheme grants deeper preferences than the original GSP programme, in exchange for the beneficiary countries ratifying twenty-seven international conventions on sustainable development, human rights and good governance (Borchert et al., 2018). There is a continuous monitoring of, and engagement with, the GSP+ beneficiaries in relation to their adherence to these commitments (European Commission, 2019).

Given the focus on sustainable development in the GSP+ scheme, we explored whether aid to GSP+ countries appears particularly focused on the sustainable development policy objectives compared to countries under the "ordinary" GSP programme.

[13] For more details and qualifications as well as additional data please see our full report with ECDPM http://respect.eui.eu/wp-content/uploads/sites/6/2019/12/RESPECT-Report-WP4–3-EU-trade-and-aid-coherence.pdf

Indeed, a somewhat higher share of EU institutions' total ODA to GSP+ countries is focused on gender, environmental or PDGG policy objectives compared to the standard GSP group, but only marginally so. A similar pattern holds for the Member States, with the exception of the gender objective for France and the environmental objective for the Netherlands, where aid to the GSP+ group appears less focused on these objectives than aid to the ordinary GSP group.

However, while aid to GSP+ countries appears somewhat more focused on the sustainable development objectives than for GSP countries, there are other country groups where the policy objectives are even more important. In particular, EU Institutions' aid to countries with an Economic Partnership Agreement (EPA) appears particularly focused on the sustainable development objectives, although the same pattern is not visible for the Member States. This is interesting given the explicit development focus of the EPAs, which are discussed in more detail by Liu and Bilal (2019) in Apiko et al. (2019). Overall, there is little coherence between the EU Institutions and the Member States, as well as a high degree of variation between the Member States themselves, in the focus on the development objectives in the aid to the relevant groups (Table 2.5).

It is not only in its unilateral preference schemes that the EU uses non-trade policy objectives conditionally, but also in its reciprocal trading arrangements. However, the depth and scope of these provisions differ between the trade agreements. A study of ninety of the EU's preferential trade agreements shows that more than 75 per cent of these agreements contain provisions on national security, environmental protection, human rights, labour rights, economic development and the right to health whereas less than 10 per cent contain provisions on, for example, minimum wage, right to freedom of belief or good governance (Lechner, 2016).

Conclusions

In this chapter, we have looked at the interrelationship between soft power, trade and trade-related aid, of the EU Institutions and the EU Member States.

We first discussed the meaning of "soft power" in detail. We noted that, for the inventor of the concept, Joseph Nye, soft power referred specifically to a power of attraction that would induce partners to see a country or bloc as an example to be copied. Nye's work stressed that the

Table 2.5 *Share of total ODA to each recipient group principally or significantly motivated by each policy objective (%)*

Trade relation with EU (2017)	Gender					Environment					PDGG				
	EUi	DEU	FRA	GBR	NLD	EUi	DEU	FRA	GBR	NLD	EUi	DEU	FRA	GBR	NLD
AA	40.3	38.6	44.3	24.9	45.7	21.6	43.0	60.4	1.9	1.6	52.9	43.0	71.8	70.7	44.5
CU	33.9	45.8	39.0	64.0	3.0	23.7	26.3	44.4	5.1	0.0	39.3	28.9	97.6	11.6	47.4
EBA	55.1	67.2	39.7	56.3	59.1	31.8	30.4	46.0	38.0	10.9	57.8	59.5	79.0	73.2	48.2
EPA	66.7	50.2	16.9	56.9	61.4	47.5	58.2	39.8	16.9	1.2	76.9	48.2	71.5	34.9	22.8
FTA	45.6	49.9	35.6	36.3	27.6	21.8	70.5	90.1	6.6	1.6	70.7	51.8	88.0	15.1	73.6
GSP	51.9	20.2	23.6	45.1	53.2	29.4	34.4	64.4	14.5	4.6	49.9	26.6	81.5	48.5	25.1
GSP+	57.5	42.9	9.7	74.4	65.4	31.8	39.4	94.4	23.6	1.5	67.7	54.9	86.7	71.4	88.8
SAA	26.4	19.6	62.9	30.7	31.0	20.2	71.1	70.8	0.1	0.0	67.3	40.1	38.4	56.2	99.7
British OCT	0.0	0.0	0.0	18.4	0.0	0.0	0.0	0.0	56.0	0.0	0.0	0.0	0.0	78.1	0.0
French OCT	0.0	0.0	0.0	0.0	0.0	0.0	0.0	1.3	0.0	0.0	0.0	0.0	16.9	0.0	0.0
No pref.	34.7	29.8	42.5	47.4	45.4	8.0	39.7	54.0	24.6	5.6	54.2	37.0	79.9	39.1	47.5
Unspecified*	47.5	50.1	19.6	26.6	39.6	32.6	47.0	51.2	21.4	6.9	59.0	52.1	75.8	29.3	25.6

* The group 'unspecified' relates to aid allocated to wider regions, such as 'Africa, regional' or 'Central Asia, regional'. As it is not possible to distinguish the individual aid recipients of such groups, we are unable to estimate the ODA per capita for this category.

use of coercion or inducement forms part of a harder form of power while the concept of "smart power" captures the complementarity between soft and hard power.

The lesson we draw is that trade and trade-related policies, such as trade-focused aid, embody incentives and carry implicit penalties, and as such these policies do not by themselves constitute soft power, but they may create it if the EU action is welcomed. Indeed, the giving of unconditional aid to country A may create a favourable perception in country B, and in so doing generate soft power. On the other hand, conditional trade preferences, or aid donations, may serve to diminish soft power if it is perceived negatively by the recipients.

We explored the coherence of trade-focused aid commitments between the EU Institutions and four key Member States (Germany, France, the United Kingdom and the Netherlands) to shed light on the extent to which the Member States project the same smart power values as the EU institutions, and the connection between the values espoused by the EU in its trade agreements and the patterns of aid given to its preferential trading partners.

Overall, we found that the correlation between EU Member States and EU Institutions' aid allocations are predominantly positive, indicating that the EU and its Member States are to some extent pulling in the same direction. Notwithstanding this, we found the degree of coherence with EU Institutions varies across the key Member States. In particular, we found Germany and France to be relatively more aligned with the EU Institutions, and increasingly so over the time period.

Overall, the degree of similarity was found to be lower with respect to the donors' distribution of aid by recipient country compared to the aid by functional category. Indeed, both the United Kingdom and the Netherlands were found to display a degree of divergence from the EU Institutions with respect to aid by recipient where the Netherlands, in particular, appeared more similar to the United States than to the EU Institutions.

Further, we found mixed evidence of the complementarity between aid policy and trade policy. The EU Institutions appeared to focus their trade-related aid on relatively closely integrated countries with the potential of future accession to the EU, but the same pattern was not observed in the aid given by the Member States.

In addition, we found aid to GSP+ countries to be somewhat more focused on the sustainable development objectives than for GSP countries, coherent with the fact that the deeper preferences in the GSP+

scheme are directly conditioned on the partner countries implementing a range of sustainable development provisions. Further, we found the EU Institutions' aid to countries with EPAs to be particularly focused on the sustainable development objectives, although the same pattern was not visible for the Member States.

Our conclusions suggest that the EU needs to develop further its thinking on complementarity among actors. One can imagine a scenario in which EU Institutions and Member States simply replicate each other's spending, in which case there would be no point in separate activity. There could also be pure "negative complementarity", with Member States doing exactly the opposite of what the institutions encourage, such as the EU incentivising regional cooperation and certain Member States encouraging unilateral actions.

But what we observe in reality is neither of these. Instead, we see what we might call "positive complementarity": the EU Institutions and the Member States appear to promote similar but not identical aims. As Nye has suggested, this can be linked to soft power in a positive way. Where there is a favourable attitude in a recipient partner to a particular donor or a particular goal it makes sense to link aid from the most favoured source and most acceptable objectives. It is worth observing that the degree of differentiation between UK and EU soft power aims does not appear to have been a major driver of Brexit. British documents reveal some tension between the United Kingdom – with a focus on aid to the poorest countries – and the Commission's interest in supporting pre-accession and neighbourhood partners. But UK official sources report that working within the EU framework was felt on balance to give the United Kingdom more rather than less leverage (see HM Government, 2013).

Our reading of the GSP and EBA experience is that there is a symbiotic relationship between soft power and smart power, as we have used the term. The existence of soft power means that in certain cases a partner is predisposed to act in a certain way and will respond without hesitation to incentives to act in that way. A successful partnership of this kind, where the donor is perceived as acting in a benign way, actually increases soft power for the future. Further, Cariforum EPA negotiators have reported that they were persuaded by the EU that the incorporation of tighter Intellectual Property Rights (IPRs) were in their own interest (Spence, 2009).

The West Africa EPA Development Programme (PAPED) experience generated complex lessons. The EU sought to use a mix of pre-existing soft power via Member State links and its own smart power package. This was partially but not wholly successful. By contrast, it is widely reported that even unconditional commitments by China to some countries in Africa causes resentment.[14]

Looking forward, one approach that the smart power strategy suggests is that the External Action Service should undertake periodic surveys of the soft power potential of the EU (as opposed to Member States which are the current focus of existing surveys) among trading partners. Such surveys might specifically look for countries that are especially admiring of EU deep integration and trade and aid policy and are therefore likely to be sympathetic to smart power strategies based on Aid for Trade and non-trade chapters (e.g. environment, labour rights) in trade agreements. In the post-Brexit era, it will be interesting to see if the United Kingdom moves in a very different direction and obtains different results in terms of influence.

References

Abbott, K. W., and Snidal, D. (2000). International Organization. *Legalization and World Politics* 54(3): 421–456.

Apiko, P., Bilal, S., Holmes, P., Liu, D., Magntorn Garrett, J., and Rollo, J. (2019). I Cannot Fund the UKTPO, ECDPM. RESPECT. http://respect.eui.eu/wp-content/uploads/sites/6/2019/12/RESPECT-Report-WP4–3-EU-trade-and-aid-coherence.pdf

Armitage, R., and Nye, J. (2007). *CSIS Commission on Smart Power: A Smarter, More Secure America*. Washington, DC: The CSIS Press.

Archibugi, D., and Filippetti, A. (2015). *The Handbook of Global Science, Technology, and Innovation*. Chichester: Wiley.

Badie, B., Berg-Schlosser, D., and Morlino, L. (2011). *International Encyclopaedia of Political Science*. Los Angeles: Sage.

Bjola, C., and Kornprobst, M. (2018). *Understanding International Diplomacy: Theory, Practice and Ethics*. 2nd ed. London: Routledge.

Borchert, I., Conconi, P., Di Ubaldo, M., and Herghelegiu, C. (2018). Trade Conditionality in the EU and WTO Legal Regimes. http://respect.eui.eu/wp-content/uploads/sites/6/2019/02/EU_conditionality_D2.2.pdf

Brazys, S., and Lightfoot, S. (2016). Europeanisation in Aid for Trade: The Impact of Capacity and Socialisation. *European Politics and Society* 17(1): 120–135.

Brown, C. (2019). *Understanding International Relations*. London: Red Globe Press.

[14] This was reported to us by African partners in our IDS China–Africa project (Gu et al., 2017).

Chitty, N., Li, J., Rawnsley, G. D., and Hayden, C. (2016). *The Routledge Handbook of Soft Power*. London: Routledge.

Commission of the European Communities (CEC) (1995). White Paper: Preparation of the Associated Countries of Central and Eastern Europe for Integration into the Internal Market of the Union. COM(95) 163 final. https://op.europa.eu/en/publication-detail/-/publication/56d29901-7861-448c-82d8–0d006ba61fc1

Commission of the European Communities (CEC) (2007). EU Code of Conduct on Division of Labour in Development Policy. COM(2007) 72 final. https://eur-lex.europa.eu/legal-content/en/ALL/?uri=CELEX:52007DC0072 https://data.consilium.europa.eu/doc/document/ST%2014470%202007%20INIT/EN/pdf

Council of the European Union (2007). EU Strategy on Aid for Trade: Enhancing EU Support for Trade-Related Needs in Developing Countries. 14470/07. https://register.consilium.europa.eu/doc/srv?l=EN&f=ST%2014470%202007%20INIT

Council of the European Union (2017). Achieving Inclusive and Sustainable Prosperity through Trade and Investment: Updating the Joint EU Strategy on Aid for Trade. 15573/17. www.consilium.europa.eu/media/32043/st15573en17-2.pdf

Commuri, G. (2012). "Are You Pondering What I Am Pondering?" Understanding the Conditions under which States Gain and Lose Soft Power. In E. Fels, J. Kremer, and K. Kronenberg (eds.) *Power in the 21st Century: International Security and International Political Economy in a Changing World*. London: Springer, pp. 43–57.

Concord (2012). EU Aid: The Facts. https://concordeurope.org/blog/2012/10/09/eu-aid-the-facts/

Development Solutions (2017). Mid-Term Evaluation of the EU's Generalised Scheme of Preferences. Final Interim Report for European Commission. https://trade.ec.europa.eu/doclib/docs/2018/october/tradoc_157434.pdf

Dunn, B. (2009). *Global Political Economy: A Marxist Critique*. London: Pluto Press.

European Commission (2019). European Union's GSP+ Scheme. https://policy.trade.ec.europa.eu/development-and-sustainability/generalised-scheme-preferences_en

Finger, J. M., and Kreinin, M. E. (1979). A Measure of "Export Similarity" and Its Possible Uses. *The Economic Journal* 89(356): 905–912.

Foucher, M. (2013). Puissance et influence: Repère et référence. In M. Foucher (ed.) *Atlas de l'influence française au XXIème siècle*. Paris: Robert Laffont/Institut français, pp. 10–17.

Gu, J., Holmes, P., Rollo, J., and Snell, S., with Mendez-Parra, M., and Procopio, M. (2017). China–UK–Africa Trilateral Cooperation on Trade and Investment: Prospects and Challenges for Partnership for Africa's Development. IDS Evidence Report 218. Brighton: IDS.

HM Government (2013). Review of the Balance of Competences between the United Kingdom and the European Union: Development Cooperation and

Humanitarian Aid Report. July. www.gov.uk/government/news/final-reports-in-review-of-eu-balance-of-competences-published

Horn, H., Mavroidis, P. C., and Sapir, A. (2010). Beyond the WTO? An Anatomy of EU and US Preferential Trade Agreements. *The World Economy* 33(11): 1565–1588.

Im, J., Ahn, E., Beck, N., Kim, J. K., and Park, T. (2017). 'Correlation Estimation with Singly Truncated Bivariate Data'. *Statistics in Medicine* (36): 1977–1988.

Kavalski, E. (2009). *China and the Global Politics of Regionalization.* Farnham: Ashgate.

Lawson, S. (2015). *Theories of International Relations: Contending Approaches to World Politics.* Cambridge: Polity Press.

Lechner, L., (2016). The Domestic Battle over the Design of Non-Trade Issues in Preferential Trade Agreements. *Review of International Political Economy.* 23 (5): 840–871.

Liu, D., and Bilal, S. (2019). Toward a Structured Approach to Support EU FTA Implementation in Developing Countries: The Case of the West Africa EPA Development Programme (PAPED). In P. Apiko, S. Bilal, P. Holmes, D. Lui, J. Mangtorn Garrett and J. Rollo, *Report on the Coherence between Europe's Trade and Development Policy.* https://respect.eui.eu/wp-content/uploads/sites/6/2019/12/RESPECT-Report-WP4-3-EU-trade-and-aid-coherence.pdf

Mann, M. (2012). *The Sources of Social Power: Volume 4, Globalizations, 1945–2011.* Cambridge: Cambridge University Press.

Nye, J. (2004). *Soft Power: The Means to Success in World Politics.* New York: PublicAffairs Books.

Nye, J. (2005). The Rise of China's Soft Power. *Wall Street Journal Asia,* 29 December. www.wsj.com/articles/SB113580867242333272

Nye, J. (2008b). Public Diplomacy and Soft Power. *Annals of the American Academy of Political and Social Science* 616 (Public Diplomacy in a Changing World): 94–109.

Nye, J. (2009). Get Smart: Combining Hard and Soft Power. *Foreign Affairs* 88(4): 160–163. www.jstor.org/stable/20699631

Nye, J. (2013). Evidence to The House of Lords Select Committee on Soft Power and the UK's Influence. www.parliament.uk/documents/lords-committees/soft-power-uk-influence/c151013Ev10.pdf

Nye, J. (2017). Soft Power: The Origins and Political Progress of a Concept. *Palgrave Communications* 3: 17008. www.nature.com/articles/palcomms20178

OECD (2018). Draft Revised Statistical Reporting Directives for DAC Statistics. DCD/DAC/STAT(2018)9/ADD2. www.oecd.org/officialdocuments/publicdisplaydocumentpdf/?cote=DCD/DAC/STAT(2018)9/ADD2&docLanguage=En

Orbie, J., and Carbone, M. (2016). The Europeanisation of Development Policy. *European Politics and Society* 17(1): 1–11. doi: 10.1080/23745118.2015.1082688

Ruffini, P. R. (2017). *Science and Diplomacy: A New Dimension of International Relations.* Cham: Springer.

Spence, M. (2009). Negotiating Trade, Innovation and Intellectual Property: Lessons from the CARIFORUM EPA Experience from a Negotiator's Perspective. UNCTAD – ICTSD Project on IPRs and Sustainable Development. Policy Brief Number 4, September.

Wilson, E. (2008). Hard Power, Soft Power, Smart Power. *Annals of the American Academy of Political and Social Science.* 616(1): 110–124.

3

Export Credit Agencies

The Consequences of Non-Transparency

KAMALA DAWAR

Background

Often unnoticed are the loans, guarantees and insurance that facilitate the sale and safe delivery of goods and services to overseas markets. Yet these financial products make international trade possible. They are as significant to the international trading system as the goods and services themselves. For trade is composed of interlocking payables and receivables; firms borrow from their suppliers and lend to their customers. This creates a trade credit chain that runs parallel to the flow of goods and services along supply chains. Without it the world economy grinds to a halt.

There has been a persistent trade finance gap, estimated at US$1.5 trillion in 2019 (ADB, 2019), which has been further exacerbated by the 2020 COVID-19 health pandemic. There are different avenues for filling this financing gap. One is through the commercial financial sector by improving the market environment for private sector investment and finance. However, private sector finance is typically not attracted to investment if the commercial or political risks are high – such as in emerging and developing countries. Instead, the richer governments have historically supported their domestic exporting companies seeking business opportunities abroad through establishing export credit agencies (ECAs). These publicly funded ECAs can address market failures by offering support for export transactions not readily offered by the private sector through either lack of availability or information asymmetries (Coppens, 2009:66) In 2020, ECAs financed $200 billion (US ExIm Competitiveness Report, 2021:34) providing significant fuel to the international trading system (Konno, 1998:95).

This chapter is based on the premise that official export finance can impact market access by facilitating firms as well as impeding those firms that do not receive official export financing. Public export support should therefore be analysed as a crucial element in the competitive interplay of the flow of goods and services. However, when governments get involved, any meaningful investigation is obstructed by the lack of information made publicly available on international trade's parallel financing market. Private financing is increasingly regulated through domestic law and internationally through the Basel Accords' liquidity and leverage requirements. These legal instruments are designed to protect against unrestrained loans and borrowing and ensure that banks have enough liquidity during times of financial difficulty. Moreover, following the 2008 Global Financial Crisis, Basel III introduced new mechanisms to improve the banks' ability to handle shocks from financial stress as well as to strengthen transparency and disclosure.

The same cannot be said for publicly financed medium-to-long term (MLT) export support measures. Despite ECA activity increasing dramatically since the 2008 financial crisis and the international market for MLT public export financing having undergone a paradigmatic shift, the twentieth-century regulatory framework remains unchanged and increasingly deficient (Hopewell, 2017; Dawar, 2020). The fragmented, partial and uneven enforcement of this regulatory framework is ill-equipped to maintain competition and prevent a race to the bottom in the terms and conditions for official export financing. It could be argued that, prima facie, the uneven application and enforcement of these two sets of rules among 115 and more diverse countries is actually contributing to the lack of a level playing field in the international trading system itself.

Yet this conclusion would be based on conjecture. The actual extent of the challenge for policy makers and law enforcement is impossible to estimate given that only partial data is available on how these ECAs operate. Scant information on individual transactions is publicly available with regard to the financing terms and conditions of their export support as well as their due diligence and impact assessments. Compounding this, World Trade Organization (WTO) Member governments are notoriously reluctant to notify their domestic subsidies under the basic WTO Subsidies and Countervailing Measures (SCM) Agreement notification requirements in the areas of subsidies and countervailing measures contained in Article 25.2 of the SCM Agreement and in Article XVI:1 of the General Agreement on Tariffs in Trade (GATT) 1994.

The inability to assess sufficient sectoral and transactional data relating to ECA activities, financing terms and conditions, Environmental, Social and Human Rights (ESHR) assessments and the extent of ECA collaboration to support specific contracts, has prevented robust evidence-based conclusions relating to both the positive and negative spill-over effects of individual public export financing instruments. It also obstructs rigorous assessments of compliance with international subsidy rules, the Organisation for Economic Co-operation and Development's (OECD) Arrangement and Common Approaches, the Paris Agreement commitments and the United Nations Sustainable Development Goals (UN SDGs). This information gap not only impacts upon good policy and rulemaking at both the domestic and international level, but also long-term social and environmental well-being.

Systematic lack of transparency undermines efforts to understand how far official export financing affects other links along international value chains and the environmental and social impacts of this support overseas. It hinders identifying where the private banking sector is being crowded out by public export financing and where there is a critical financing gap that ECAs need to fill through additionality – as the lender of "last" resort. At a time when governments are short of resources due to the costs of the pandemic response, even greater transparency is required to ensure crisis measures are targeted and encourage competition based on the price and quality of the goods or services themselves, rather than their publicly funded financing terms. Access to data serves to better understand how best to deploy limited public export financing in an increasingly knowledge- rather than goods-based economy.

With the objective of examining the policy implications of the lack of information on officially financed export support, this chapter first sets out an analysis of the limits of publicly available information on international MLT export financing. It then submits that this lacuna merely perpetuates the inadequacy of the current international rules-based system for regulating official export support.

Transparency in Official Export Credit Support (*Not*)

Domestic ECA Self-Reporting

The source of data on ECA activity originates at the domestic level, in the ECA itself. The first public information point is the ECA annual reporting and financial accounting publications. Some governments providing official export financing have enacted legal provisions pertaining to ECAs that require each agency to report progress on its authorisations and specific areas of activity in its annual reports. Cross-comparison is difficult due to different domestic reporting methods. These are self-reported documents and, as a result, their accounting and reporting methodologies vary both from agency to agency and from country to country.

The United Kingdom's Export Finance (UKEF), for example, prepares its annual reports in line with HM Treasury's Government Financial Reporting Manual (FreM). The UKEF annual reports include a full set of commercial-style accounts showing information about the performance and turnover for the year. The data include details of the guarantees, loans and insurance policies issued, a business commentary and the annual report of the Export Guarantees Advisory Council. The information on export credit support provides the name of the exporter or investor; the name of the buyer, airline, operating lessor or borrower; the goods or services covered and the products' maximum liability in pounds sterling. However, the terms, tenor or conditions of this public export financing are not available for any of these individual transactions. This lack of data, along with the self-reporting nature of these accounts, prevents verifiable assessments of the impact of these support measures on competition along supply chains, and compliance with both the OECD Arrangement and Common Approaches, as well as the WTO SCM.

Indeed, UKEF is under scrutiny for operating without a "cap" on the amount of funding it can provide for fossil fuel projects abroad. The findings of the House of Commons Environmental Audit Committee (UK House of Commons EAC, 2019) inquiry noted that UKEF spent £2.4 billion on fossil fuel-related projects in low- and middle-income countries between 2013 and 2018, as compared to £200 million on clean power. There were also differences between how UKEF allocates overseas energy funding for developed nations and developing nations. During financial year 2017/18, 96 per cent of the agency's energy support for high-income countries went to support renewables, while the proportion for low- and middle-income nations stood at just 0.6 per cent. The EAC report concluded that UKEF risks "locking" low-income nations "into high-carbon dependency" for years to come, by removing financial risks from fossil fuel projects in developing nations (UK House of Commons EAC, 2019).

Further, the Corporate Standard of the GreenHouse Gas (GHG) Protocol and accounting principles classify direct and indirect GHG emissions into three "scopes".[1] UKEF does not calculate Scope 3

[1] Scope 1 includes "Direct emissions from own or controlled sources"; Scope 2 includes "Indirect emissions from the generation of purchased electricity, steam, heating and

emissions, although they are being calculated in the private sector using the GHG Protocol and advocated by the ECAs such as Export Development Canada (EDC). If full accounting and transparency were required, UKEF would follow the GHG principles to report on the forecast and actual, full scope of emissions of all individual projects it supports, as well as the portfolio totals, in a single comparative format. However, as with the terms and conditions of individual transactions, UKEF does not report on its emissions at a portfolio level, or on each project in a single location.

In the United States, the Export–Import Bank (US ExIm) is established as an independent self-sustaining agency, although its loans are backed by the government and it is subject to the provisions of the 1990 Federal Credit Reform Act.[2] The US ExIm annual reports provide consolidated financial statements and yearly data on total authorisations, authorisations for small businesses and authorisations by market. They do not publicly provide transactional data or specific information on terms and conditions for public export support. One analysis of the US ExIm accounting methods for calculating gains and losses concluded that the choice of method was significant because using a different method yields diametrically opposite results. In 2014, the Congressional Budget Office (CBO) estimated the budget effects of the ExIm Bank from 2015 through 2024 using Fair Credit Reporting Act (FCRA) standards[3] as well as Fair-Value standards. The CBO found that using the FCRA standards showed a $14 billion positive revenue effect of the ExIm Bank on the federal budget, whereas the Fair-Value method showed a $2 billion *loss* of revenue when both were measured in 2015 dollars (de Rugy and Leventhal, 2019). The Fair-Value method of accounting is used by the private sector because it takes market risks into consideration, unlike ExIm's FCRA method.

In France, the government transferred its guarantee from COFACE, a private insurer, to Bpifrance, which is a government bank, in December 2016. Bpifrance now offers a direct state guarantee as opposed to COFACE's guarantee on behalf of the French state. This enhances France's export credit support, making it more accessible to commercial

cooling consumed by the reporting company"; and Scope 3 covers "All other indirect emissions that occur in a company's value chain" Greenhouse Gas Protocol, Corporate Value Chain (Scope 3) Accounting and Reporting Standard.

[2] Public Law (PL) 101-508.

[3] Fair Credit Reporting Act (FCRA), 15 U.S.C. § 1681 et seq.

banks in the context of a challenging regulatory regime through circumventing the capital adequacy rules applicable to commercial banks. Under the Basel III standards, commercial banks such as COFACE need to hold additional capital and to undertake initiatives to address maturity mismatches between their assets and liabilities.

Bpifrance Assurance Export is mandated by the state[4] to manage and deliver, under its control, on its behalf and in its name, the public export guarantees of Article L. 432-1 of the Insurance Code. Bpifrance Assurance Export has a right to request from a customer all documents it may be entitled to demand in connection with its "know-your-customer" procedures.[5] This includes all documents concerning the transaction to be covered and it can authorise checks with respect to the truth and accuracy of the declarations and compliance with obligations. Bpifrance is moreover entitled to provide the competent government authorities with all information or, in general, all available facts in connection with the transaction and its performance. However, when it comes to publicly accessible data, the Bpifrance Annual Reports present an aggregate overview consisting of consolidated balance-sheets, including consolidated profits and loss, net income, gains and losses and variations in shareholders' equity.

Article I. In another OECD Participant country – Germany – the absence of mandatory reporting of projects that have been awarded an export guarantee remains a fundamental barrier to transparency. However, it is legally required by the protection of business secrets codified in Paragraph 20 of the Verwaltungsverfahrensgesetz, VwVfg (Germany's Administrative Procedures Act) and Paragraph 203 on the violation of personal secrets codified in the Strafgesetzbuch, StGB (Germany's Criminal Code). Euler Hermes prepares the applications for approval in an interministerial committee, which consists of the economics ministry (leading ministry), financial and development ministry and the foreign office. The ministries must then take a unanimous decision. In accordance with German business confidentiality protection, project data is published only with approval by the exporter or the bank financing the project. Euler Hermes publishes project information about guarantees but provides only aggregate contract value categories. If companies are requesting a credit guarantee in excess of €1 billion, the German parliament's budget committee must be informed. Otherwise, the parliament agrees an overall annual budget ceiling for all guarantees, called the statutory cover limit, within which the interministerial committee enjoys

[4] In accordance with Article L. 432-2 of the Insurance Code.

[5] Know Your Customer is a customer compliance system. See https://knowyourcustomer.com/about-us/

discretion. This has resulted in reports that Germany's economics ministry has denied parliamentarians access to the exact figures that would reveal which firms received the biggest allocations of Euler Hermes guarantees (Schäfer, 2008).

If levels of disclosure are patchy among OECD Arrangement ECAs, for both the terms and conditions as well as ESHR impacts, this is merely amplified in non-OECD Arrangement ECAs. In China, four institutions – Sinosure, China ExImbank, China Development Bank (CDB) and Agricultural Development Bank of China – play a coordinated role in supporting China's foreign trade development with the strategy of "go-abroad", safeguarding the security of national economy and promoting economic growth and employment. All these institutions have quasi-ministerial status. China's loan agreements have caused various concerns, particularly in its Belt and Road Initiative (BRI): the 2013 global infrastructure development strategy, whereby the Chinese government invests US$575 billion in seventy economies geographically located along BRI transport corridors.[6] If completed, BRI transport projects have the potential to increase trade and reduce poverty.

However, there are significant risks common to many major infrastructure projects: debt, poor procurement, stranded infrastructure and ESHR risks. The foundation upon which to begin to design strong measures to mitigate these risks is increased transparency. Currently there are allegations that China is systematically pursuing a policy of "debt trap diplomacy", signing contracts with its developing country government counterparties that allow it to seize strategic assets and undermine their sovereignty when debtor countries run into financial problems (Parker and Chefitz, 2018), while other commentators question the veracity of these claims (Bräutigam and Kidane, 2020). The random annual reports available in English provide a consolidated financial statement, balance sheets, income statements, cash flow statements and statements of changes in owners' equity. Individual transaction data is unavailable on the countries to which its clients export, the products those companies export, the exporters' home states, the primary borrowers and, of course, the terms and conditions.

One black letter law analysis of the legal terms of China's foreign lending has found that Chinese contracts increasingly contain unusual confidentiality clauses that bar borrowers from revealing the terms or

[6] www.worldbank.org/en/topic/regional-integration/brief/belt-and-road-initiative

even the existence of the debt (Gelpern et al., 2021). The research suggests that Chinese lenders seek advantage over other creditors through the use of collateral arrangements such as lender-controlled revenue accounts and commitments to keep the debt out of collective restructuring. This is unlike OECD Arrangement Participants, who have elected to use the 1956 Paris Club to find coordinated and sustainable solutions to the payment difficulties experienced by debtor countries. This analysis of Chinese contracts concludes that the inclusion of cancellation, acceleration and stabilisation clauses in these contracts could potentially provide lenders influence over their debtors' domestic and foreign policies.

China is not unique in failing to publish detailed information about its lending terms. There is no uniform public disclosure standard or practice for bilateral official lenders, although many governments and most multilateral institutions publish information about their lending, but at varying levels of detail, and only share such information with a subset of other creditors (see Table 3.1). The following section examines the monitoring and disclosure requirements applicable to EU Member States' ECAs. This is the most comprehensive, binding regulatory framework governing ECA activity, and could therefore be perceived to be the current gold standard.

Transparency and Monitoring under the Legal Framework Regulating EU ECAs

Pursuant to Article 207 of the Treaty on the Functioning of the European Union (TFEU), the EU has exclusive competence in the area of common commercial policy, which includes official export financing. The Commission's mandate is to ensure that ECA activity is conducted in accordance with the principles and objectives of the Union's external action (Article 207.1 TFEU). This mandate is clear in the area of short-term credit support. The Commission has provided guidelines to EU Treaty rules in its Short-Term Export Credit Communication. These set out the Commission's interpretation of the areas where official ECAs cannot compete with the private market. The EU State Aid rules under Articles 107–109 TFEU additionally operate to ensure that public interventions through short-term ECA products such as export guarantees and bonds, do not distort competition and trade inside the EU. The EU state aid rules require notification to the Commission and are closely monitored. However, medium-to-long term export credit support

China Exirnbank *(all contracts after 2014)*	LMA template *(33% of the blanks in our sample)*	Islamic Development Bank *(all 20 contracts)*	Agence Française de Développement (AFD) *(2 out of 10 contracts)*
The Borrower shall keep all the terms, conditions and the standard of fees hereunder or in connection with this Agreement strictly confidential. Without the prior written consent of the Lender, the Borrower shall not disclose any information hereunder or in connection with this Agreement to any third party unless required by applicable law.	Each Finance Party [defined as lenders] agrees to keep all Confidential Information [enumerated items] confidential and not to disclose it to anyone, save to the extent permitted by Clause 36.2 (Disclosure of Confidential Information) [and Clause 36.3 (Disclosure to numbering service providers)], and to ensure that all Confidential Information is protected with security measures and a degree of care that would apply to its own confidential information. The Agent and each Obligor agree to keep each Funding Rate . . . confidential and not to disclose it to anyone, save to the extent permitted by paragraphs . . . below. . . . The Agent and each Obligor acknowledge that each Funding Rate . . . is or may be price-sensitive information and that its use may be regulated or prohibited by applicable legislation including securities law relating to insider dealing and market abuse and the Agent and each Obligor undertake not to use any Funding Rate . . . for any unlawful purpose.	All of the bank's documents, as well as its correspondence and records, need to be kept confidential by the borrower.	The Borrower shall not disclose the contents of the agreement without the prior consent of the Lender to any third party, unless required by law, applicable regulation or a court decision.

The China Exirnbank confidentiality clause excerpted here binds the sovereign debtor. It applies to the entire agreement and, potentially, to a broader set of dealings between the debtor and China Exirnbank "in connection with" the contract. On the other hand, the clause contains a carve-out that would allow the sovereign debtor to make disclosure required by law. It is unlikely, however, that this carve-out would be broad enough to allow a debtor to disclose China Exirnbank contract terms to its Paris Club creditors, since the Paris Club process and output are at best "soft law."
Source: Gelpern et al. (2021).

provided by EU Member States' ECAs are not normally notified to the Commission as state aid for it is deemed to comply with the OECD Arrangement terms and conditions (see Box 3.1), although export credit insurance is governed by the 1998 Directive on Harmonisation of the Main Provisions Concerning Export Credit Insurance for Transactions with Medium and Long-term Cover.

The European Parliament (EP) has exercised its role in common commercial policy to engage with other EU institutions in a larger reporting and policy coherence exercise on official export financing. To this end, the EP has placed a particular emphasis on the implementation of the OECD Common Approaches and the ethical international agreements which apply to the operations of EU Member States' ECAs. This greater engagement also aims to ensure compatibility between ECA activities at the Member State level and the EU's obligations pursuant to TFEU Article 3.5(5) and Article 21.1, which uphold the values of respect for human rights and policy coherence for development, the fight against climate change and the principles of international law.

The main instrument for monitoring Member States' ECA activity is Article 5 Regulation (EU) 1233/2011. This requires all Member States to screen applications for export credit support from the perspective of environmental and associated risk, following the OECD Common Approaches and other EU obligations. Annex 1 stipulates that each Member State shall make available to the Commission an Annual Activity Report in order to step up transparency at Union level on assets and liabilities, claims paid and recoveries, new commitments, exposures and premium charges. Further, Member States shall describe how environmental risks, which can carry other relevant risks, are taken into account in the officially supported export credit activities of their ECAs. The Commission shall then produce an annual review for the European Parliament based on this information, including an evaluation with respect to the compliance of the Member States' ECAs with Union objectives and obligations.

These Member States' Activity Reports were only made available through a freedom of information request to AsktheEU.org. The response to this request indicated that only after the Commission has concluded the review of the reports and transmitted its evaluation report to the EP that access to the requested reports might be considered.[7] This

[7] www.asktheeu.org/en/request/request_for_annual_activity_repo#incoming-16720

can take up to three years. The Activity Reports are underwhelming. They are based on a questionnaire and the answers largely replicate or directly reference the ECA's Annual Reports. These, as discussed earlier, are largely aggregate figures based on different reporting methodologies and constrained by confidentiality clauses. An overview of the Member States' Activity Reports provided from 2011 up to 2016 all reported they were in full compliance with the OECD Arrangement, the Common Approaches guidelines and therefore EU law. Accordingly, the European Commission has also consistently reported full compliance with EU objectives and obligations, including under the OECD and WTO SCM. Only in the very first Annual Review in 2012 did the Commission explicitly disclose that: "It is difficult to define a precise benchmark for measuring 'compliance' in EU law" (7.3.2014 COM(2014) 123 final:6).

Understandably, the Commission's light-touch evaluation approach has led to concern. Upon receiving the first annual report from the Commission on the Activities of Member States' Export Credit Agencies, the European Parliament issued a resolution (European Parliament Resolution P7_TA(2013)0291).[8] This stressed that the annual reports of the Member States, along with the Commission's evaluation of these reports, did not yet satisfy the Parliament's intention to be able to make an assessment as to whether the Member States' export credit activities are in compliance with the Union's foreign policy goals, as enshrined in Articles 3 and 21 TFEU, and the treatment of environmental risks in the calculation of ECA premiums. The EP Resolution recommended that the Council Working Group on Export Credits and the Commission consult with the European External Action Service (EEAS) on developing a common methodology, with public consultation, for meaningful reporting on TFEU Article 21 compliance, and on the application in the EU of certain OECD guidelines in the field of officially supported export credits.

This Resolution was followed by a formal complaint to the European Ombudsman by ECAWatch, a coalition of non-governmental organisation monitoring export credit agency activities. Their submission

[8] European Parliament resolution of 2 July 2013 on the first annual report from the Commission to the European Parliament on the activities of Member States' Export Credit Agencies (2012/2320(INI)). www.europarl.europa.eu/doceo/document/TA-7-2013-0291_EN.pdf

protested that the Commission had failed to put in place adequate benchmarks and compliance tests in the context of its third annual review of the activity reports of the ECAs for 2013 (Correspondence Case 212/2016/JN, 2016).[9] Further, that the Commission had failed to assess thoroughly export credit agencies' compliance with EU objectives and obligations, in particular with respect to human rights and environmental protection.

The Ombudsman's investigation sided with the complainant, opining that the annual reviews prepared by the Commission so far do not meet the requisite standard. In the absence of a transparent explanation of the method applied and of the considerations leading to the Commission's conclusions, the Ombudsman reasoned that the Commission has committed maladministration under Article 41 of the EU Charter of Fundamental Rights and the principles of good administration (European Ombudsman Recommendation Case 212/2016/JN, 2016).[10]

The Commission maintains its defence that the current reporting process reflects what can reasonably be achieved within the confines of the limited reporting obligations contained within the regulation. As it stands, EU Member States are free to have a range of diverse export credit systems in place. Annex 1 of Regulation 1233/2011 respects this diversity by leaving the manner and methodology of reporting to individual EU Member States. The Commission interprets this to mean that it is not required to verify such information.

As a result, without factual evidence that EU law is not respected in the context of a Member State's export credit programme, the Commission has no case to launch an investigation. This is a Catch-22. The Commission is dependent on the individual Member State to provide the factual information indicating non-compliance which the Commission can use to launch an investigation. The domestic transparency deficit caused by the self-reporting nature of ECA activities is validated by the lack of substantive evaluation undertaken by the Commission. As a result, the Commission has to rely disproportionately

[9] The European Commission's failure to evaluate the compliance of Member States Export Credit Agencies with the EU's objectives and obligations, in particular on human rights. Correspondence Case 212/2016/JN, 2016. www.ombudsman.europa.eu/en/doc/correspondence/en/67998

[10] Recommendation of the European Ombudsman in case 212/2016/JN on the European Commission's annual reviewing of Member States' export credit agencies at www.ombudsman.europa.eu/en/recommendation/en/95605

on investigations of infringements initiated by complaints from civil society, such as ECAWatch, which do not have access to sufficient information to make evidence-driven assessments.

Transparency under the OECD Arrangement and Common Approaches

Participants in the 1978 OECD Arrangement have agreed to discipline their export credit activities in line with the terms of the Arrangement (Box 3.1). The Arrangement applies to all official support for exports of goods and/or services, or to financial leases with repayment terms of two years or more. This is regardless of whether official support for export credits is given by means of direct credit and financing, refinancing, interest rate support, guarantee or insurance. Special sectoral guidelines apply to ships, nuclear power plants, aircraft and project finance transactions. The Arrangement does not apply to military equipment and agricultural products.

Reflecting its age, the OECD Arrangement is called a "gentlemen's agreement" between an invitation-only club of the richer countries.[11] It is a soft law instrument, without enforceable rights and duties (Guzman and Meyer, 2010). Compliance relies heavily on the attraction of cooperation in order to avoid a subsidy war and the inevitable race to the bottom in terms and conditions. Rather than an enforcement mechanism, the main deterrent to non-compliance is a form of "self-help" available under Article 18, which permits "matching" the terms of another offer from an ECA – operating either inside or outside the OECD Arrangement. The matching clause provides that a Participant must verify, notify and provide other Participants and the Secretariat information on their official support for individual transactions. Non-Participants, on the other hand, are only able to obtain information on a reciprocal basis from the individual Participant on a specific export credit offer. This limited disclosure hinders any comprehensive independent evaluation of the use of matching and its impact on competition, as well as their compliance with international subsidy rules and SDGs.

[11] Australia, Canada, the European Union, Japan, Korea, New Zealand, Norway, Switzerland, Turkey, the United Kingdom and the United States.

The implementation of the OECD Recommendation on Common Approaches[12] is similarly monitored primarily through information self-reported by the adherents to the Recommendation for all projects

BOX 3.1 MAIN DISCIPLINES OF THE OECD ARRANGEMENT

The OECD Arrangement's main disciplines limiting the terms and conditions of official supported export credits set the **minimum cash down-payment** of credit required for each transaction at 15 per cent of the export contract value.

Countries are classified under two categories based on World Bank thresholds.[13] The **maximum repayment terms** are five years[14] for Category 1 countries and ten years for Category 2 countries.[15]

The 1998 Knaepen Package determines the **minimum risk premium rates** by:

(1) the country risk category;
(2) the time at risk;
(3) the quality of ECA cover, in terms of whether it is a direct loan, guarantee or insurance; and
(4) the percentage of ECA cover.

Minimum **interest rates** for official financing support[16] by the Participants are Commercial Interest Reference Rates (CIRRs),[17] intended to reflect commercial rates and adjusted monthly.

The Arrangement also incorporates the 1991 Helsinki Package, which prohibits tied[18] and partially untied aid for richer developing countries, as well as for projects which should be financed commercially. It also sets minimum concession levels for transactions that incorporate tied aid credits and grants.[19]

12 Recommendation of the Council on Common Approaches for Officially Supported Export Credits and Environmental and Social Due Diligence (the "Common Approaches") (TAD/ECG(2012)5).

13 Countries that are graded by the IBRD are in Category 1; Category 2 consists of all other countries.

14 With eight and a half years after prior notification.

15 The maximum repayment term for conventional power plant is twelve years.

16 Official Financing support includes direct credits/financing, refinancing or interest rate support.

17 CIRRs have been established for thirteen currencies, the majority of which are based on either the five-year government bond yields or on three-, five- and seven-year bond yields, according to the length of the repayment period.

18 Tied aid is aid tied to the purchases from the donor country.

19 Fifty per cent concessionality level for the poorest Least Developed Countries (LDCs) as classified by the UN, and 35 per cent concessionality level for all other developing countries.

BOX 3.1 (*CONT.*)

The Participants in the OECD Arrangement have also produced a series of OECD Recommendations on Common Approaches[20] to undertaking environmental and social due diligence to identify, consider and address the potential environmental and social impacts and risks relating to applications for officially supported export credits as an integral part of Members' decision-making and risk management systems. Specifically, these include ESHR risks, sustainable lending risks through the OECD Principles and Guidelines to Promote Sustainable Lending Practices and the Provision of Official Export Credits to Low-Income Countries; and corruption risks through the OECD Council Recommendation on Bribery and Officially Supported Export Credits.

supported that had a potentially high (Category A) or medium (Category B) negative environmental or social impact (Recommendation, VIII). The OECD Secretariat monitors implementation through compilation of reporting by the members (Recommendation, VIII:49). However, as with the EU analysis, this self-reporting exercise lacks public transparency, independent monitoring and verification. It has led to concerns regarding the lack of enforceability of such voluntary commitments, as well as the loopholes in their content, as discussed earlier with regard to UKEF. Of particular concern here is that the classification of project applications according to the risk of adverse environmental and social impacts is made by the ECA itself (Brynildsen, 2011; Amnesty International, 2013; BankWatch, 2017).

US ExIm Bank's Comparative Data

The continuation of the US ExIm Bank's functions is subject to periodic extensions that must be granted by Congress.[21] This involves intense bipartisan lobbying (Hopewell, 2017) and the Bank publishes an additional annual report to US Congress on "Global Export Credit Competition". The US ExIm annual competitiveness report is an

[20] The current OECD Recommendation of the Council on Common Approaches for Officially Supported Export Credits and Environmental and Social Due Diligence (the "Common Approaches"), was adopted on 28 June 2012 and revised by the OECD Council on 6 April 2016 (OECD/LEGAL/0393).

[21] 12 USC 635 et seq.

advocacy tool and the methodologies used to compile data from various sources are not verifiable.

Over the past decade, US ExIm's competitiveness reports have been increasingly highlighting the "weaponisation" of official export financing and the aggressive competition from new non-OECD Participants such as China and India. The data suggests that over the decade, OECD Arrangement activity has been displaced by non-Arrangement activity among OECD Participants as well as by non-Participants. Prior to the pandemic, in 2019, total activity provided under the rules of the OECD Arrangement totalled approximately $76 billion, which is only 34 per cent of total export and trade-related finance.[22] In 2020 this had fallen; less than a third of official export credit support was issued under the OECD Arrangement terms and conditions (source US ExIm Competitiveness Report, 2021:26).

Table 3.2 further indicates that among the top ECA providers in 2020, all but China and India were Participants of the OECD Arrangement and all but China were European countries. The volume of official export support being provided by non-OECD Participant ECAs raises questions about the lack of a level playing field for ECAs to compete on due to the shrinking scope and volume of official export financing activity taking place under the OECD Arrangement terms. Yet the availability of information on these complex developments is preventing analysis of direct and indirect impacts and the design of smarter regulation.

Gaping Information Gaps

Additionality: Filling the Financing Gap

Most ECAs operate under the principle of "additionality" by seeking to provide public support only if the transaction would not go forward without it. This is the lender of last resort principle. Additionality requirements aim to ensure that ECAs do not "crowd-out" the private financial sector and waste taxpayers' money. For example, in the United Kingdom, the mission of UK Export Finance is to ensure that no viable UK export fails for lack of finance or insurance, while operating at no net cost to the taxpayer. In the United States, the concept and definitive

[22] Report to the U.S. Congress on Global Export Credit Competition, June 2020. For the period 1 January–31 December 2019, p. 17 as well as Report to the U.S. Congress on Global Export Credit Competition, June 2021. For the period 1 January–31 December 2020. www.exim.gov/news/reports/competitiveness-reports

Table 3.2 *Top ECA MLT providers in 2020*

Billions USD*		
1	China**	18.0
2	France***	12.1
3	Germany	8.6
4	Italy	8.4
5	Korea	5.0
6	Sweden	4.7
7	United Kingdom	3.4
8	Denmark	2.8
9	Belgium	2.5
10	India	2.3
11	Canada	2.2
12	Netherlands	1.9
13	United States	1.8
14	Spain	1.8
15	Finland	1.1

** As reported in EXIM's methodology section, EXIM estimated China's official MLT export credit volumes through open-source research and third-party research in English and Mandarin. EXIM estimated Sinosure's volumes based on this research and data found in Sinosure's 2019 Annual Report.
*** Roughly $8 billion of Bpifrance's new aircraft contracts are for aircraft that will be delivered in the future.
Source: US ExIm Competitiveness Report (2021).

meaning of the word "additionality" has varied. The current guidance for US ExIm is to "neutralize the effect of such foreign credit on international sales competition" and/or "supplement and encourage, and not compete with, private capital" (primarily Section 2(b)(1)(B) of the Export–Import Bank Act of 1945). However, given the lack of transparency surrounding individual official export financing transactions, it is typically impossible to evaluate when ECAs crowd out rather than crowd in private finance, or to assess the additionality of a single transaction against a counterfactual to determine value for public money.

A singular research opportunity presented itself when the US ExIm temporarily lost its ability to underwrite loans of a significant size between 2015 to 2019. This allows for assessments of the performance of US ExIm before and after it lost the ability to underwrite loans of significant size. The lower transaction cap led to a significant decrease in new loans, loan guarantees and working-capital approvals from $21 billion in 2015, to $3.6 billion in 2018. Data from financial years 2007–2014 indicates that pre-quorum, 70 per cent of all US ExIm loan guarantees and 35 per cent of total authorisations went to Boeing. In 2014, Boeing constituted 40 per cent of US ExIm's financial commitments, a few major corporations such as John Deere and Caterpillar comprised 35 per cent, while only 25 per cent of ExIm's financial commitments went to small businesses (de Rugy and O'Sullivan, 2014).

Needless to say, post-quorum, US exports did not collapse. Rather, the big-ticket beneficiaries of the US ExIm Bank gained easy access to capital markets, and as a result the continued ability to finance their exporting activities (de Rugy and Leventhal, 2019). According to the International Trade Administration (ITA), in 2014, the United States exported $1.7 trillion in goods. By 2018, this figure had risen very slightly to $1.8 trillion. There was no major change despite a 72 per cent drop in the ExIm Bank's financing during that time. The level of exports in 2018, when the ExIm Bank's financing was at a minimum, was $266 billion higher than in 2012, when the ExIm Bank's financing was at its peak (de Rugy and Leventhal, 2019). Many previously supported firms were able to access other financing sources. For example, in 2014, before the loss of its quorum, the aid directed to Boeing was nominally valued by the ExIm Bank at over $8 billion. By 2018, the amount of this aid had fallen to zero due to the lack of quorum in place.

Yet, significantly for US taxpayers, from 2014 to 2017 Boeing's profits and stock prices actually increased even though the company was not being supported by US ExIm and had to shop for export financing in the marketplace. Boeing had a record year in 2018 with sales of $101.1 billion, including an increased number of aircraft exported. Boeing has stated that it is attracting new capital and innovative ways to access new financial markets, including outside investors, such as Marsh and McLennon, to set up an entirely new financing company for its products. This study strongly suggests that the ExIm Bank may not be providing additionality in all of its transactions (de Rugy and Leventhal, 2019). If the ExIm Bank was filling an existing financing gap, Boeing would not have been so easily able to find the lost $8 billion in export financing without the ExIm Bank and achieve record sales.

OECD Flexibilities: Finance without Accountability

Under the OECD Arrangement, Participants may finance up to 85 per cent of an export contract's value regardless of the level of domestic content that contract contains. Foreign content consists of any portion of an export that originates outside the ECA's, the exporter's and the foreign buyer's countries. Subject to this rule, Participant ECAs are free to implement a content policy that supports its own domestic firms and to help internationalise domestic suppliers. ECAs have two content-related policies they can adjust to maximise flexibility. First, they can lower the minimum domestic content an export contract must contain to qualify for maximum allowable support. Second, ECAs are free to determine what qualifies as eligible domestic content, based on national interest or value-added. This broader concept encompasses factors such as overall company exports rather than a single transaction or the dividends and royalties associated with a given transaction. For example, in 2017, Servizi Assicurativi del Commercio Estero (SACE) in Italy agreed to provide full support to buyers of Boeing 787 aircraft, although the Boeing 787 only contains approximately 14 per cent Italian content (US ExIm Competitiveness Report, 2021:32).

The broader national-interest calculation is that as the ECA maximises its support for an exporter's competitiveness, the exporter will accordingly support domestic employment and growth. This is a shift away from transaction-specific considerations in favour of long-term strategic assessments of how an ECA can contribute to macroeconomic expansion and overall national employment. Using national-interest or value-creation concepts offers a more flexible, but far less transparent approach towards their transactional assessment for support.

In addition to flexing the Arrangement rules, some OECD Participant ECAs also try to circumvent them. For example, many ECAs now provide a market window that offers pricing competitive with the commercial market. As a result, a market window transaction will not necessarily result in lower financing costs when compared with financing provided under the OECD Arrangement. Rather, market windows offer ECAs more flexibility on tenor, down-payments and fees because these transactions are not covered by OECD rules and circumvent their requirements. So, even if they are provided at costs higher than the

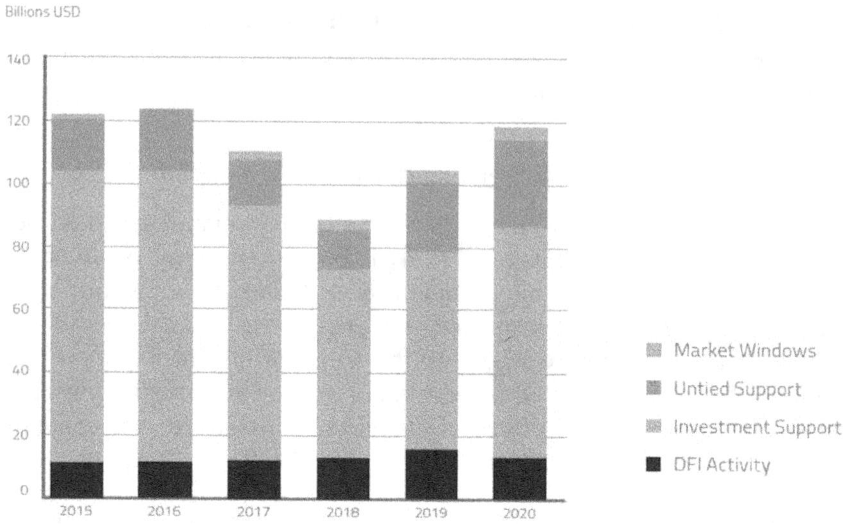

Figure 3.1 Trade-related (non-export credit) activity from OECD and non-OECD countries
Source: US ExIm Competitiveness Report (2021).

OECD Arrangement, there are less onerous requirements in the terms and conditions offered under market window programmes.

Various OECD Participants are also increasingly providing investment financing. Together, providing more than $35 billion in investment support in 2017 (US ExIm Competitiveness Report, 2021:19). This financing is untied, in that there may not be any international trade of goods or services. Nevertheless, untied financing can lead to procurement contracts or other benefits. By taking an equity stake in a foreign entity, domestic companies can potentially drive future procurement or play a role in the selection of an engineering, procurement and construction contractor. Technically, untied investment financing does not fall under the Arrangement and appears to be a reaction by some OECD Participants to promote national interest in the face of increased activity by non-OECD Participants, such as China's BRI strategy. Investment financing helps buyers mitigate some of the due diligence burdens associated with identifying suppliers from unfamiliar markets that would be necessary for tied financing. Given the diverging approaches in using untied financing, its competitive implications vary as widely as their ESHR impacts.

Another non-Arrangement activity is the use of development finance to support private-sector entities that wish to do business in foreign developing markets for developmental purposes (see Figure 3.1).

Development Finance Institutions (DFIs) offer untied support. They are seen to be competitive because they can offer financial components such as direct equity authority or equity support and local currency financing that some ECAs cannot offer.

Although DFI aid is untied while ECAs traditionally are tied, both can have similar "national interest" mandates by seeking to support domestic exporters through a whole-of-government approach. This blurring of development and export support mandates has caused accountability concerns. In the United Kingdom, for example, the process that led to the decision to merge the Department for International Development and the Foreign and Commonwealth Office to create the Foreign Commonwealth and Development Office (FCDO) was itself criticised by parliament for lack of transparency, consultation and accountability:

> For the Government to deliver on its stated aim of more accountable development spending with a greater focus on the national interest, it should establish and deliver on a clear strategy for communicating its interpretation of the "national interest" to Parliament, institute regular reporting to Parliament, and be explicit in the ways in which the FCDO will help deliver it.
>
> (UK House of Commons Foreign Affairs Committee, 2020:3)

More widespread are the allegations that the China Development Bank (CBD), a stated DFI, is competing with foreign ECAs. Unlike other DFIs, CDB only finances Chinese exports by providing loans to foreign importers for the purchase of Chinese goods and services; Chinese content should not be less than 50 per cent and there is a requirement for customers to purchase Sinosure export credit insurance when using CDB's buyer's credit programme (US ExIm Competitiveness Report, 2021:33).

The growing ECA activity indicated here that is not regulated by the OECD Arrangement and Common Approaches is by default, governed by the multilateral WTO SCM. The following section assesses the efficacy of this binding agreement in maintaining competition in the provision of official export credit support and promoting sustainable development.

The WTO Agreement on Subsidies and Countervailing Measures

The WTO agreements provide the multilateral legal ground-rules for international commerce, guaranteeing member countries important trade rights. They bind the government's *pacta sunt servanda* to keep their trade policies within agreed limits (Marrakesh Agreement,

Article II).[23] WTO Members are automatically subject to the SCM. Under the WTO SCM, Article 1.1(a)(1) stipulates that a subsidy exists if there is a financial contribution by a government or any public body within the territory of a Member, or there is any form of income or price support (Article 1.1(a)(2)) and a benefit is thereby conferred. Subsidies prohibited under the WTO SCM Agreement Article 3 include subsidies contingent in law or fact, whether solely or as one of several other conditions, upon export performance. The SCM's Annex I Illustrative List of export subsidies clarifies what can be considered to be a prohibited export subsidy. If the measure at issue is banned by the List, a Member does not have to demonstrate that the measure falls within the scope of Article 3.1(a) SCM. Of relevance to official export credit support are the inclusion of Item (j) on export guarantees and insurance and Item (k) on export credit subsidies as prohibited export subsidies on the Illustrative List.

The second paragraph of Item (k) provides an implicit safe haven to those export credits provided in compliance with the requirements of the OECD Arrangement.[24] The WTO Panel Report for Brazil – Export Financing Programme for Aircraft noted the linkage between the OECD Arrangement and the WTO SCM rules, stating that: "The second paragraph of Item (k) provides that 'an export credit practice' which is in conformity with the 'interest rate provisions' of the OECD Arrangement shall not be considered an export subsidy prohibited by the SCM Agreement."[25] The Article 21.5 Implementation Appellate Body Report further opined that although Article 15 of the OECD Arrangement defines the minimum interest rates applicable to the officially supported export credits as the Commercial Interest Reference Rates (CIRRs), it is not the only benchmark to assess the material advantage of an export subsidy. However, the Member has to provide evidence from comparable transactions in the marketplace.[26]

[23] The Marrakesh Agreement Establishing the World Trade Organization. https://treaties.un.org/doc/Publication/UNTS/Volume%201867/volume-1867-A-31874-English.pdf

[24] Panel Report (16 July 2001). Brazil – Export Financing Programme for Aircraft – Second Recourse by Canada to Article 21.5 of the DSU. WT/DS46/RW/2.

[25] Panel Report (14 April 1999). Brazil – Export Financing Programme for Aircraft. WT/DS46/R. WT/DS46/R. ¶¶1.1–1.10.

[26] Brazil – Export Financing Programme for Aircraft: Recourse by Canada to Article 21.5 of the DSU; Report of the Appellate Body (WT/DS46/AB/RW) and Report of the Panel (WT/DS46/RW).

The application of the Item (k) paragraph two "safe harbour" is not guaranteed in the case of "matching" under the OECD Arrangement, discussed earlier. In the Brazil – Export Financing Programme for Aircraft dispute, the Panel found that while it recognized that matching of derogations is permitted under the OECD Arrangement, this did not alter the fact that both the original derogation and the matching remain, by the Arrangement's own terms out of conformity with the provisions of the Arrangement.[27] Item (k) paragraph 2 on safe harbour has been interpreted narrowly.[28] It is available only for those forms of export credit support to which the interest rates provisions of the OECD Arrangement are applicable – that is, direct credits. It does not apply to export credit support in the form of pure cover (Item (j)), when it is provided to exporters on terms more favourable than the market rate. This is even if it conforms fully to the minimum premium and other disciplines in the OECD Arrangement. Some commentators argue that, in theory, even export credit support benefiting from the safe harbour remains vulnerable (i) to WTO challenge if it causes certain enumerated forms of economic harm to other WTO Members' interests – so-called adverse effects; and (ii) to unilateral countervailing duty action if injury to another country's domestic industry is shown (Coppens and Friedbacher, 2015).

Yet disputes involving an export credit subsidy in the WTO remain rare. The only two cases that have directly addressed this are the Canada–Brazil Aircraft cases, which are over fifteen years old. Evaluating compliance with this complex set of legal requirements is based on the need for greater transparency. To bring a successful WTO challenge to suspected export credit subsidy programmes, the requesting party needs to make a prima facie case that, first, the other government provides export financing; second, that the financing is contingent on export performance; and third, that the rates at which the financing is provided are below market rates. Having made this evidence-based claim, the burden of demonstrating that the official export credits comply with the WTO SCM, or qualify for the safe harbour, shifts to the responding party. The paucity of information that exists on these fast-paced but murky transactions undermines the ability of the SCM to regulate ECA activity convincingly.

[27] Panel Report, Canada – Aircraft (Article 21.5 – Brazil), ¶5.125; Panel Report, Canada – Aircraft Credits and Guarantees, ¶7.169.

[28] Panel Report, Canada – Aircraft Credits and Guarantees. ¶7.177.

The systemic challenge that needs further understanding is that the SCM applies to goods but not services, in an increasingly knowledge-based economy; it is based on the outdated assumption that trade involves goods that are produced in one country and sold to another. Transnational export credits defy this tradition. There is much discussion as to whether subsidies provided to a recipient that is not "in the territory" of the government granting the support are even caught by Article 1 ASCM (Hopewell, 2019). Yet the rise in official export credit activity demonstrates that states are internationalising their use of export subsidies for commercial or strategic advantage. The SCM does not account for the complex impacts, both positive and negative, such support has on global competition and trade in goods and services within the context of international value chains (Hoekman, 2016). Understanding these complex impacts, regulating them appropriately and providing clear public policy space for legitimate official export support will require, from the outset, reliable and comprehensive data analysis.

The WTO SCM agreement requires that Members submit a new and full notification of all specific subsidies relating to all goods sectors, provided by any level of government, every three years, with updated notifications due in the intervening years.[29] In the interests of transparency, Members are also encouraged to notify that they have not provided any specific subsidies. Notification does not prejudge the legal status of any notified measure.[30] The number of Members making subsidy notifications is low (IMF, OECD, World Bank, and WTO, 2022). Various WTO Members have submitted Communications to the WTO since March 2019 calling for the establishment of new procedures to enhance transparency and strengthen notification requirements under WTO Agreements, specifically in the context of the pandemic (WTO Ottawa Group, 2020).

Neither Litigation nor Negotiation

Despite concerns raised about economic impacts of official export financing activities, there are no recent disputes over an export credit subsidy in the WTO. This suggests that the increasingly time-consuming nature of the WTO dispute settlement procedure is unable to respond effectively to the fast pace of largely non-transparent export financing transactions.

[29] Notifications of Specific Subsidies. Article 25.1 of the SCM Agreement.
[30] SCM Agreement Article 25.7.

Moreover, enforcement under the WTO SCM is conducted on a bilateral basis, dependent on investigations from injured Members of the WTO. Without the necessary transparency to understand on a transactional basis economic impacts, injuries and compliance, any challenge may trigger a wave of tit-for-tat retaliation.

Instead, the United States launched negotiations with China and thirteen other governments through the Strategic and Economic Dialogue, in 2012, to find some agreement on guidelines to govern export credit financing. The International Working Group on Export Credits (IWG) was established "to make concrete progress towards a set of international guidelines on the provision of Official Export Financing that, taking into account varying national interests and situations, are consistent with international best practices" (UK Export Finance, 2012–13:34; CAPEXIL, 2017).

The first plenary meeting of the IWG took place in 2012. Many delegations in principle supported the view that the overall objective should be to eventually agree on a "successor undertaking" to the current OECD Arrangement, in the sense of Item (k) of Annex I of the SCM. Little progress was demonstrated until September 2020, when the G12 Heads of Export Credit Agencies issued its first-ever G12 joint statement that the meeting was a productive and *transparent exchange* highlighting all ECA efforts to stabilise the availability of working capital and export credit in a volatile international market environment. However, this was followed by a U-turn in November 2020 with the announcement that the EU and ten other delegates of the IWG had suspended their participation in the IWG discussions. As a result, the regulation of official export credit support remains ill-suited to govern twenty-first century global realities.

Evaluating ECA Activity: Patchy Data, Patchy Rules

The underlying theme of this chapter is that greater transparency in official export financing is the base requirement for any attempt to create more relevant and inclusive rules to maintain the level playing field. Information disclosure, dissemination, monitoring and auditing is a vital element of good governance. Such data can provide timely information on unfair competition, sustainable lending and debt distress. Emergencies such as the 2008 financial crisis or the COVID-19 pandemic led many governments to rapidly introduce rafts of new support aimed at both the financial and non-financial sectors. The terms and conditions of these transactions are a matter of global public interest. Emergency measures have in some cases taken precedence over competition rules and good governance principles. Excessive secrecy over publicly funded export support ultimately undermines the quality of public decision-making and prevents checks on abuse of public power, to the detriment of society and governance.

Transparency requirements and clearly defined policy space for legitimate government support instruments serve to provide the context for a positive assessment of certain measures of support, and also preclude the possibility that action and remedies are taken (Howse, 2009; Rubini, 2015). Without these, it is not possible to distinguish between those export subsidies that are vital to fulfil domestic policy objectives and those that governments use to support certain firms or domestic industries to give them an unfair advantage over both international and other domestic competitors. There is therefore both an enlightened and a self-interested rationale for governments to negotiate more comprehensive rules based upon widely accepted transparency and monitoring requirements for publicly funded export credit interventions – to the benefit of many and not the few.

References

Amnesty International (2013). *A History of Neglect UK Export Finance and Human Rights*. London: Amnesty International UK.

Asian Development Bank (ADB) (2019). Brief No. 113, September.

BankWatch Network (2017). ECAs Go to Market: A Critical Review of Transparency and Sustainability at Seven Export Credit Agencies in Central and Eastern Europe. December.

Boehm, E. (2019). Justin Amash Wants to Kill the Zombified Remains of the Export–Import Bank. Reason 29/4/2019. https://reason.com/2019/03/28/justin-amash-wants-to-kill-the-export-im/

Brautigam, D., and Kidane, W. (2020). China, Africa, and Debt Distress: Fact and Fiction about Asset Seizures. China Africa Research Initiative Policy Brief No. 47/2020.

Brynildsen, Ø. S. (2011). Exporting Goods or Exporting Debts? Export Credit Agencies and the Roots of Developing Country Debt. European Network for Debt and Development. www.eca-watch.org/sites/default/files/exportinggoods.pdf

CAPEXIL (2017). Background Note | International Working Group (IWG) on Export Credit. http://capexil.org/background-note-iwg-on-export-credit/

Chauffour, J.-P., and Farole, T. (2009). Trade Finance in Crisis: Market Adjustment or Market Failure? Policy Research Working Paper Series 5003, The World Bank.

Coppens, D. (2009). How Much Credit for Export Credit Support under the SCM Agreement? *Journal of International Economic Law* 12(1): 63–113.

Coppens, D., and Friedbacher, T. (2015). A Tale of Two Rules: The Intersection Between WTO and OECD Disciplines on Export Credit Support, The Future of Foreign Trade Support – Setting Global Standards for Export Credit and Political Risk Insurance. In A. Klasen and F. Bannert (eds.), *The Future of Foreign Trade Support: Setting Global Standards for Export Credit and Political Risk Insurance*. London: Global Policy.

Council Directive 98/29/EC of 7 May 1998 on Harmonisation of the Main Provisions Concerning Export Credit Insurance for Transactions with Medium and Long-Term Cover.

Dawar, K. (2020). Official Export Credit Support: Competition and Compliance Issues. *Journal of World Trade* 54(3): 373–395.

de Rugy, V., and Leventhal, J. (2019). ExIm Bank: A Comparative Analysis of Pre- and Post-Quorum Lending. Mercatus Centre Policy Brief, April. www.mercatus.org/media/69821/download

de Rugy, V., and O'Sullivan, A. (2014), The US Export–Import Bank: A Review of the Debate over Reauthorization, MERCATUS RESEARCH. www.mercatus.org/research/research-papers/us-export-import-bank-review-debate-over-reauthorization

Gelpern, A., Horn, S., Morris, S., Parks, B., and Trebesch, C. (2021). How China Lends: A Rare Look into 100 Debt Contracts with Foreign Governments. Peterson Institute for International Economics, Kiel Institute for the World Economy, Center for Global Development, and AidData at William & Mary. Working Papers 21-7, May 2021. www.piie.com/sites/default/files/documents/wp21-7.pdf

Guzman, A. T., and Meyer, T. L. (2010). International Soft Law. *Journal of Legal Analysis* 2: 171–173.

Hoekman, B. (2016). Subsidies, Spillovers and WTO Rules in a Value-chain World. *Global Policy*, 7(3), 351–359.

Hopewell, K. (2017). When Market Fundamentalism and Industrial Policy Collide: The Tea Party and the US Export–Import Bank. *Review of International Political Economy* 24(4): 569–598.

Hopewell, K. (2019). Power Transitions and Global Trade Governance: The Impact of a Rising China on the Export Credit Regime. *Regulation & Governance* 15: 634–652.

Howse, R. (2009). Do the World Trade Organization Disciplines on Domestic Subsidies Make Sense? The Case for Legalizing Some Subsidies. In K. Bagwell, G. Bermann, and P. Mavroidis (eds.), *Law and Economics of Contingent Protection in International Trade* (pp. 85–102). Cambridge: Cambridge University Press.

IMF, OECD, World Bank, and WTO (2022). Subsidies, Trade, and International Cooperation. Prepared by staff of IMF, OECD, World Bank, and WTO www.wto.org/english/news_e/news22_e/igo_22apr22_e.pdf

Konno, H. (1998). From Simple to Sophisticated: The Export Credit Arrangement. In *The Export Credit Arrangement: Achievements and Challenges 1978/1998*. Paris: OECD Publishing.

Parker, S., and Chefitz, G. (2018). Debtbook Diplomacy. Paper, Belfer Center for Science and International Affairs, Harvard Kennedy School, 24 May. www.belfercenter.org/publication/debtbook-diplomacy

Rubini, L. (2015). Rethinking International Subsidies Disciplines: Rationale and Possible Avenues for Reform. E15 Initiative. Geneva: International Centre for Trade and Sustainable Development (ICTSD) and World Economic Forum. www.e15initiative.org/

Schäfer, K. (2008). Bankrolling Climate Change: Why It Is Time to End Hermes Flights of Fancy. European ECA Reform Campaign. Briefing Paper 6.

UK Export Finance (2012–2013). Export Credits Guarantee Department Annual Report and Accounts. https://assets.publishing.service.gov.uk/government/uploads/system/uploads/attachment_data/file/207721/ecgd-ukef-annual-report-and-accounts-2012-to-2013.pdf

UK House of Commons Environmental Audit Committee (2019). UK Export Finance, Nineteenth Report of Session 2017–19 Report. https://publications.parliament.uk/pa/cm201719/cmselect/cmenvaud/1804/1804.pdf

UK House of Commons Foreign Affairs Committee (2020). Merging Success: Bringing together the FCO and DFID. Government Response to Committee's Second Report. Sixth Special Report of Session 2019–21. https://committees.parliament.uk/publications/2704/documents/26878/default/

US ExIm (Export-Import Bank of the United States) (2021). Reports to US Congress on Global Export Credit Competition (Competitiveness Report). https://img.exim.gov/s3fs-public/reports/competitiveness_reports/2020/EXIM_2020_CompetitivenessReport_Web-Ready_Single%20pages.pdf

WTO Ottawa Group (2020). 2020 Statement of the Ottawa Group: "Focusing Action on Covid-19", WT/GC/217, communicated to the WTO General Council. 16 June. https://docs.wto.org/dol2fe/Pages/SS/directdoc.aspx?filename=Q:/WT/GC/217.pdf

4

The Effects of Non-Trade Provisions in Trade Agreements on Bilateral FDI

HUGO ROJAS-ROMAGOSA

Introduction

Preferential trade agreements (PTAs) have been estimated to increase bilateral FDI between the signing countries (Anderson et al., 2019; Kox and Rojas-Romagosa, 2020). However, there is significant heterogeneity between PTAs (Horn et al., 2010). PTAs differ by number and combinations of trade-related provisions, and by varying degrees of legal enforceability for these provisions (Dür et al., 2014; Hofmann et al., 2017; Mattoo et al., 2020). In addition, and with increasing frequency, several non-trade issues (NTIs) are also incorporated in PTAs (Lechner, 2016). These include provisions on political and civil rights (CPR), economic and social rights (ESR) and environmental protection (ER). Given the overall intrinsic heterogeneity in PTAs, it is relevant to analyse which PTA characteristics are driving the increase in bilateral foreign direct investment (FDI) flows after signing a trade agreement.

Given the legal complexity of PTAs and the level of detail incorporated in the agreements, it is common practice to use indexes and summary indicators to capture different degrees of variation between PTAs.[1] The most commonly used summary indicator is the PTA depth index from the Design of Trade Agreements (DESTA) database (Dür et al., 2014). Using seven broad provision categories, it classifies PTAs using an index that ranges from one to seven, depending on how many of these broad provisions are present in a specific PTA. The higher the index, the deeper the PTA agreement is, while those with fewer provisions are defined as shallow PTAs. Using this PTA depth index, Kox and Rojas-Romagosa (2020) find that the precise composition of the trade agreement does not

[1] See for example: Dür et al. (2014); Lechner (2016); Hofmann et al. (2017). PTAs are legal texts that can run into several hundred pages, with not only different provisions and enforcing mechanisms, but also with different levels and depth of legal detail.

have a significantly different effect than signing the agreement itself. The average effect of implementing any PTA is to increase bilateral FDI by around 30 per cent, while signing the deepest PTAs (with a depth index of seven), increases FDI by around 35 per cent. This slightly larger FDI impact, however, is not robust to different specification, and hence Kox and Rojas-Romagosa (2020) do not find conclusive empirical evidence that deeper PTAs have any additional effect on bilateral FDI. On the other hand, Kox and Rojas-Romagosa (2020) do find that belonging to the EU single market has a very large impact – increasing bilateral FDI by 135 per cent – as well as signing a bilateral investment treaty (BIT) – with around a 40 per cent increase.

This chapter expands the analysis in Kox and Rojas-Romagosa (2020) to empirically test the specific relation between NTIs and bilateral FDI. Accordingly, we also employ a structural gravity model of FDI, together with bilateral FDI data from the United Nations Conference on Trade and Development (UNCTAD, 2014). The model includes country-pair fixed effects to control for observable and non-observable specific country-pair time-invariant FDI determinants. We then include time-variant policy indicators, which control for membership of the EU single market, the presence and depth of PTAs (Dür et al., 2014) and for the presence of a BIT.[2]

To analyse the effect of non-trade provisions on bilateral FDI, we use the NTI indexes constructed by Lechner (2016). These indexes summarise the NTI provisions contained in PTAs over time and, in conjunction with the presence of a PTA, allow us to estimate the potential effect of NTIs on bilateral FDI. Lechner (2016) constructs two types of indexes for the three broad categories of NTIs: civil and political rights, economic and social rights, and environmental protection. The first set of indexes are constructed using the latent trait analysis (LTA) and the second set adds all the individual NTI provision in each of the three broad NTI categories.

A priori, it is not clear how the inclusion of non-trade provisions in PTAs can affect bilateral FDI. On the one hand, stronger commitments on labour and environmental protection, for example, can hinder the entry (or expansion) of multinational enterprises (MNEs) into certain

[2] BIT data are taken from the UNCTAD data on international investment agreements (UNCTAD, 2019). Furthermore, BITs can be classified between those in-force and those that have only been signed (but not enforced). This data was compiled by Valentino Desilvestro, who kindly shared it with us.

countries by increasing operational and compliance costs. On the other hand, MNEs with strong corporate responsibility and social awareness policies will prefer these stronger commitments on non-trade issues as part of their own global policies and public relations stance. Therefore, the magnitude and sign of the effect of the inclusion of NTIs in PTAs on bilateral FDI is an open empirical question.

To the best of our knowledge, this is the first study that empirically examines the relation between NTI provisions in PTAs and bilateral FDI values. We find that, in general, NTI provisions have, if any, a positive relation with bilateral FDI. The CPR index has a positive, significant and robust relation with bilateral FDI. However, the other two indicators, economic and social rights and environmental protection, usually have positive coefficient signs, but they are not robust to different specifications. This implies that we do not find any negative FDI effects of including more and/or stronger non-trade provisions in trade agreements. Thus, we conclude that if NTIs have any relation with bilateral FDI, it is positive.

This result can be driven by countries that already have relatively strong institutions, such as good governance, strong rule of law and property rights. For instance, Gamso and Grosse (2021) note that PTAs might become more important to attracting FDI when the country has relatively weak property rights. Moreover, it is likely that countries that already have strong environmental protection, civil and political rights, and labour and social rights have more incentives to include NTI provisions in any PTA they negotiate and sign. Therefore, the positive relation we find between NTI provisions and bilateral FDI can be generated by pre-existing non-trade policies already implemented that are not directly related to the PTA effects. In our gravity specification, however, these host-country institutional differences are controlled by destination-time fixed effects, as long as these institutional differences are not changing over the years our data covers (2001 to 2012).[3] On the other hand, Blonigen and Piger (2014) find that host-country institutional variables have small inclusion probabilities as FDI determinants in their Bayesian approach.[4] Therefore, within our methodology, we can establish correlation, but not causality, between more NTI provisions in PTAs and

[3] Using a more elaborate gravity approach that deals with country-specific institutions, Beverelli et al. (2018) do find robust empirical evidence that stronger institutions promote international trade. However, a similar analysis has not been conducted for FDI.

[4] They do find that trade agreements have a high probability inclusion as FDI determinants, which is in line with the results in Kox and Rojas-Romagosa (2020).

positive effects on bilateral FDI. Our results, however, do find empirical evidence that including stronger non-trade provisions does not have a negative relation with bilateral FDI.

This chapter is organised as follows. The next section explains our analytical framework and econometric specification. The data is presented and our main structural gravity results are shown in the following two sections. The final section concludes.

Analytical Framework

Although the gravity equation fits FDI data reasonable well, a micro-founded FDI gravity model does not yet exist – that is, there is no similar FDI equivalent to the trade-gravity model of Anderson and van Wincoop (2003). In other words, there is no micro-based tractable model that specifically identifies gravity variables as the sole determinants of FDI patterns (Blonigen, 2005). On the other hand, several papers have theoretical models explaining the relations between trade, FDI and the operations of multinational corporations (Bergstrand and Egger, 2007, 2010; Ramondo and Rodríguez-Clare, 2013; Anderson et al., 2019, 2020). However, these particular models are too complex and data-demanding for real empirical testing, and therefore only allow for calibrated exercises.

Gravity Model for FDI

Given these theoretical limitations, in this study we follow Kox and Rojas-Romagosa (2020), and we deliberately choose a partial equilibrium FDI gravity model that explains the main push and pull factors for FDI and also accounts for absolute and relative bilateral FDI frictions. This model specification means that we do not test the interrelation between PTAs, trade and FDI, or the FDI diversion effects of PTAs. However, using this approach has the advantage that we avoid the endogeneity bias related to employing trade and FDI data in the same regressions. Bergstrand and Egger (2007, 2010) state that both trade and FDI flows are generated by the same 'common process' and this can mis-specify the estimations when including both variables simultaneously.

Our gravity model builds on the knowledge capital interpretation of FDI.[5] In particular, we employ the FDI gravity specification from Kox

[5] Other papers using this approach include Bergstrand and Egger (2007, 2010); Anderson et al. (2019, 2020).

and Rojas-Romagosa (2020), which is a stand-alone partial-equilibrium model for exploring the direct impacts of different PTA designs on bilateral FDI. This model is represented by the following equation system:[6]

$$FDI_{ij}^{stock} = \omega_{ij} \frac{\alpha Y_i \beta Y_j}{P_i \prod_j} \tag{4.1}$$

$$P_i = \left[\sum_{j=1}^{N} \left(\frac{z_{ij}}{\prod_j} \right)^{(1-\sigma)} \frac{Y_j}{Y} \right]^{\frac{1}{1-\sigma}} \tag{4.2}$$

$$\prod_{ij} = \left[\sum_{i=1}^{N} \left(\frac{z_{ji}}{P_i} \right)^{(1-\sigma)} \frac{Y_i}{Y} \right]^{\frac{1}{1-\sigma}} \tag{4.3}$$

where FDI_{ij}^{stock} are the bilateral FDI stocks originating from country i and hosted in country j.[7] The relative openness of country j to FDI from country i is represented by ω_{ij}, which has values between 0 and 1.[8] Thus, if $\omega_{ij} = 1$, country j is fully open for entry of technology capital from country i, while in the case of $\omega_{ij} = 0$, no technology capital originating from country i is admitted. FDI flows are positively affected by both the size (GDP) of the origin country (Y_i) as well as the destination country (Y_j). The parameters $\alpha > 0$ and $\beta > 0$ are both gravity proportionality factors that indicate how strongly the bilateral FDI stocks react to the economic masses of, respectively, the origin and the destination country. For example, the ratio Y_j/Π_j can be regarded as a proxy for country j's potential absorption capacity for FDI-related technology capital from country i. Equation 4.1, therefore, provides the main determinants of bilateral FDI stocks.

Equation 4.2 defines the inward multilateral resistance term (P_i) of the gravity trade model. It consistently aggregates and averages all country-specific FDI friction costs z, after weighting them by the relative economic size of each country. These bilateral FDI friction costs include the effects of distance and having different languages, among others.

[6] Time indexes are suppressed in this representation. For further details on the model see Kox and Rojas-Romagosa (2020).

[7] We follow the common practice in the literature and use bilateral FDI stock data, which are more widely available and reliable than FDI flow data. In addition, FDI stocks are a better analytical fit to the knowledge capital stock concept (Anderson et al., 2019).

[8] Note that this variable is the inverse to FDI-related entry barriers or frictions.

$Y = \sum Y_j$ is world output or world GDP, used to normalise the size of each Y_j, and σ is the elasticity of substitution from the constant elasticity of substitution (CES) functions, which provides the opportunity costs of investing in other countries. To complete the full FDI gravity system, Equation 4.3 defines the outward multilateral resistance term (Π_j). It consistently aggregates and averages all bilateral costs of country j versus all other countries by relative country size (Y_i/Y).

It is important to recall, moreover, that our methodology cannot identify the causal relation between NTI provisions and bilateral FDI. The political motivation and decision process to include non-trade provisions in a particular PTA can be determined, at least partially, by the current MNEs already established in the country, the institutional framework of both countries and any legal interrelations that can affect both FDI and a set of non-trade issues. This reverse-causality link between existing bilateral FDI and the NTI included in a PTA creates potential endogeneity issues. Hence, we can establish the correlation between NTI provisions in PTAs and changes in bilateral FDI, but cannot establish a causal link between them.

As explained, it is not clear, a priori, how strong non-trade provisions can affect bilateral FDI. For certain MNEs it can represent an increase in the FDI entry barriers (ω) and/or increase FDI cost frictions (z). On the contrary, for MNEs that prioritise corporate social and environmental responsibility, these provisions can reduce these entry barriers and related costs, since it provides international recognition and prior commitment to enforce NTIs. Our empirical evaluation will then indirectly evaluate what the average value of these entry and friction costs are, and hence how NTIs affect bilateral FDI.

Main Regression Equation

The structural model of Equations (4.1) to (4.3) is then applied to a data panel (with time t) using the following econometric specification:

$$FDI_{ijt} = exp\left[\gamma_1 \mathbf{POL}_{ijt} + \mu_{it} + \mu_{jt} + \mu_{ij}\right] + \epsilon_{ijt} \qquad (4.4)$$

where FDI_{ijt} is the inward FDI stock from country of origin i (the partner country) to country of destination j (the reporting country) in period t.[9]

[9] In our main specification we use yearly FDI data. For sensitivity analysis we also use 3-year FDI averages.

Our main variables of interest are included in the vector $\mathbf{POL}_{ijt}$. These are time-variant bilateral policy variables (e.g. PTAs, NTIs and bilateral investment treaties). We also include a full set of fixed effects. First, μ_{it} are time-varying source-country fixed effects that control for the outward multilateral resistance terms and other specific origin-country variables. Second, μ_{jt} are time-varying destination-country fixed effects that account for the inward multilateral resistance terms and other country-specific characteristics of the destination country. Third, μ_{ij} are the set of country-pair fixed effects that absorb all time-invariant gravity covariates from t_{ij} along with any other time-invariant determinants of FDI costs that are not observable. For instance, this last set of fixed effects controls for bilateral FDI determinants, such as distance, common language, common law systems and cultural similarities, among others. Finally, ϵ_{ijt} is a combined error term.

Equation (4.4) is our main estimating equation and in this specification it is key to identifying the relevant country-specific time-variant policy variables. In particular, it is key to isolating the effect of particular policies, which can be correlated with each other. In the case of NTIs, this is particularly challenging, since they are only present when a PTA is signed, and therefore, if no PTA indicator is included in the regressions, the NTI coefficient can absorb the effects of the trade provisions of the PTA. Therefore, we employ several combination and additional policy variables – membership of the EU single market and BITs – to better identify the policy effects of each variable.

To estimate this specification we also follow a number of best practices regarding the structural gravity equation (Yotov et al., 2016):

- We employ a pseudo-Poisson maximum likelihood (PPML) estimator to effectively deal with zero bilateral FDI flows and accounts for the presence of heteroscedasticity in FDI data (Santos Silva and Tenreyro, 2006). Thus, we are careful to distinguish between real zero FDI (flows or stocks) and missing (or non-reported, suppressed) data.[10]

[10] Note however, that the quality of the bilateral FDI is problematic on this issue. In particular, the UNCTAD (2014) has a large number of missing information regarding most country pairs and even though for some cases there is a clear distinction between zeros and missing data, we expect that many of the missing data are actual zeros. This is particularly problematic regarding the bilateral information between small countries that are in different continents. However, we refrain from assigning zero values to missing information as this will add measurement errors to the data.

- Use panel data to be able to include country-pair fixed effects and account for any unobservable time-invariant FDI and other FDI barriers. Using these country-pair fixed effects has been proven to be a better measure of the bilateral costs than the standard set of gravity variables (Egger and Nigai, 2015; Agnosteva et al., 2014). Moreover, there is also a potential endogeneity problem regarding the relation between signing PTAs and existing FDI.[11] In this respect, the use of country-pair fixed effects can partially deal with the endogeneity of PTAs by accounting for the observable and unobservable linkages between the endogenous trade policy covariate and the error term (Yotov et al., 2016).
- Include origin-time and destination-time fixed effects to properly account for multilateral resistance terms in panel data gravity estimations (Olivero and Yotov, 2012). Both these fixed effects also absorb the country size variables (Y_{it} and Y_{jt}) from the structural gravity system in Equations (4.1–4.3), in addition to all other observable and unobservable time-varying country-specific characteristics, including different national policies, institutions and exchange rates (Yotov et al., 2016).
- We follow Heid et al. (2015), and in the context of FDI, we estimate the structural gravity model using both international and intra-national bilateral data.[12] Hence, we account for the effect of non-discriminatory domestic policies, which can influence domestic capital stocks and inward FDI stocks simultaneously. This also allows for theoretically consistent identification of the effects of bilateral policies and for a bias-free estimation of the effects of PTAs on FDI.[13]

It is important to note that the empirical results from Kox and Rojas-Romagosa (2020) show that using country-pair fixed effects, as well as domestic (intra-national) capital stocks, are key for the empirical results. Neglecting to include these elements results in biased and unreliable estimations.

Data

Data availability is a serious issue with regard to FDI (IMF, 2003) and only a few sources offer consistent time series for bilateral FDI flows. In this study we use UNCTAD's Bilateral FDI Statistics (UNCTAD, 2014), which provides systematic FDI data for 206 countries, covering inflows, outflows, inward stocks (instock) and outward FDI stocks (outstock). The UNCTAD data is collected mainly from national sources when available. If not available, it is complemented with data from partner

[11] In other words, PTAs are more likely between partners that already have intense economic relations.

[12] Intra-national investment is proxied by using the capital stock in each country.

[13] See Yotov et al. (2016) for an equivalent explanation regarding trade flows. In addition, this specification can also solve the "distance puzzle" by accounting for foreign and domestic distances.

countries (mirror data) as well as data from other international organisations.[14] This database has available information for the years 2001 to 2012, all in US$ millions.[15]

We use different policy variable data sources. First, to analyse the presence and depth of PTAs we use the Design of Trade Agreements (DESTA) database (Dür et al., 2014). This database has systematically collected data on more than 700 agreements, and ranks each PTA by the presence of seven different provisions: full tariff reductions (with few exceptions), provisions on common standards, services trade provisions, competition provisions, provisions on public procurement, provisions on investment and provisions on intellectual property rights (IPRs). Using these provisions, DESTA generates a PTA depth index that ranges from one to seven, depending on how many provisions are present in each trade agreement.

Some adjustments have been made to the original DESTA database. The most important one relates to the EU, since DESTA does not consider the EU's single market as a PTA. One can assume that all EU country pairs have a deep PTA (with value seven) with each other. However, the EU single market provides broader and deeper economic integration than any existing PTA. The EU's single market is the largest project of economic integration among sovereign states.[16] Its legal and institutional setting ensures that the EU single market provides substantially less friction for bilateral trade and FDI than the deepest PTA. Therefore, in our analysis, we also distinguish the EU single market by using a dummy variable.[17] Moreover, we also adjust the DESTA database so each new EU member state automatically inherits the past PTAs negotiated by the EU. Thus, upon the date of accession of each new member state, we adjust the DESTA data to reflect that these new member countries are also part of the previously negotiated EU PTAs.

[14] For instance, the OECD's International Direct Investment Statistics database and FDI data from the IMF.

[15] There is a small proportion (less than 3%) of stock values in the UNCTAD database that are negative. This issue is mainly explained by changes in intra-company loans and changes in asset valuations. We replace these negative values with zeros in our data. See Kox and Rojas-Romagosa (2020) for further details and explanations.

[16] Among others, broad integration is provided by the four fundamental principles of the EU's single market: free movement of goods, capital, services, and labour. In addition, it entails a customs union and common external trade policy, a large number of EU-wide regulatory bodies, and the enforcement of EU law through the European Court of Justice.

[17] Here we account for the year of accession of new member states: 2004 for ten new member states, 2007 for Bulgaria and Romania, and 2014 for Croatia.

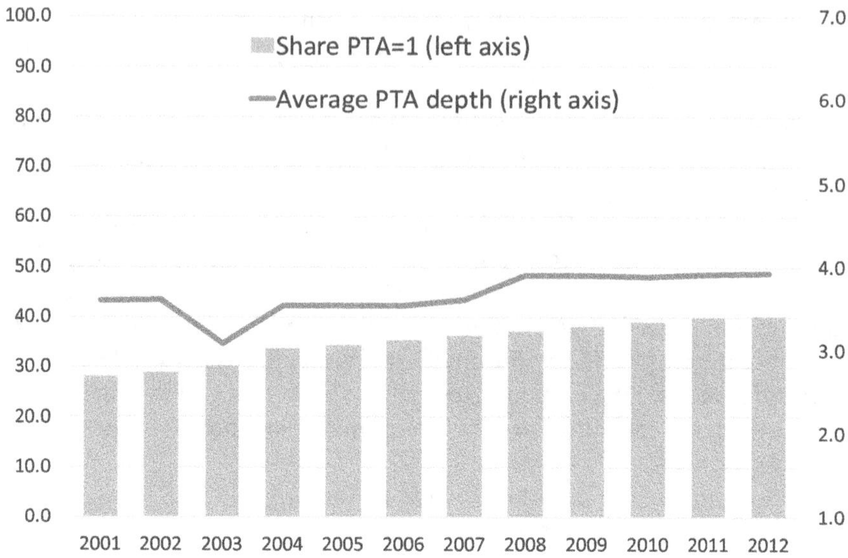

Figure 4.1 PTA presence and depth between 2001 and 2012
Source: Own elaboration using DESTA database.

To account for the existence of bilateral investment treaties we employ the indicator (dummy variable) from the original UNCTAD data on international investment agreements (UNCTAD, 2019). Here we distinguish between BITs that have just been signed and those that are signed and effectively in force.[18]

Combining the UNCTAD bilateral FDI data with the DESTA database provides us with more than 100,000 observations and around 8,500 unique country pairs for twelve years (2001–2012). As has been previously documented (Dür et al., 2014; Miroudot and Rigo, 2019), the cumulative number of active PTAs, as well as the depth of PTAs, has been increasing over time. For our sample period, Figure 4.1 shows an increase in the share of active PTAs (from around 28 per cent of total observations in 2001, to 40 per cent in 2012). We also observe that the PTA depth has experienced a less pronounced increase, moving from a depth average of 3.6 to 3.9.

[18] We thank Valentino Desilvestro for sharing the compiled and processed BIT data extracted from the UNCTAD website.

Furthermore, Table 4.1 shows the frequency of different PTA depths. First, we observe that around two-thirds of all observations (and of all country pairs) have no active PTAs during this period. When there is an active PTA, the most common depth levels are one and seven (both with around 28 per cent of total observations). When we look at country pairs, however, the most common depth level is seven (29 per cent). However, this is driven by EU member states, since country pairs within the EU single market represent 21 per cent of the total PTAs. Once we account for the EU single market, the most common depth level is three (24 per cent). The EU, moreover, is part of 2,263 PTAs (either as one or both partners), and this represents 68 per cent of all the active PTAs during this period. Excluding the country pairs within the EU single market, the most frequent depth levels for EU trade agreements are three (30 per cent) and seven (20 per cent).

We also look at the individual provisions that constitute the DESTA depth index. We find that the standards provisions is the most common, present in 88 per cent of all PTAs, followed by full tariff reductions (73 per cent). The services, public procurement and competition provisions are present in around half the PTAs, while the least common provisions are the IPRs (34 per cent) and investments (39 per cent). Table A4.1 in the Appendix shows the most frequent provision combinations by PTA depth level. There we observe that when only one provision is present (depth 1), the standards provisions account for 70 per cent of the cases, with the full tariff reductions accounting for 23 per cent. Since these two provisions are the most common, it is not surprising that for PTAs with two provisions, this combination (standards + full tariffs) accounts for 95 per cent of the cases. However, when three provisions are present, the most common combination does not include them, and the combination with services, competition and investment represents 29 per cent of the cases. For PTAs with depth level four, the most common combination is standards, full tariffs, services and competition (80 per cent). For PTA depth levels of five and six, the most common combinations exclude IPRs, which is also the least common of all the provisions.

The presence and intensity of non-trade issues is measured by the NTI indexes constructed by Lechner (2016). She classifies all individual NTI provisions (data-points) into three broad categories: civil and political rights, economic and social rights, and environmental protection. The first set of indexes uses the latent trait analysis to aggregate individual NTI data-points (each coded 0 and 1). The core purpose of the LTA is to measure the difficulty of each non-trade individual provision getting selected into a particular PTA. For instance, the provisions with fewer

Table 4.1 *Main characteristics for the presence and depth of PTAs between 2001 and 2012*

	All observations			Country pairs[a]			Country pairs with EU as partner		
With:	total	share (%)	share (%) if PTA = 1	total	share (%)	share (%) if PTA = 1	total	share (%)	share (%) if PTA = 1
No PTA	67,780	64.9		5,183	61.0		2,410	51.6	
PTA (dummy = 1)	36,680	35.1		3,320	39.0		2,263	48.4	
PTA Depth = 1	10,373	9.9	28.3	438	5.2	13.2	210	4.5	9.3
PTA Depth = 2	6,030	5.8	16.4	556	6.5	16.7	139	3.0	6.1
PTA Depth = 3	4,095	3.9	11.2	785	9.2	23.6	669	14.3	29.6
PTA Depth = 4	2,035	1.9	5.5	210	2.5	6.3	145	3.1	6.4
PTA Depth = 5	2,721	2.6	7.4	203	2.4	6.1	141	3.0	6.2
PTA Depth = 6	1,176	1.1	3.2	163	1.9	4.9	35	0.7	1.5
PTA Depth = 7	10,250	9.8	27.9	965	11.3	29.1	924	19.8	40.8
EU – single market	6,570	6.3	17.9	693	8.2	20.9	693	14.8	20.9
Depth = 7, excl. EU-sm	3,680	3.5	10.0	272	3.2	8.2	231	4.9	20.0
Total	104,460	100.0	100.0	8,503	100.0	100.0	4,673	100.0	100.0

[a] Excluding same country pairs.

Source: Own estimations using DESTA database.

Table 4.2 *NTI indexes, averages for all PTAs and EU PTAs*

	All PTAs	EU PTAs
CPR (sum)	6.02	7.11
ESR (sum)	7.21	7.76
EP (sum)	5.17	5.46
CPR (LTA)	3.78	4.20
ESR (LTA)	3.79	3.99
EP (LTA)	3.68	3.85

Source: NTI indexes taken from Lechner (2016).

observations across PTAs receive higher weights (e.g. human rights conditionality clauses), whereas the provisions with many observations receive lower weights – such as the exception clause, which nearly all PTAs have. The second set of indexes (SUM) simply sums up all the individual NTI provisions by each of the three broad NTI categories.

In total we have NTI information for 33,242 observations, which represents around 91 per cent of all the observations in our sample when a PTA is present. In addition, around 92 per cent of the NTI indexes have positive (non-zero) values. This means that most PTAs in our analysis have at least one NTI provision. Table 4.2 shows the average values for the different NTI indexes for all PTAs and when only EU PTAs are considered. We observe that ESR provisions are the most common (based on the SUM index), followed by CPR and EP. For the EU PTAs the ranking is the same, but the average number of provisions is higher for all three categories. The difference is larger for CPR: the EU PTAs have almost one CPR provision more than an average PTA. The LTA indexes also show that NTI provision in EU PTAs are more important than average PTAs. However, for the EU PTAs, the CPR provisions have a higher LTA index than the ESR, so CPR provisions are more highly ranked than when using the simple sum of provisions. To sum up, the EU has stronger NTI provisions in their PTAs and, in particular, this difference is more pronounced regarding CPR provisions.

When we analyse the evolution of the NTI indexes over our timeframe (2001 to 2012) we find that the indexes have been relatively stable over time (see Figure 4.2). All indexes experienced a decrease between 2004 and 2007, but rebound in the later years. The SUM indexes (upper row in Figure 4.2) show small increases for the ESR and EP indexes.

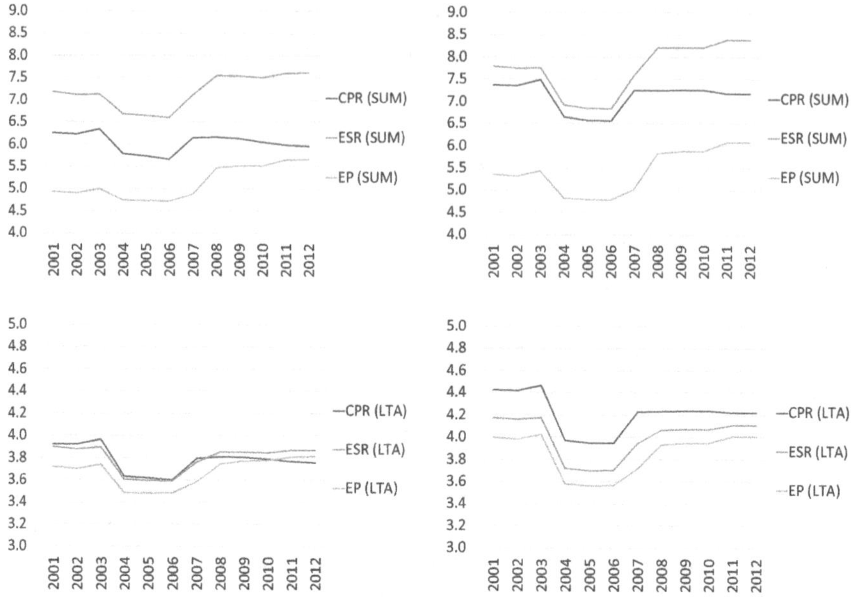

Figure 4.2 NTI indexes: yearly averages for all PTAs (left) and EU PTAs (right)
Source: NTI indexes taken from Lechner (2016).

While the LTA indexes (lower row) have more even values over time. On the other hand, we see that the indexes are higher for the EU PTAs. The main difference relates to the CPR index, which is higher for the EU PTAs, in particular for the LTA indexes.

The simple correlations between the bilateral FDI stocks and our policy variables is presented in Table A4.2 in the Appendix. First, we observe that the presence of PTAs (dummy) and the PTA depth index have a high correlation of 0.8. Hence, to avoid multi-correlation issues, we do not employ them simultaneously in our regressions. Second, the correlation between the six NTI indexes and the PTA variables is also high (between 0.72 and 0.89). This issue is related to the large number of country pairs without a PTA (around two-thirds) and we only have positive NTI values if a PTA is present. To deal with this, we also run separate regressions using only the sub-sample where PTAs are present. In this way, we can isolate the effect of NTIs from that of the other trade issues included in PTAs. Finally, we also observe that the correlation between the NTI indexes is very high (0.93 on average), and hence we regress each of the three broad indexes separately.

FDI Gravity Results

In this section we present our main empirical results based on the FDI gravity specification defined in Equation 4.4 using yearly bilateral FDI stock data and the NTI indexes constructed by Lechner (2016). Following the findings in Kox and Rojas-Romagosa (2020), we include intra-national capital stocks to account for the effect of non-discriminatory domestic policies and for a bias-free estimation of the effects of PTAs on FDI.[19]

Civil and Political Rights (CPR)

Table 4.3 shows the results when regressing bilateral FDI stocks against the CPR (LTA) index.[20] We observe that the CPR (LTA) index is positive and significant when included as the only specific country-pair time-variant policy, but also when combined with the PTA indicator, membership of the EU single market and enforced BITs.[21] We also find here that membership of the EU single market is a robust indicator of increased bilateral FDI between EU member states. On the other hand, signing a BIT has a positive coefficient but is not robust to different specifications.

When using the full sample, however, we also observe that the PTA dummy variable is not significant. This can be related to multicollinearity issues between the PTA and the NTI variables discussed earlier. To avoid this issue, we run separate regressions using a sub-sample that only includes observations where a PTA is present. These results are shown in the last three columns in Table 4.3. We find again that the CPR index is positive and significant using this sub-sample. Note that we also add here a regression including the PTA depth index, which turns out to have a lower correlation (0.43 on average) with the different NTI indexes for the sub-sample of active bilateral PTAs (see Table A4.3 in the Appendix). In this case, the PTA depth indicator has a negative coefficient, which is surprising but not at odds with the findings in Kox and Rojas-Romagosa (2020) that this depth indicator is not robust, while

19 To estimate the PPML regressions we use Zylkin's STATA ado files (cf. Larch et al., 2017), which provide a much faster estimation than the normal STATA command.

20 Note that as shown by Fally (2015), using PPML in conjunction with country-time and country-pair fixed effects generates a near-perfect fit of the data (i.e. $R^2 = 1$). Thus, this statistic is non-informative for our PPML estimates and we do not report it in any of our regression results.

21 Most results are similar when using either in-force BITs or BITs that are only signed. Therefore, in what follows we only show results with the in-force BIT indicator.

Table 4.3 *Gravity regressions using yearly inward FDI stocks and the CPR (LTA) index*

	Full sample			Only if PTA present		
	(1)	(2)	(3)	(4)	(5)	(6)
CPR (LTA)	0.201***	0.192***	0.249***	0.487***	0.314***	0.330***
	(0.033)	(0.052)	(0.044)	(0.067)	(0.066)	(0.066)
PTA dummy		−0.073				
		(0.186)				
PTA depth			−0.0417			−0.108***
			(0.027)			(0.036)
EU single market		0.617***	0.427***		0.765***	1.064***
		(0.089)	(0.147)		(0.132)	(0.171)
BIT (in force)		0.137	0.368***		−1.099***	−1.079***
		(0.092)	(0.092)		(0.326)	(0.305)
Observations	74,377	74,377	74,377	25,803	25,803	25,803

Notes: Dependent variable: FDI inward stocks. PPML estimations using country-pair clustering of standard errors, in parentheses: *** $p < 0.01$, ** $p < 0.05$, * $p < 0.1$. Origin-country-time (μ_{it}), destination-country-time (μ_{jt}), and country-par (μ_{ij}) fixed effects are not reported. PTA_dummy and PTA_depth are taken from the DESTA database.
Source: Own estimations using UNCTAD bilateral FDI and NTI indexes from Lechner (2016).

the presence of a PTA is. Using this sub-sample we find again a positive effect of the EU single market, but now the BIT indicator has a negative sign. This last effect can be related to the low correlation between signing a PTA and signing a BIT, which are usually substitutes and not complements – that is, countries that sign PTAs usually do not have the need to sign BITs (see Kox and Rojas-Romagosa, 2020).

When we use the CPR additive (SUM) index – which sums up all individual CPR provisions in the PTAs – we find very similar results (see Table 4.4). The magnitude of the positive relation of the CPR index is easier to interpret using the SUM index,[22] where we can translate the

[22] Interpreting the results using the LTA index is less straightforward, since this is by construction a relative index that accounts for the difficulty of some provisions being included or not in a trade agreement.

Table 4.4 *Gravity regressions using yearly inward FDI stocks and the CPR additive (SUM) index*

	Full sample			Only if PTA present		
	(1)	(2)	(3)	(4)	(5)	(6)
CPR (SUM)	0.142***	0.133***	0.114***	0.168***	0.134***	0.140***
	(0.017)	(0.019)	(0.019)	(0.021)	(0.021)	(0.021)
PTA dummy		0.0264				
		(0.117)				
PTA depth			-0.021			-0.083**
			(0.017)			(0.034)
EU single market		0.572***	0.486***		0.766***	0.993***
		(0.091)	(0.114)		(0.134)	(0.168)
BIT (in force)		0.227**	-0.174		-0.943***	-0.836***
		(0.092)	(0.108)		(0.292)	(0.254)
Observations	74,377	74,377	74,377	25,803	25,803	25,803

Notes: Dependent variable: FDI inward stocks. PPML estimations using country-pair clustering of standard errors, in parentheses: *** $p < 0.01$, ** $p < 0.05$, * $p < 0.1$. Origin-country-time (μ_{it}), destination-country-time (μ_{jt}), and country-par (μ_{ij}) fixed effects are not reported. PTA_dummy and PTA_depth are taken from the DESTA database.

Source: Own estimations using UNCTAD bilateral FDI and NTI indexes from Lechner (2016).

impact on the dependent variable (inward FDI), using the formula: $V = \left(exp^{\hat{\gamma}} - 1\right) * 100$, where V is the FDI effect (in percentages) and $\hat{\gamma}$ is the estimated coefficient of the NTI index. Using this formula and the CPR (SUM) coefficients in Table 4.4, we find that including the CPR provisions is associated with an overall increase on bilateral FDI stocks of around 15 per cent.

Economic and Social Rights (ESR)

The results for the ESR index are presented in Table 4.5. The ESR index has a positive sign, but it is only significant when regressed alone or in

Table 4.5 *Gravity regressions using yearly inward FDI stocks and the ESR (LTA) index*

	Full sample			Only if PTA present		
	(1)	(2)	(3)	(4)	(5)	(6)
ESR (LTA)	0.055**	−0.014	0.006	0.0392	0.267***	0.079**
	(0.022)	(0.024)	(0.034)	(0.037)	(0.038)	(0.0335)
PTA dummy		0.302***				
		(0.060)				
PTA depth			0.0397			−0.006
			(0.027)			(0.036)
EU single market		0.709***	0.877***		0.793***	0.872***
		(0.089)	(0.145)		(0.134)	(0.170)
BIT (in force)		0.328***	0.378***		0.187	−0.202
		(0.091)	(0.094)		(0.163)	(0.156)
Observations	74,377	74,377	74,377	25,803	25,803	25,803

Notes: Dependent variable: FDI inward stocks. PPML estimations using country-pair clustering of standard errors, in parentheses: *** $p < 0.01$, ** $p < 0.05$, * $p < 0.1$. Origin-country-time (μ_{it}), destination-country-time (μ_{jt}), and country-par (μ_{ij}) fixed effects are not reported. PTA_dummy and PTA_depth are taken from the DESTA database.

Source: Own estimations using UNCTAD bilateral FDI and NTI indexes from Lechner (2016).

some combinations with other policy variables in the sub-sample that only includes active PTAs.

When using the additive (SUM) index (see Table 4.6) the ESR index is no longer significant in the PTA-only sub-sample. Hence, in contrast to the CPR index, we find that the ESR does not have a robust impact on bilateral FDI.

Environmental Protection (EP)

When we use the EP index, again we find positive and significant effects in some specifications, but not for all. Table 4.7 shows the results using the LTA index, where the EP index is only significant when regressed

Table 4.6 *Gravity regressions using yearly inward FDI stocks and the ESR additive (SUM) index*

	Full sample			Only if PTA present		
	(1)	(2)	(3)	(4)	(5)	(6)
ESR (SUM)	0.023**	-0.001	-0.006	0.012	-0.019	0.022
	(0.010)	(0.011)	(0.014)	(0.015)	(0.017)	(0.014)
PTA dummy		0.280***				
		(0.061)				
PTA depth			0.048**			-0.009
			(0.024)			(0.036)
EU single market		0.707***	0.919***		0.909***	0.880***
		(0.089)	(0.136)		(0.134)	(0.170)
BIT (in force)		0.377***	0.304***		-0.467**	-0.222
		(0.092)	(0.092)		(0.193)	(0.157)
Observations	74,377	74,377	74,377	25,803	25,803	25,803

Notes: Dependent variable: FDI inward stocks. PPML estimations using country-pair clustering of standard errors, in parentheses: *** $p < 0.01$, ** $p < 0.05$, * $p < 0.1$. Origin-country-time (μ_{it}), destination-country-time (μ_{jt}), and country-par (μ_{ij}) fixed effects are not reported. PTA_dummy and PTA_depth are taken from the DESTA database.
Source: Own estimations using UNCTAD bilateral FDI and NTI indexes from Lechner (2016).

alone or in the sub-sample with active PTAs in combination with the PTA depth index.

Table 4.8 presents the results for environmental protection provisions when using the additive (SUM) index. As before, we find that the EP index is only significant for a sub-set of the specifications.

To sum up our main results. We find that only the CPR index has a positive, significant and robust relation with bilateral FDI. The other NTI provisions – ESR and EP – have positive and significant relations, but these results are not robust to different specifications. It is important to observe that we do not find a single specification where there are negative and significant relations between any of the three NTI indexes and bilateral FDI.

Table 4.7 *Gravity regressions using yearly inward FDI stocks and the EP (LTA) index*

	Full sample			Only if PTA present		
	(1)	(2)	(3)	(4)	(5)	(6)
EP (LTA)	0.0453**	−0.012	−0.001	0.037	−0.011	0.209***
	(0.020)	(0.023)	(0.032)	(0.053)	(0.115)	(0.042)
PTA dummy		0.311***				
		(0.059)				
PTA depth			0.044			0.025
			(0.027)			(0.030)
EU single market		0.708***	0.897***		0.789***	0.772***
		(0.088)	(0.143)		(0.151)	(0.162)
BIT (in force)		0.393***	0.373***		−0.309	−0.024
		(0.093)	(0.094)		(0.474)	(0.155)
Observations	74,377	74,377	74,377	25,803	25,803	25,803

Notes: Dependent variable: FDI inward stocks. PPML estimations using country-pair clustering of standard errors, in parentheses: *** $p < 0.01$, ** $p < 0.05$, * $p < 0.1$. Origin-country-time (μ_{it}), destination-country-time (μ_{jt}), and country-par (μ_{ij}) fixed effects are not reported. PTA_dummy and PTA_depth are taken from the DESTA database.
Source: Own estimations using UNCTAD bilateral FDI and NTI indexes from Lechner (2016).

Sensitivity Analysis

We perform different sensitivity tests to check our main results. First, we run our regressions using three-year average FDI stocks, instead of yearly FDI data. This specification smooths the FDI series – which can be driven in some countries by single-year large FDI investment – but it also reduces the number of observations. We find that using this specification, the number of positive and significant NTI indexes increases with respect to our main results.[23] Again, there are no significant and negative

[23] Results available upon request.

Table 4.8 *Gravity regressions using yearly inward FDI stocks and the EP additive (SUM) index*

	Full sample			Only if PTA present		
	(1)	(2)	(3)	(4)	(5)	(6)
EP (SUM)	0.019*	−0.014	−0.011	0.012	0.055*	0.025
	(0.010)	(0.010)	(0.016)	(0.028)	(0.021)	(0.025)
PTA dummy		0.330***				
		(0.049)				
PTA depth			0.058**			−0.008
			(0.025)			(0.034)
EU single market		0.705***	0.958***		0.865***	0.898***
		(0.088)	(0.136)		(0.135)	(0.168)
BIT (in force)		0.254***	0.370***		−0.137	−0.241
		(0.089)	(0.094)		(0.155)	(0.159)
Observations	74,377	74,377	74,377	25,803	25,803	25,803

Notes: Dependent variable: FDI inward stocks. PPML estimations using country-pair clustering of standard errors, in parentheses: *** $p < 0.01$, ** $p < 0.05$, * $p < 0.1$. Origin-country-time (μ_{it}), destination-country-time (μ_{jt}), and country-par (μ_{ij}) fixed effects are not reported. PTA_dummy and PTA_depth are taken from the DESTA database.
Source: Own estimations using UNCTAD bilateral FDI and NTI indexes from Lechner (2016).

coefficients, which indicates that NTI provisions have, if any, a positive relation with bilateral FDI.

The UNCTAD data also provides information on bilateral FDI in- and outflows. However, the FDI flow series has large yearly fluctuations and also a relatively large number of negative values.[24] To deal with this issue, we use four-year averages to provide information on the medium-term FDI flows, which will be more suitable to account for policy changes. Using these FDI flow data, we find that the NTI provision results are very

[24] See Kox and Rojas-Romagosa (2020) for more information about the FDI flow series.

similar to our main results: the CPR index has positive, significant and robust relation with bilateral FDI flows, while the other two indexes find positive and significant relations, but only for some specifications.[25]

Finally, we estimate our main specifications excluding the 'domestic inward' stocks taken as the country's capital stock data. Kox and Rojas-Romagosa (2020) found that not accounting for these intra-national capital stocks, which control for the effect of non-discriminatory domestic policies, critically changes the estimations. In our case, we also find that not accounting for these domestic inward stocks creates significant changes in our results. In particular, some of the NTI indexes become negative and significant. Thus, we find that it is critical to include the intra-national capital stocks to obtain a bias-free estimation of the relation between PTAs on FDI and to control for the effects of non-discriminatory trade policies.

Conclusions

Non-trade policy objectives are becoming more common in trade negotiations and provisions with NTIs are frequently included in preferential trade agreements. This trend relates not only to enhanced public scrutiny of trade policy, but also to the idea that soft power mechanisms, including trade agreements, can help achieve some of these objectives. In principle, there are several reasons why including stricter provisions on civil, political, economic and social rights, as well as more environmental protection measures, might directly affect FDI flows. On the one hand, MNEs with strong corporate responsibility and social awareness policies will prefer stronger commitments on non-trade issues to bolster their own global policies, international image and public relations stance. On the other hand, some of these NTI provisions can increase operational and compliance costs, which can hinder the entry or expansion of MNEs in these countries. The magnitude and sign of the effect of the inclusion of NTIs in PTAs on bilateral FDI is thus an open empirical question.

Using the structural gravity methodology from Kox and Rojas-Romagosa (2020), we estimate the expected relation between the NTI provisions included in preferential trade agreements and bilateral FDI. The empirical results are based on past FDI effects derived from different

[25] Results available upon request.

PTA treaties and the provisions they included. To account for NTI provisions, we use the indexes constructed by Lechner (2016), who divides non-trade issues into three broad categories: civil and political rights, economic and social rights and environmental protection.

We find that including NTI provisions on PTAs does not have a negative correlation with bilateral FDI. If there is any relation at all, it will be positive and mainly related to the inclusion of civil and political rights. This positive relation, however, can be the result of initial or changing institutional conditions in the country that facilitate and/or incentivise the inclusion of NTI provisions in the trade agreement in the first place.

The rising inclusion of provisions safeguarding labour rights and standards, environmental protection, and other economic and political rights in trade agreements is in itself a positive development. These non-trade provisions have the potential to reduce negative effects of increased trade and FDI flows, while preserving a fluid international trading and investment system. The results of our study show that the rising number of non-trade provisions in recent PTAs did not have a negative correlation with bilateral FDI flows. In this regard, the positive impact of having more provisions to uphold higher economic, political and environmental standards has a positive correlation, if any, with larger bilateral FDI flows. These results suggest that most MNEs are not hindered, and are probably encouraged, to continue or start investing in countries where these provisions have been included in the PTAs that affect their international activities.

References

Agnosteva, D., J. E. Anderson, and Y. V. Yotov (2014). "Intra-national trade costs: Measures and aggregation," NBER Working Paper 19872, National Bureau of Economic Research.

Anderson, J. E., M. Larch, and Y. V. Yotov (2019). "Trade and investment in the global economy: A multi-country dynamic analysis," *European Economic Review*, 120: 103311.

Anderson, J. E., M. Larch, and Y. V. Yotov (2020). "Transitional growth and trade with frictions: A structural estimation framework," *The Economic Journal*, 130: 1583–1607.

Anderson, J. E. and E. van Wincoop (2003). "Gravity with gravitas: A solution to the border puzzle," *American Economic Review*, 93(1): 170–192.

Bergstrand, J. H. and P. Egger (2007). "A knowledge-and-physical-capital model of international trade flows, foreign direct investment, and multinational enterprises," *Journal of International Economics*, 73(2): 278–308.

Bergstrand, J. H. and P. Egger (2010). "A general equilibrium theory for estimating gravity equations of bilateral FDI, final goods trade, and intermediate trade flows," in *The Gravity Model in International Trade: Advances and Applications*, ed. by P. V. Bergeijk and S. Brakman, Cambridge: Cambridge University Press, 29–70.

Beverelli, C., A. Keck, M. Larch, and Y. V. Yotov (2018). "Institutions, trade and development: A quantitative analysis," CESifo Working Paper 6920, Center for Economic Studies and the Ifo Institute (CESifo).

Blonigen, B. (2005). "A review of the empirical literature on FDI determinants," *Atlantic Economic Journal*, 33(4): 383–403.

Blonigen, B. A. and J. Piger (2014). "Determinants of foreign direct investment," *Canadian Journal of Economics*, 47(3): 775–812.

Dür, A., L. Baccini, and M. Elsig (2014). "The design of international trade agreements: Introducing a new database," *Review of International Organizations*, 9(3): 353–375.

Egger, P. and S. Nigai (2015). "Structural gravity with dummies only: Constrained ANOVA-type estimation of gravity models," *Journal of International Economics*, 97(1): 86–99.

Fally, T. (2015). "Structural gravity and fixed effects," *Journal of International Economics*, 97(1): 76–85.

Gamso, J. and R. Grosse (2021). "Trade agreement depth, foreign direct investment, and the moderating role of property rights," *Journal of International Business Policy*, 4: 308–325.

Heid, B., M. Larch, and Y. V. Yotov (2015). "A simple method to estimate the effects of non-discriminatory trade policy within structural gravity models," Mimeo, University of Bayreuth.

Hofmann, C., A. Osnago, and M. Ruta (2017). "Horizontal depth: A new database on the content of preferential trade agreements," Policy Research Working Paper 7981, World Bank, Trade and Competitiveness Global Practice Group.

Horn, H., P. C. Mavroidis, and A. Sapir (2010). "Beyond the WTO? An anatomy of EU and US preferential trade agreements," *World Economy*, 33(11): 1565–1588.

IMF (2003). "Foreign direct investment trends and statistics," Working Paper, October, International Monetary Fund, Statistics Department.

Kox, H. L. M. and H. Rojas-Romagosa (2020). "How trade and investment agreements affect bilateral foreign direct investment: Results from a structural gravity model," *World Economy*, 43(12): 3203–3242.

Larch, M., J. Wanner, Y. V. Yotov, and T. Zylkin (2017). "The currency union effect: A PPML re-assessment with high-dimensional fixed effects," Working Paper 2017-07, Drexel University School of Economics.

Lechner, L. (2016). "The domestic battle over non-trade issues in preferential trade agreements," *Review of International Political Economy*, 23(5): 840–871.

Mattoo, A., N. Rocha, and M. Ruta (2020). *Handbook of Deep Trade Agreements*, Washington, DC: World Bank.

Miroudot, S. and D. Rigo (2019). "Preferential trade agreements and multinational production," RSCAS Working Papers 2019/14, European University Institute, Robert Schuman Centre for Advanced Studies, Global Governance Programme.

Olivero, M. P. and Y. V. Yotov (2012). "Dynamic gravity: Endogenous country size and asset accumulation," *Canadian Journal of Economics*, 45(1): 64–92.

Ramondo, N. and A. Rodríguez-Clare (2013). "Trade, multinational production, and the gains from openness," *Journal of Political Economy*, 121(2): 273–322.

Santos Silva, J. and S. Tenreyro (2006). "The log of gravity," *Review of Economics and Statistics*, 88(4): 641–658.

UNCTAD (2014). "Bilateral FDI statistics 2014," Database accessed in August 2018, United Nations Conference on Trade and Development, http://unctad.org/en/Pages/DIAE/FDI%20Statistics/FDI-Statistics-Bilateral.aspx.

UNCTAD (2019). "International investment agreements navigator," Investment Policy Hub, database accessed in July 2019, United Nations Conference on Trade and Development, https://investmentpolicy.unctad.org.

Yotov, Y. V., R. Piermartini, J.-A. Monteiro, and M. Larch (2016). *An Advanced Guide to Trade Policy Analysis: The Structural Gravity Model*, Geneva: World Trade Organization.

Appendix

Table A4.1 *Most frequent provisions by PTA depth level*

	Most frequent PTA provision combination					
With:	First	Share (%)	Second	Share (%)	Third	Share (%)
PTA Depth = 1	Standards	69.8	Full tariffs	23.3	Services	5.8
PTA Depth = 2	Full tariffs + standards	94.9	Investment + Services	1.3	Full tariffs + Services	1.2
PTA Depth = 3	Investment + Services + Competition	29.3	Full tariffs + Standards + IPRs	15.4	Full tariffs + Standards + Procurement	14.7
PTA Depth = 4	Full tariffs + Standards + Services + Competition	79.8	Full tariffs + Standards + Services + Procurement	6.5	Full tariffs + Standards + Investment + Competition	5.0

Table A4.1 (*cont.*)

	Most frequent PTA provision combination					
With:	First	Share (%)	Second	Share (%)	Third	Share (%)
PTA Depth = 5	All except: Investment + IPRs	40.9	All except: Procurement + IPRs	26.6	All except: Investment + Competition	23.9
PTA Depth = 6	All except: IPRs	43.6	All except: Competition	36.6	All except: Procurement	15.8

Source: Own estimations using DESTA database.

Table A4.2 *Simple correlations between bilateral FDI and main policy variables, full sample*

	Variable:	1	2	3	4	5	6	7	8	9	10	11
1	FDI bilateral stocks	1										
2	PTA depth	0.10	1									
3	PTA dummy	0.06	0.80	1								
4	EU single market	−0.01	0.68	0.40	1							
5	BIT only signed	0.04	0.12	0.12	0.02	1						
6	BIT enforced	0.05	0.16	0.14	0.06	0.89	1					
7	CPR (lta)	0.09	0.79	0.87	0.46	0.16	0.17	1				
8	CPR (sum)	0.11	0.75	0.79	0.44	0.17	0.18	0.98	1			
9	ESR (lta)	0.10	0.85	0.89	0.47	0.14	0.15	0.97	0.92	1		
10	ESR (sum)	0.15	0.85	0.77	0.45	0.13	0.15	0.90	0.90	0.95	1	
11	EP (lta)	0.11	0.82	0.87	0.37	0.15	0.16	0.96	0.92	0.98	0.95	1
12	EP (sum)	0.17	0.75	0.72	0.24	0.15	0.16	0.84	0.85	0.89	0.95	0.94

Sources: UNCTAD bilateral FDI, DESTA and Lechner (2016).

Table A4.3 *Simple correlations between bilateral FDI and main policy variables, sub-sample when PTA is present*

	Variable:	1	2	3	4	5	6	7	8	9	10
1	FDI bilateral stocks	1									
2	PTA depth	0.09	1								
3	EU single market	–0.04	0.65	1							
4	BIT only signed	0.06	0.07	–0.05	1						
5	BIT enforced	0.07	0.13	0.00	0.91	1					
6	CPR (lta)	0.08	0.32	0.25	0.19	0.18	1				
7	CPR (sum)	0.10	0.31	0.23	0.21	0.20	0.96	1			
8	ESR (lta)	0.11	0.51	0.26	0.09	0.10	0.86	0.79	1		
9	ESR (sum)	0.16	0.61	0.24	0.09	0.11	0.73	0.73	0.91	1	
10	EP (lta)	0.13	0.40	0.05	0.13	0.13	0.83	0.78	0.93	0.89	1
11	EP (sum)	0.18	0.43	–0.07	0.15	0.15	0.63	0.66	0.79	0.90	0.91

Sources: UNCTAD bilateral FDI, DESTA and Lechner (2016).

5

How EU Trade and Cooperation Policies Stimulated China to Go Green

JACQUES PELKMANS

Introduction

Linking EU values to EU trade policy has become a prominent feature. Although there were occasional linkages between EU trade policy and 'values' before 2009, a systematic linking between the two became mainstream with the Lisbon Treaty, especially Art. 21, Treaty on the European Union. This approach was refined and articulated in 2015 with the Commission's policy paper 'Trade for All, Towards a More Responsible Trade and Investment Policy' (European Commission, 2015). The new approach raises questions regarding the nature and effectiveness of these linkages (for a critical overall approach, see Pelkmans, 2021b). The RESPECT project has attempted to address a wide range of these questions.[1] In pursuing such research, it is crucial to distinguish two policy tools for promoting the linkages: living up to bilaterally or multilaterally agreed *legal commitments* to specified values, and bilateral or multilateral *cooperation*. The first is found in free trade areas (FTAs) where the two or more parties agree on legal texts specifying the 'values', often called non-trade-policy-objectives (NTPOs), such as human rights, sustainable development, responsible business in world trade and 'good' governance. A border case is Generalised System of Preferences-plus (GSP+), a unilateral instrument employed by the EU, with the number and ambition of the commitments for the GSP+ countries set by the EU, without negotiation.[2] There are also multilateral agreements and 'standards' which have various forms of common enforcement.

[1] The RESPECT project under H2020 is executed by a large consortium of research centres and scholars. Details about the project and all publications so far (over three years) can be found at www.respect.eui.eu

[2] The EU may well assist the relevant countries in accomplishing the needed commitments.

The other path of promoting these linkages is without any bilateral legal basis. This study falls into that category. In these numerous bilateral cases, there is no FTA and promoting values may well turn out to consist of a rather 'soft' form of EU policy, usually 'cooperation'. In many bilateral trade and investment relations the EU maintains, the emphasis is on World Trade Organization (WTO) mechanisms of consultation and commercial diplomacy. In some instances this is complemented by development programmes, or specific projects. On the whole, such bilateral relations tend to be weak and unsystematic. Adding 'cooperation' is usually symbolic and limited. It is rare that 'cooperation' is regarded as a substitute for legal commitments about values in, say, FTAs. Except in the case of China. This chapter studies the effectiveness of EU–China cooperation in environmental policies and the mitigation of climate change over twenty-five years, from 1995 to 2020.[3] This cooperation can be seen as an extension or complement of EU trade policy in that the NTPOs of environment and climate are pursued in China. The hypothesis is that, over this long period of time, the EU has helped to stimulate a process of convergence in 'green' policies and outcomes in China. In order to verify this hypothesis three related but separate research questions are posed:

1. What is the process of convergence between the EU and China in the status of environment and climate factors, as captured by **relevant sustainable development [SD] indicators**.
2. What is the process of convergence in environmental and climate-related **policies** between the EU and China over the period 1995–2020?
3. Have EU trade policy and cooperation vis-à-vis China with respect to sustainable development **systematically pursued** the NTPOs of environment and climate mitigation since the late 1990s and has this pursuit been **effective** in supporting a process of convergence?

The convergence referred to is best considered as a gradual process. It should be remembered that China of the mid-1990s was very much a developing country. It is only due to the exceptional growth of the country that this is no longer the case. Although sustained high economic growth catapulted the country to upper-middle-class status, if not developed status, by 2021, and more than 800 million people were lifted out of extreme poverty – an unbelievable achievement – there were also

[3] The chapter draws heavily from a lengthy exercise in the framework of RESPECT going into considerable detail about indicators, Five-Year Plans and policies as well as numerous cooperative activities between the EU and China (see Pelkmans, 2021a).

very high costs of this super-growth. As recently as 2019 the Organisation for Economic Co-operation and Development still speaks of 'growth at all costs' (OECD, 2019). Much of these costs can be found in the areas of environment and climate. Stimulating China to gradually converge with the EU in these respects is therefore crucial for Chinese citizens, farmers, nature (including forests and soil), but selectively also for other countries due to the reduction of negative externalities, in particular the mitigation of climate change. The initial neglect of or lack of interest in 'going green' can even be regarded as distorting international trade, given the systematic avoidance of the costs of pursuing 'green policies' that otherwise tends to be incorporated in the prices of goods and services. This amounts to a direct rationale for regarding these NTPOs as 'trade-related'.

The next section provides a snapshot of China's environmental and climate status around the mid-1990s based on indicators and setting out constraints and emerging policies, followed by a bird's-eye view of twenty-five years of bilateral and multilateral cooperation between the EU and China in the green policies of sustainable development. The next section addresses the first research question in steps. We then look at policies and commitments, China's policies before and after 2015 ('green growth' as the basis for 'ecological civilization') as well as a carefully derived taxonomy of all thirty-seven 'green' elements in a sustainable development chapter à la the Economic Partnership Agreement (EPA) (between Japan and the EU) which China can be expected to support. This analysis provides the answer to the second research question. The final section attempts to answer the third research question.

China's Not-So-Green Status in the Mid-1990s

The status of China's environment and climate issues in the mid-1990s is based on two authoritative reports by the World Bank, with co-authorship of Chinese specialists[4] and support from China's main environmental agency at the time (NEPA). Some core indicators on environment and on climate from China of the mid-1990s will be set out, but before doing so, it should be noted that China may have plenty of coal, but limited resources otherwise. A few indicators are:

[4] On the environment (non-climate), mainly air and water, see World Bank (1997); and on climate questions, see Johnson et al. (1996).

(a) China has nearly 20 per cent of the world's population but barely 7 per cent of arable land
(b) Agricultural land per capita is only 28 per cent of the world's average
(c) Forests and wilderness (in 1995[5]) per capita is only 15 per cent of the world's average
(d) Water resources per capita are one-third of the world average
(e) In energy resources, it is a major net importer of oil and gas, and recently this includes liquefied natural gas (LNG).

With respect to air pollution, particulates[6] as well as sulphur (SO_2), nitrogen oxide (NOx), volatile organic compounds (VOCs) and carbon monoxide are the damaging emissions for humans. In China in the 1990s, both industrial boilers (inefficient and with low smokestacks) and small household stoves were culprits: industrial boilers consumed 33 per cent of China's coal and emitted an even higher percentage of ground-level pollution in cities; households consumed only 15 per cent of coal but contributed an amazing 30 per cent to ground-level pollution. Between 1985 and 1995, particulate concentrations in cities had fallen significantly, but in large cities they were still four times the maximum World Health Organization (WHO) guideline, whereas in smaller cities they were some three times that guideline. It was therefore still very unhealthy. As to SO_2, the decline (in concentration) was small, and in big cities the level was still two and a half times the maximum WHO guideline, again far from healthy. When citizens entered their homes, stepping out of the air pollution, they were often worse off because indoor air quality was (especially in winter[7]) very poor. Altogether, citizens suffered disproportionately from respiratory diseases, the leading cause of death in rural areas and the third cause in cities. There was also a serious lead problem (especially for children), resulting from industrial emissions and from leaded patrol, as only one-half of petrol production was unleaded. Negative externalities across China and beyond – so no longer local only – were caused by long-range transportation of sulphur, resulting in acid rain, damaging agriculture, ecosystems and materials.

Water pollution in China in 1995 was very serious as well. Some 40 per cent of monitored sections of rivers flowing past cities did not meet

[5] The year matters because around that time China initiated a massive long-term reforestation programme.

[6] Both fine (less than 10 microns) and ultrafine (less than 2.5 microns).

[7] Due to combustion of raw coal and wood for cooking and heating. By 1995, Chinese citizens had increasing access to gas for the home and, if coal was still used, to cleaner coal and more efficient briquettes.

minimum quality levels. Water shortages complicated matters further, as upstream cities or others often stopped the water flow in order to extract water, thereby causing relatively greater pollution downstream. Municipal and industrial wastewater were at first hardly treated; since the early 1990s, this had been improving for industrial waste of regulated industries but not for municipal wastewater. In agriculture, intensive use of nitrogen fertilizer and pesticides was a source of serious water pollution. Pesticides added to this, causing a problem for birds. Chemical oxygen demand (COD) pollution in water often originated from larger livestock farms, since meat production on farms increased greatly. About half of the monitored rivers in northern China did not even meet the lowest standard for water, making it unsuitable even for irrigation. Only 8 per cent was grade 3, the minimum standard for contact with humans.

Furthermore, there were other environmental issues such as environmental degradation in the form of soil erosion, land degradation, deforestation and desertification, with one study estimating the costs at 5 per cent of GDP (Smil, 1996, as quoted in the World Bank, 1997, p. 23). This compares to a cost of 8 per cent of Chinese GDP in 1995 for air and water pollution, as discussed earlier. Hence, a staggering roughly 13 per cent of GDP is at stake, and this does not include the costs of carbon dioxide (CO_2) emissions (which are summarized later). In a simulation up to 2020 under a 'business-as-usual' scenario, and taking into account the projected increase in income, the cost of 8 per cent of GDP rises to a cost of 13 per cent of GDP. The latter would consist of 600,000 premature deaths per year, 5.5 million cases of chronic bronchitis, more than 5 billion restricted activity days and 20 million cases of respiratory illness each year. Thus, even if human considerations were to assume a lower priority, it would still be in the Chinese interest to address these huge social and health costs as a major burden on the economy.

When it comes to greenhouse gas (GHG) emissions – primarily CO_2 – in 1990 China emitted about half of the US total and of the European total (equal at the time) but far less per capita than the US CO_2 emissions per capita (only some 12 per cent[8]). But between 1990 and 1995, CO_2 emissions in China went up by nearly 300 metric tonnes of carbon (mtC), some two-thirds, reaching 800 mtC; and, at the time, a baseline

[8] Over 30 per cent in the case of the EU (as the EU has much lower emissions).

scenario for 2020 estimated some 2,200 mtC under plausible assumptions. If this simulation were to have been roughly correct, in order to keep the level of *global* CO_2 emissions constant at the 1990 level, the rest of the world would have had to *decrease their emissions by roughly one-third* merely to let the Chinese grow that much. This inference alone can be seen as a strong encouragement for the EU to engage with China in joint solutions, projects, dialogues and so on, to help China onto a radically different path.

The 2,200 mtC simulation for 2020 results from an astounding increase in coal used, jumping from some 1.3 billion tons of raw coal in 1995 to 3.1 billion tons. This must imply, when considering policy in the late 1990s, an expectation of incredible surges of SO_2 emissions and of particulates by 2020 if no strategy were to be applied. However, the baseline scenario already includes market-induced improvements in energy efficiency over twenty-five years, *without* any new strategy, primarily due to changes in economic structure. These changes result from a lesser emphasis on heavy industry, better performing equipment when replacing capital goods, the rise of (much less polluting) services in overall GDP and improvement of heating and cooking inside households given higher incomes.[9] These implied improvements ensure that, by 2020, rather than 10,000 mega tonnes of coal equivalent (mtce), 'only' 3,300 mtce of energy use is the model outcome, most of which is coal. Interestingly, a daring simulation of three options for reducing GHG emissions by 2020 is presented: high energy efficiency (330 mtC lower), alternative energy (low-carbon-intensive fuels and renewables, with the warning that, with the state-of-the-art of 1995, these would be more costly than coal – note that coal at the time was not taxed directly) or via emissions (up to 237 mtC less) and afforestation (to be undertaken aggressively for a long period, reducing GHG by 221 mtC). The upshot would be that GHG emissions would, over twenty-five years, only slightly less than double. However, all three options are demanding and invite international aid and open trade in environmental goods as much as possible, according to the World Bank team. Thus, there is a development motive for donors but just as much a direct (commercial and climate) interest for the EU, for example, to step in and find effective

[9] In the simulation, it means that input–output coefficients would alter over time, leading to lower energy use.

ways to support if not intensify the Chinese attempts to address these environmental and climate challenges.

Altogether, the baseline around 1995 for the environment and climate is highly problematic and – given the very high growth path China was determined to continue – outright worrying. In terms of EU–China cooperation, still in its infancy, the divergence between the two in indicators and in strategic perspective could hardly be greater.

Twenty-Five Years of EU–China 'Green' Cooperation: A Bird's-Eye View

Over the last twenty-five years, the EU and China have cooperated bilaterally and multilaterally. The latter is too often overlooked. If the EU and China were to have a deep and comprehensive FTA with a sustainable development chapter, a considerable part of what would look like bilateral commitments would in fact be converging multilateral commitments of both parties referred to in the FTA. In the absence of a FTA, the very same multilateral commitments matter just as much to China and the EU. The next sections deal with multilateral agreements in environmental and climate matters, and cover bilateral 'green' cooperation over two distinct periods.

Multilateral 'Green' Convergence between China and the EU

In EU FTAs there are references to at most a handful of MEAs (multilateral environmental agreements), whereas China has ratified no fewer than twelve MEAs, including all those that matter in EU FTAs. That does not include fisheries and timber, where the EU has undertaken important activities (with increasing cooperation from China), but no MEAs exist. In other words, with respect to multilateral environmental obligations, China has legally agreed to commitments far beyond what has so far been specified in EU FTAs. China and the EU have accomplished full convergence in MEAs. Because China was still a developing country when ratifying certain treaties, in some cases its obligations might temporarily be less stringent than those of the EU. In fact, these twelve MEAs cover much more, since today these MEAs also come with eleven substantive 'amendments', three extra protocols and four supplementary treaties or agreements (see Pelkmans, 2021a, table 2). A summary is provided in Table 5.1.

Table 5.1 *MEAs: convergence between China and the EU*

No	MEA	Treaty title	Ratified CH / EU
1	CITES	(Washington) Convention on international trade in endangered species of wild fauna and flora	Yes / yes
2	London Convention on Marine Pollution	London Convention on the prevention of marine pollution by dumping wastes and other matter (linked to the International Maritime Organisation)	Yes / yes
3	Vienna Ozone Convention	Vienna Convention for the protection of the ozone layer	Yes / yes
4	Montreal Protocol	Montreal Protocol on substances that deplete the ozone layer (precision of Vienna Convention)	Yes / yes
5	Basel Convention	Basel Convention on the control of transboundary movements of hazardous wastes and their disposal	Yes / yes
6	Ramsar Convention	Ramsar Convention on wetlands of international importance, esp. waterfowl habitat	Yes / yes
7	Biodiversity	Convention on Biological Diversity (CBD)	Yes / yes
8	Nuclear safety	Vienna Convention on nuclear safety	Yes / yes
9	Combating desertification	(Paris) UN Convention to combat desertification in those countries experiencing serious drought and/or desertification particularly in Africa (UNCCD)	Yes / yes
10	Climate change	UN Framework Convention on Climate Change (UNFCCC), 1997 Kyoto Protocol + Paris	Yes / yes
11	Stockholm Convention	Stockholm Convention on POPs (persistent organic pollutants)	Yes / yes
12	Rotterdam Convention	Rotterdam Convention on the prior informed consent procedure for certain hazardous chemicals in international trade	Yes / yes

Note: for further details, see Pelkmans (2021a, table 2); in addition, there are many amendments, extra protocols and supplementary treaties, and all of these have also been ratified by China; also the Kigali amendment of the Montreal Protocol (on 17 June 2021) without as yet a licensing system for HFCs (fluor-related substances).

It is exceedingly rare to find a specification about so many MEAs. It is comforting that – even without a FTA – China's and the EU's positions and international commitments overlap so much that the term 'convergence' seems fully justified. Even when, in a few cases, obligations for China come with some delay (e.g. the Kyoto Protocol before the Paris Treaty, see point 10 in Table 5.1; the Kigali amendment on phasing out HFCs, see point 4 in Table 5.1).

EU–China Bilateral 'Green' Cooperation

EU–China bilateral 'green' cooperation began in 1995 with the Commission's first paper on EU–China, following the EU's decision to launch a New Asia Strategy in 1994.[10] The 1995 paper mentions the emergence of a working group (what would later become a policy dialogue):

> The environmental challenge faced by a rapidly developing China has been recognized by the Chinese government in its 'Agenda21' follow-up programme of the [1992] Rio summit, with its accompanying list of specific projects leading to sustainable development. The problems faced by China in the environmental field are partly systemic – a low awareness of the long-term consequences of inaction – partly technological, and partly that China does not believe that it can afford the costs of high environmental standards. Of critical importance is the need to integrate environmental considerations into other areas of policy, such as economic planning. A new working group has been set up to discuss how the EU can best help Chinese efforts. We need to identify a coherent European contribution in a field where there is multiplicity of signals from the Chinese side. (Snyder, 2009, pp. 352–353)

The quote shows clearly that the EU intention results from development considerations, with China in a recipient position. There is no suggestion yet of a genuine common interest or an EU-specific interest.

Another eight years of gradually intensifying dialogues, exchanges and policy papers (see Pelkmans, 2021a, section 5.4), accompanied by a range of conferences, projects or other activities, would follow until the two partners decided to establish an ambitious 'strategic and comprehensive

[10] For the New Asia Strategy, COM (94)314 of 13 July 1994, see Snyder (2009, pp. 310 and 320–339); for the 1995 paper see COM(1995)279, entitled 'A long-term policy for China-Europe relations', as reproduced in Snyder (2009, pp. 340–369).

partnership' at the EU–China Summit of 2003. During those eight years the partners were actively engaged in bilateral efforts to create or bolster capacity in energy and environment, besides almost permanent diplomatic efforts to approximate their positions on a range of sustainable development issues. One can also notice a shift away from a development perspective to common interests or convergence: 'with the current shift ... away from traditional development projects towards *sectoral interventions which are increasingly aligned with EU policies*, a greater degree of involvement of line ministries is required' (Snyder, 2009, COM (2003)533, p. 478; emphasis added).

From 2003 to 2019 inclusive a significant intensification of joint activities as well as a widening of the scope can be observed. Numerous activities have been organised and an exhaustive survey would be impossible in the present context. A single heading may well refer to many joint activities at various levels, including highly practical ones.[11] In this period, seven major energy activity streams have been set up, a number of them of a multi-annual nature and with loaded agendas. The EU–China Energy Dialogue, dating back to 1994, is now part of the annual summit, and often connected to the EU–China energy conference with business. The European Investment Bank (EIB) is also involved. One of the seven activity streams consists of the ambitious and multi-faceted EU–China Roadmap on energy cooperation concluded in 2016 and ran to the end of 2020 (see Pelkmans, 2021a, table 4 and related text). This agenda is concerned with a range of activities on energy demand, energy supply and cross-cutting issues (even including harmonisation) and with a strong emphasis on energy efficiency.

Another ten activity streams were concerned with the environment directly. This has been headed by the EU–China Ministerial Dialogue on environmental policy since 2003. Other important items include, for example, the EU–China Clean Development Mechanism (CDM) facilitation project, the Environmental Governance Programme (2011–2015) and the EU–China Environmental Sustainability Programme, which was specifically linked to the attainment of the targets in China's twelfth

[11] One major example is the EU–China Trade Project II from 2010 to 2016, which aimed to support the Chinese government's trade reform and sustainable development agenda. Focusing mainly on customs and regulatory issues (including technical standards as well as SPS), it also dealt with sustainable development under 'cross-cutting issues'. One among several of the 400 activities in this massive project is the EU–China Low Carbon Economy platform; also Green Smart Cities was dealt with.

Five-Year Development Plan 2010–2015. As recently as in 2021 (despite the sanctions on both sides and the Comprehensive Agreement on Investment being suspended), the EU and China invigorated the newly established High-Level Environmental and Climate Dialogue with a new ambitious programme of twelve areas of cooperation.

CDM is a market mechanism helping developing countries to finance climate mitigation measures in companies. Developed countries under the Kyoto Protocol (Annex 1 countries) were allowed to purchase CO_2 reductions in developing countries, including China at the time (2005 and later). The EU and China worked closely together. By April 2012 China had approved no fewer than 3,935 projects, ensuring some 50 per cent of the world CDM market in terms of projects whilst the EU exercised roughly half the world demand for certified emission reductions. The EU–China commercial interaction was intense. Besides CO_2 reduction, a range of other benefits was observed, including co-benefits for SO_2, particulate matter (PM)2.5 and NOx. Later on drawbacks emerged, including the strong suspicion that – given that windfall profits could be made – end-of-pipe technologies were employed solely for profit reasons.[12]

The EU–China climate partnership of 2005 deserves a special mention, not only because it still exists and has generated several action plans (for detail, see Pelkmans, 2021a, Box 9)[13] but it has engendered important policy moves by China. Joint Statements at summit level were made in both 2010 and 2015, the latter being crucial as a preparation for the Paris Conference of the Parties (COP) leading to the Paris Climate Treaty under the UNFCCC. The switch that China made in moving away from the position under the Kyoto Protocol – holding that OECD countries were responsible for most of the cumulative emissions from the past two centuries, and hence that developing countries, such as China in 1997, did not have to share the full burden of mitigation – was softened considerably, which was critical for the Paris agreement. In a Memorandum of Understanding in 2018, the EU agreed to help China

[12] Pelkmans (2021a, box 10) explains in far greater technical and economic detail this CDM facilitation.

[13] One on clean coal (with China hoping that coal production could be maintained in one way or another, but the project did not demonstrate the breakthrough innovation hoped for) and one on energy efficiency and renewables. Other technical cooperation occurred on methane recovery, hydrogen and power transmission.

with its domestic emission trading system, which was suffering from some teething problems.

EU–China 'Green' Convergence, Measured by Indicators

The first research question is about green convergence measured by indicators: fact-based, not policy-based or guided by hazy perspectives about strategies. In the following sub-sections, the (relatively few) indicators of three successive Five-Year Plans will first be discussed, followed by a more sophisticated analytical view over two decades. Then, a more detailed analysis of the most recent indicators of both climate and environment will be presented, and an attempt will be made to answer the first research question.

Fifteen Years of Chinese Planning on Sustainable Growth

The tenth, eleventh and twelfth Five-Year Plans reflect a slow process of growing awareness of 'green' issues. However, China was clearly struggling and, largely, still stuck in existing patterns as well as addicted to reckless growth. Beginning with the 10th Five-Year Environmental Plan (2001–2005), there is an attempt to show that indicators will move in the right direction, even when that hardly seems credible. In a table of fourteen (non-CO_2-related) indicators, a range of targets barely decreases by 2005 and their actual realisation in 2005 is highly uneven (see Pelkmans, 2021a, table 5): four targets were plain failures (the worst being SO_2), some were successful (for example, industrial COD) and some were just about met (ex. industrial dust). Several indicators were not in the list in the first place (ex. precise measurement of particles in various classes). It should be noted that CO_2 and other GHGs are not reported in this plan.

The eleventh Plan has a different set-up, is largely qualitative and is much less fact-based. There are numerous announced investments in programmes, detailed inspections, closure of facilities (e.g. dangerous mines) and tougher regulations. The text is sprinkled with smart labels which tell citizens nothing concrete and comprise no verifiable targets: examples include the creation of 2,000 'environment-beautiful towns', the 'Blue Sea initiative' in the Bohai sea, and the development of the 'socialist new countryside'. The Plan contains (i) a list of nine 'key environmental projects' (four with hard targets), (ii) a priority list of ten environmental science and technology innovations, and (iii) ten priorities for the development of the environmental protection industry.[14] The list of fourteen indicators has shrunk to five very sensitive ones, for which targets over five years improve by no more than between 2 to 10 per cent (see Pelkmans, 2021a, table 6).[15] Again, there is no attention to CO_2 at all. However, the *overall* eleventh Plan for national economic and social development was brought out and both tone and assessment are rather different. After first emphasising energy efficiency (suggesting an improvement of 20 per cent), harsh criticism follows, spiced with frank remarks:

> the productive force is not developed and some enduring deep-level development-restricting contradictions still exists: farmland, fresh water, energy and important mineral resources are relatively insufficient, ecological environment is relatively vulnerable, economic structure is irrational, the task to resolve the three dimensional rural issues is very arduous, employment pressure is still great . . . In the rapid development of the Tenth Five Year Plan period, some new major problems emerged: uncoordinated investment and consumption relationship, blind expansion of some industries, superfluous capacity, slow transformation of economic growth mode, excessive energy resource consumption, aggravated environmental pollution, continuous expansion of the development gap between urban and rural areas and between regions and income difference between some social members and backward development of social causes; . . . [it ends with the observation of] the co-existence of strategic opportunity and contradiction. (Pelkmans, 2021a, p. 5)

These frank observations clarify well what the enormous challenges were for China at the time and the realisation that these not-so-green developments were utterly unsustainable.

In the energy chapter (chapter 12 of the Plan), coal is still treated in a relaxed way insofar as the climate is concerned. It explicitly confirms having 'coal as the basis to realize pluralistic development'. The short passage on developing coal in an 'orderly' fashion calls to 'strengthen coal resource exploration . . . and enhance coal recovery'.[16] The concerns expressed are about the safety of mines and miners (fully justified, as it was a major problem in China); hence the closure of 'coal mines without

[14] For the latter, ranging from water pollution prevention and control technologies and equipment to 'special reagent and materials' such as membrane materials.

[15] Moreover, note that both for COD and SO_2, 2010 targets are far higher than the previous plan had hoped to accomplish by 2005.

[16] In a complex sentence with many aspects placed together, it also plans to 'reduce impact of coal mining on ecological environment', without any further detail.

safe production conditions and with resource and environmental destruction'. No word here about SO_2 in and near cities and industrial centres, or about CO_2 when using coal. However, it is followed by a section called 'all-out development of renewable energy resources'. Coal is still the linchpin of industrial development and heating in the China of 2006–2010 and otherwise the solution is sought in technology and renewables, *not* in reducing coal exploration *or* in taxing coal or the emissions arising from its use.

The tone, detail and ambition of the twelfth Five-Year Plan (2011–2015) are quite different. The tone is often that of plain instructions or commands or indeed prohibitions. The scope and details of the twelfth Five-Year Plan for Environmental Protection are impressive. Unlike previous Plans, practically everything is covered and the number of intentions is huge. Although 'all the targets and key tasks of environmental protection identified in the 11th Plan have been achieved', the tone of the twelfth Plan is alarming throughout, best illustrated by a lengthy list of frank admissions of environmental shortcomings and deficiencies as well as deep concerns about China's environmental degradation. The Plan begins with a comparison of 'major' indicators between the eleventh and the twelfth Plans.[17] One observes little progress in urban and domestic COD but a major improvement in industrial COD. From the respective Plans it can be understood that agricultural COD has grown (in particular, due to large-scale livestock farms) into a major issue but without disposing of hard data. Assuming that the reduction of industrial COD has continued (as is suggested in texts), agricultural COD can be 'guesstimated' as roughly 800–900 (x 10,000 tons), and it is likely to be costly to reduce this significantly. As far as SO_2 is concerned, after the failure in 2005, the eleventh Plan target was realised (with a reduction of 11 per cent) but the twelfth Plan expects only an 8 per cent reduction – this is probably due to the continued increase of the use of coal in China. Coal remains 'shielded' from genuine cuts. This coal addiction has to do with low prices for coal (as negative externalities are not priced in) but increasingly also with the rapidly rising Chinese imports of energy. Shielding coal requires strategic choices comprising (a) structural change (e.g. phasing out outdated production capacity of iron and steel, non-ferrous metals, building materials, chemicals, paper-making and dyeing and tannery), (b) a stronger move to

[17] More detail on the twelfth Plan is found in Pelkmans (2021a).

introduce desulphurisation and denitrification in the coal sector and encouragement elsewhere, (c) dust removal facilities in coal-fuelled power plants and, for example, steel, and (d) a great boost of the renewables sector. It is interesting to note the attention to biodiversity, the more systematic 'whole-process management' of environmental risk, the dramatic clean-up (and liability for) old heavy-metal sites, curbing the high incidence of heavy metal pollution accidents, the strengthening of the legal system and of environment economic policies, and finally the strong encouragement of the environmental protection industry. Altogether, it would seem to be appropriate to conclude that the twelfth Plan signifies a turning point, at least in planning.

Assessing Chinese 'Green Growth' over Two Decades

As shown in the previous sub-section, the Five-Year Plans are at best only selectively helpful in assessing Chinese 'green' growth since (say) 1995. In order to discern overall trends in indicators and recognise how these trends are related, a more analytical approach is needed. Based on a recent OECD study produced in cooperation with the DRC (Development Research Centre) of the State Council of China (Linster and Yang, 2018), such a perspective can be described in summary form.

In Figure 5.1 some telling long-run environmental trends in China are depicted. The focus is on industry,[18] long the main culprit of environmental damage by far. One finds that industry was (in 1990) overwhelmingly the principal generator of waste[19] and that was still the case in 2014. It has improved considerably in wastewater discharges. With respect to SO_2, Figure 5.1 confirms that industrial SO_2 was stubbornly increasing, with much larger volumes in 2014. The same goes for CO_2 emissions – the high share coming from industry still increased and the volumes grew multi-fold by 2014. Although energy efficiency in China strongly improved over the twenty-five years, the share of industrial energy consumption nevertheless increased, mainly due to very high economic growth. The GDP spoke shows that all this happens with a constant share of industry in GDP (of some 40+ per cent) between 1990 and 2014.

Most striking are the Chinese productivity indicators. Whereas energy productivity is around 60 per cent of the average OECD level, and carbon

[18] Defined as manufacturing, mining and quarrying, and energy.

[19] Even though agricultural waste was not included in the statistics, the industrial shares are too high.

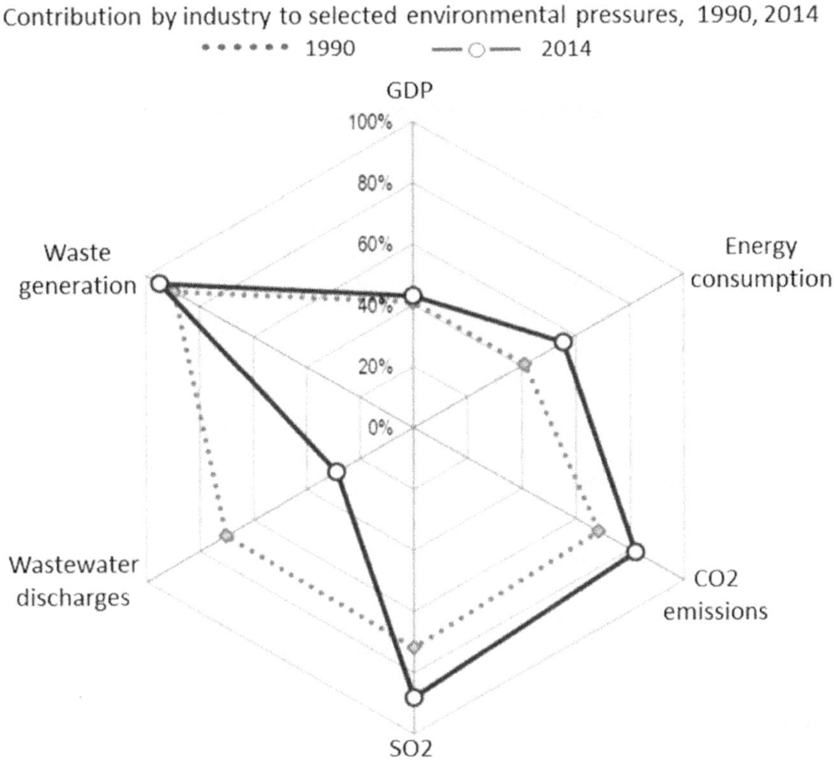

Figure 5.1 Environmental profile of Chinese industry. Contribution by industry to selected environmental pressures, 1990 vs 2014
Sources: Linster and Yang (2018); *Report on the State of the Environment in China* (various issues); *Environmental Data Handbook*; *China Statistical Yearbook on Environment*; IEA's *World Energy Balances database*; *CO_2 Emission from Fuel Combustion database.*

productivity at some 45 per cent, material productivity is only some 23 per cent and overall productivity about one-fifth of the OECD level. The yardstick used here is multi-factor productivity adjusted for negative environmental impacts. A telling illustration is the generation of $1,000 of GDP in 2015: whereas China uses 180 ktoe (kilo tonne of oil equivalent) of primary energy and 1,930kg of materials other than energy, the OECD on average uses only 110 ktoe of primary energy (some 60 per cent) and only 420kg of materials (just 23 per cent); moreover, the OECD emits 260kg of CO_2 from this energy use and China 540kg, more than double. Less noticed is the recent extreme reliance on imports of such resources: according to Linster and Yang (2018), China relied on imports for more than half of its supplies of oil, gas, iron ore, copper, lead and zinc in 2011; by 2014, China consumed nearly half the world's metals.

Although energy productivity[20] has steadily improved, it is clearly below that of the BRICS (Brazil, Russia, India, China, South Africa) countries and even further below the OECD average. Thus, efficiency gains should be stepped up and coal must be urgently capped and reduced. The coal cap by 2020 foreseen in the thirteenth Plan was 4.1 billion tonnes, which is unbelievably high (and even higher than the 3.1 billion tonnes obtained in the simulation done in the late 1990s). China has long committed to lower its carbon intensity (CO_2 emissions per unit of GDP, here 2005 level) by some 60+ per cent (in 2030 and by 40 per cent by 2020) but when GDP rises very fast this measure remains completely unrelated to the negative externalities inside and outside China.

The inefficiency of materials consumption is extreme and, in turn, this has led to very large waste flows. Thus, the (non-energy) material productivity of China is comparable to Canada (a resource country, whereas China is not) but only some 7–8 per cent of that in the United Kingdom or Japan and some 15 per cent or so of that in France or Korea.

Figure 5.2 shows that SO_2 and CO_2 emissions increased in China both absolutely and relatively between 1990 and 2014. Official NOx data is only available as from 2006. The rise of CO_2 and SO_2 during the 1990s was steep, implying that the situation in 2000 was already problematic. Figure 5.2 (left side) clarifies the enormous tasks China faces when combining future economic growth and decoupled trends of CO_2, NOx and SO_2. The high SO_2 level of 2000 was only returned to – after a surge – in 2012 and has since been slowly declining, thereby beginning to reduce – after a lag – the acid rain problem as well as related problems of air quality.

But the trend of NOx is sharply up and the 2015 level is still more than 60 per cent higher than in 2000. The very rapid increase of CO_2 emissions hugs the steeply rising trendline for energy, which is predominantly coal. This trendline is below the GDP trend (so, energy growth and CO_2 emission growth are decoupled from GDP growth) but that is little consolation when CO_2 emissions continue to increase so rapidly, from already high initial levels.

[20] Defined as how much GDP is generated from one unit of energy.

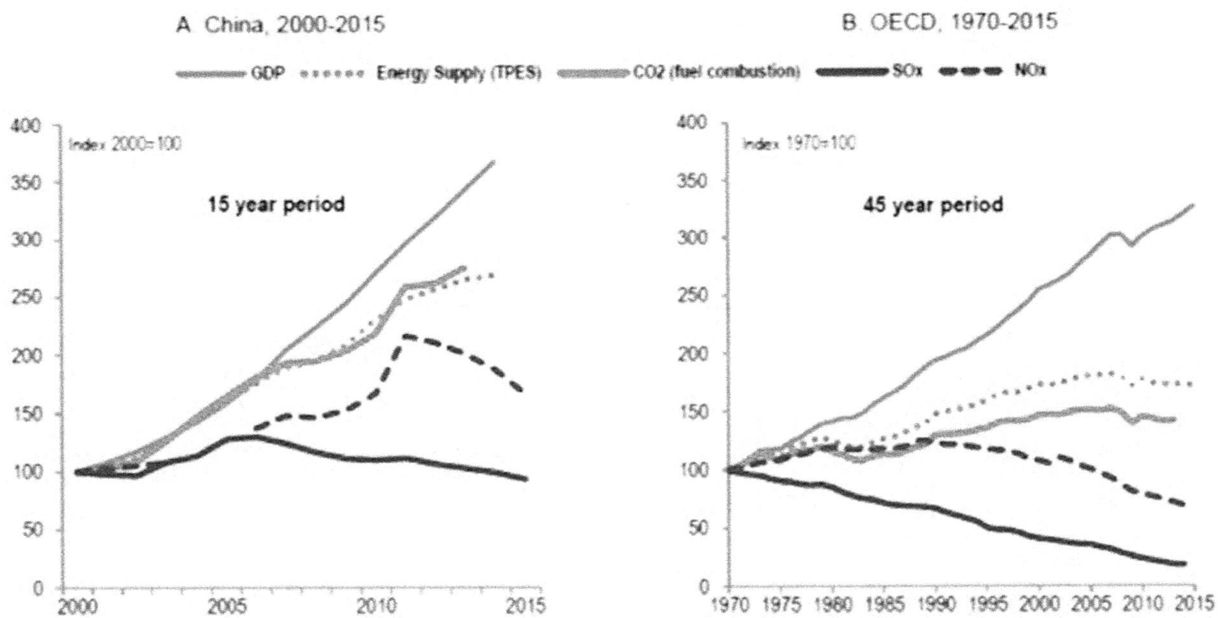

Figure 5.2 China and the OECD: environmental trends and economic growth
Source: Linster and Yang (2018); data from the *OECD, the IEA, and the Ministry of Ecology and Environment.*

Air quality is another major problem in China. Since 2013 (and even before) China has attempted to impose air quality standards based on the high WHO threshold (far higher than the EU).[21] A high WHO threshold for fine particulates (2.5 PM) is 35 micrograms (μg)/cubic metre (m3), most OECD countries have much lower thresholds, and hence better air quality. In December 2016, however, the levels of PM 2.5 concentration in thirty Chinese cities were a multiple of the high threshold, from almost four times the WHO threshold to as much as eight times (see Linster and Yang, 2018, p. 25, figure 14). The health toll in terms of respiratory diseases must be quite high. Recent studies suggest a similar or worse adverse impact[22] than in the 1990s.

But there is good news too (see Linster and Yang, 2018, pp. 29–31). The OECD environmental policy stringency index (indicating strictness of environmental laws) for China has moved sharply upwards since about 2010 and is beginning to approach OECD levels. However, the index does not measure enforcement. Environmentally related tax revenues rose very steeply in 2007/8 and stayed roughly at that level for the following eight years, close to the OECD revenues as a percentage of GDP. Both appear to be a genuine break with the past: tougher rules and pricing negative externalities had long been called for. Another item of good news is the rapid development of green technologies. Unfortunately, it is hard to 'read' the quality of Chinese patents, unless they are tested by the European Patent Organisation (EPO) in the EU, but the rise of patented inventions in this field in China is around tenfold since 2000. Wind and solar industries are booming and are leading in the world. They already produced some 15 per cent of Chinese energy in 2015.

Do Indicators Point to China's 'Ecological Civilisation'?

Since around 2015 there has been a new urgency in China's policy circuits, expressed in Xi's 'ecological civilisation'. The question is whether this shows up in the indicators. In letting the data speak, the following is

[21] For SO_2, NO_2, PM10, PM2.5, CO and O_3.

[22] A prominent example is provided in a leading survey by Jin et al. (2016, p. 2). A quote is telling: 'The ambient air quality pollution in China has been estimated by the Global Burden of Disease to lead to 1.2 million premature deaths from one year's (2010) exposure in China, and in multiple studies to cause annual economic losses equivalent to between 1% and 7% of China's GDP.'

a dry enumeration of the most recent indicators (2018, 2019 and 2020), beginning with climate indicators, followed by air and water.

On climate, selective quotes about China can be misleading. Until very recently, China remained silent on coal, but the country has meanwhile committed to peak with its CO_2 emissions by 2030 or earlier. Its willingness to cap coal output and use is nevertheless in doubt for three reasons. First, both in 2018 and in 2019 China added new coal-fired power, and again in 2020. Second, in these years it added extra CO_2 emissions. Third, Chinese state-owned banks continued to lead the world in the financing of new coal-fired plants all over the world, not least in the Belt-and-Road. Only in 2021 did China publicly commit to terminate such loans. On the other hand, in 2018 China added no less than 43 per cent of extra renewables capacity globally, in addition boosting electric vehicles (cars, buses). China is also active in adding nuclear power plants (seven in the last few years), obviously without operational CO_2 emissions. Moreover, China has had an ambitious (re)forestation programme since 1996 and expects to continue it beyond 2030, adding 7 percentage points of forest to China's surface (from 16 to 23 per cent).[23]

Nevertheless, the coal issue is pertinent. Whereas historically (over two and a half centuries) China has emitted less CO_2 per capita than the EU and the United States, its share in the world's total CO_2 emissions is 28 per cent (nearly double the United States and nearly triple the EU), its share of world coal consumption in 2018 was 50.5 per cent and its carbon intensity is the highest in the world (0.37, with the EU at 0.16).

With respect to air and water, China is improving from a very low level. If air pollution is measured by its two principal causes – SO_2 and NOx – the EPI (Environment Performance Indicator) of 2018 ranked China 177 of 180 countries (Yale Environment Center and World Economic Forum, 2019, p. 46), which sharply contradicts the sunny messages from the China State Council (2018).[24] The thirteenth Five-Year Plan comprised a reduction target for SO_2 and NOx of 20 per cent for 2020 (over 2015) and the co-benefits of CO_2 reduction should also help air quality. Indeed, the EPI of 2020 shows improvement: the ranking shifts up to 137. However, more often than not, accomplishing these

[23] With co-benefits such as working against floods, reducing soil erosion and combating desertification.

[24] The Council announces 'remarkably improved air quality and a much greater sense of happiness for the people'.

targets will not be sufficient to achieve the Blue Skies the State Council says it wants for the people.

The damage caused by widespread water pollution and the problematic quality of drinking water or even water for irrigation is considerable. In combination with the structural water shortage the country is suffering from, the challenges for a strategy of remediation of water in China are no less than daunting. A summary of the crucial shortcomings will be provided here but this is done in analytical and policy terms. However, such terms hardly convey an appropriate picture of the practical issues and fears of citizens confronted with 'black and odorous' waters (in cities), greenish lakes and rivers due to eutrophication, some rural communities refusing to eat the agri-products they produce and sell due to the polluted irrigation water they use, numerous creeks and small rivers feeding the big rivers in China (such as the Yangtze River) which no longer carry water and the anxiety of citizens and workers along big rivers knowing of thousands of unreported sewage outlets spilling straight into the river or lakes. In some areas of China, chronic exposure to water pollution has led to the emergence of hundreds of 'cancer villages'.

An authoritative and independent[25] China Water Assessment by the Asian Development Bank (2018) identifies many water issues,[26] including severe water pollution, aquatic ecosystem degradation, low water-use efficiency and insufficient water services.

Nearly 10 per cent or so of flows or lakes consists of water of such low quality that it simply cannot be used for anything; parts of other water sources can only be used for (say) irrigation and constrains flexible solutions. Altogether, water pollution and overuse are a serious hindrance to development and, worse, a major health issue causing the premature deaths of many and illnesses for others. Producing cheaply at such health costs is plainly distortive globally and the same is true when generating such environmental damage.

Answering the First Research Question

The first research question is whether and to what extent *indicators* reveal that China and the EU converge in terms of environment and

[25] But in cooperation with the Ministry of Water Resources.

[26] As well as unaddressed water shortages, weak water-related disaster mitigation capacities and weak water governance (in a country so short of water), an issue also emphasized by the World Bank.

climate mitigation. The relevant period is from 1995 to 2020. The answer to this double query has to start with the initial deterioration in China of practically all indicators of the environment and climate. The sharp contrast with the EU in the first decade or fifteen years of this period – even longer for GHGs – amounts to clear divergence, not convergence. One explanation is paramount: exceptional economic growth 'at all costs', driven by the desire to rapidly move the country towards developed economy status and the determination to lift hundreds of millions out of extreme poverty. The pattern seemed more like a U-curve. In other words, China began to converge only after first letting both environment and climate issues get out of hand.

By far the worst performance was linked to the use of coal, the CO_2 and SO_2 emissions caused, and the dreadful air quality. The coal addiction seems to have been a conscious choice, presumably also influenced by industrial and mining pressures as well as regional lobbying. The enormous negative externalities this caused over time, especially for public health, not to speak of the broader costs to society, were first ignored and later treated with little more than lip service. When interventionist policy became unavoidable, the options favoured were in the technological domain: end-of-pipe techniques such as filters for denitrification and desulphurization, and the aggressive development of renewables in electricity generation. Only recently has the taboo on taxation and on the rise in coal prices finally ended. The peak in CO_2 has not been reached yet. China's insistence that carbon intensity is falling rapidly should be acknowledged but is little consolation when CO_2 emissions – already the highest in the world – are still increasing. Air quality standards (if measured by SO_2 and NOx) are amongst the worst in the world and have only very recently begun to be addressed. Water standards are slowly beginning to improve as well, albeit still too selectively. Water pollution – with extremely worrying indicators – has been ignored or down-played for a very long time, although investments in infrastructure and new legislation have helped somewhat. Waste is now being addressed more effectively, after serious investments in treatment.

On the other hand, China is very active in sustained reforestation, with strong results, and in the swift expansion in renewables, generating 20 per cent of electricity in 2020. It has become a world leader in electric vehicles and lithium batteries. Expansion in nuclear energy also helps to support climate policies.

Therefore, on the basis of the indicators, one can conclude that China has stopped initially divergent trends and moved them into a converging direction but a firm conclusion would need still more recent data and clear, credible targets for 2025 or 2030 that are actually met.

EU–China 'Green' Policy Convergence after Several Decades

This section is divided into two parts: first, a range of China's green policies, such as soil protection, air quality, water quality, GHGs (linked to the National Determined Contributions, NDCs, under the Paris Treaty), responsible business initiatives, sustainable forestry and timber trade, sustainable fishing and China's green industrial policy, are inspected; second, a very different exercise is attempted: the thought experiment that China would have a FTA with the EU, including the same sustainable development chapter as in EPA, and verify which of the thirty-seven 'green' commitments China would already agree with or already be committed to. This exercise is another way of 'measuring' green policy convergence. In addition, in checking China's first ever sustainable development chapter, the relevant section of the recent draft CAI treaty is inspected. Both exercises have to be brief for reasons of space.

Assessing 'Green' Policy Convergence between the EU and China

Within the confines of this chapter, it is not possible to discuss eight domains of China's 'green policies' in detail and do justice to all aspects. Inevitably, therefore, in a single overview, policies have to be sketched with respect to their main characteristics and given a simple rating for the impact on convergence (see Table 5.2).

Table 5.2 shows clearly that China is 'under way'. But its initial position in several of the listed domains was so bad that even by 2020 the legacies are not easy to overcome. There are vested interests, too, and the formidable costs of cleaning up are rightly feared. In addition, whether for reasons of energy security or low costs or both, coal remains in a protected position, although capping the volume or raising its price are no longer fully taboo. Therefore, the ranking – never a hard measure, of course – is still not so positive. Stopping bad policies is one thing, undoing the damage quite another. This overview is a snapshot of around 2020. It goes without saying that this process of convergence has to be assessed over time. Some areas have targets for 2030 which inspire optimism about more convergence (e.g. forestry, soil quality, water quality, renewables).

Table 5.2 *Assessing the contribution of eight 'green' policies in China in 2020*

No	Policy domain	Characteristics of policy domain	Rating
1	Soil quality	New stricter law in 2018, with near-exhaustive massive new data collection (e.g. seven heavy metals in soil) and legal responsibilities for remediation; risk-based approach; target 2030 – 95% of land safe to be used (in 2020 some 16–20% is polluted); costs are astronomical, one estimate 10% of GDP only for period 2016–2020	Quite negative for convergence; U-turn only recently
2	Water quality	New water pollution and control law (2017), with three 'red lines' (cap on total water use; hard efficiency targets for industry for 2020 and 2030, as well as for irrigation; drastic upgrading of water quality); non-trivial improvement of surface water realised by 2020; huge enforcement efforts (e.g. discovery of 60,000 secret sewage outlets near Yangtze and Taihu; 19,000 near Bohai Sea); lots of water still wasted, water and land erosion no less than 31% of total land area and increasing worries about deep groundwater pollution	Negative
3	Air quality	New stricter air pollution law (2015); focus on 6 pollutants (with PM 2.5 and SO_2 in the lead); between 2015 and 2019 indicators down for PM 2.5 (28%), CO (27%) and SO_2 (56%, amazing) but ozone up by 11%; yet evidence of domestic pollution havens in 'coal bases'; technology approach doubtful, filters not suitable for ozone and NO_2, whilst limited for SO_2; still, PM 2.5 *levels* still very far above OECD levels and above max. WHO thresholds	Negative (U-turn only very recently)
4	GHGs mitigation	China's 2020 NDC for Paris not impressive (but met); i.e. peak CO_2 emissions before 2030, reduce carbon intensity by 60+% in 2030 (but see above, section on green convergence), renewables share in 2030 to 20% and increase forest stock (by 4.5 bn m3 in 2030); together not consistent with goal of Paris; 'soft'	Negative

Table 5.2 (*cont.*)

No	Policy domain	Characteristics of policy domain	Rating
		2020 coal cap on 58% of consumption; so far little control of rapid rise of non-CO_2 GHGs (methane, N20 and HFC), possibly in 2030 to 25% GHG equivalent	
5	'Responsible business' initiatives	CSR (Corporate Social Responsibility) increasing in China since 2003 (but never bottom-up); from 2021, some 3,000 firms must publish CSR reports based on relatively strict (Hong Kong) standards, but extractive industries do not align with widely accepted standards on e.g. exposure of corruption	Positive
6	Sustainable forestry & timber trade	Since 2009 EU–China BCM[a] on FLEG[b] aiming to combat illegal logging and derived trade whilst promoting sustainable development; China huge importer and exporter, from fifteen voluntary partnership agreements/FLEGT countries too; Chinese Timber Legality Verification System developed + monitoring; in 2020 China fully prohibited purchase, transport and processing of illegal wood; trialogue EU–Indonesia/China, trialogue with Africa in the making	Positive
7	Sustainable fisheries	Besides super-growth in aquaculture in China, China fishing with DWF[c] in the Pacific coastal areas and around Africa; Chinese underreporting to the Food and Agriculture Organization (FAO) in 2012 twelve times (report to the European Parliament; EU–China fisheries cooperation via three High-Level Dialogues (since 2010), plus WG on IUU);[d] 2018 Blue Partnership for the Oceans on sustainable fisheries; murky contracts with African countries to be substituted with international (EU-driven) standard; WTO group on fisheries subsidies still stuck (before Kazakhstan WTO ministerial);	On balance, probably neutral, but issues outstanding

		Reg. 1005/2008 imposes strict controls (with import certificates) on EU imports from third countries, with 'red cards' (bans) – China exports a lot of fish to the EU and hence cooperates, but how far?	
8	Green industrial policies	Starting from the quest (e.g. to the EU) for support of 'green technologies' under the tenth Plan, and adding to its hydro strategy, China has stressed green industrial policies; renewables, e-cars, e-scooters, e-buses; battery factories supporting green tech; phenomenal growth (with subsidies and regulation); UN Environmental Programme says Chinese investment in renewables 2010–2019 amounts to $758bn; cost cuts in solar so radical that the biggest EU anti-dumping case ever (for €22bn) was terminated halfway through the period as it hindered the green transition in the EU; subsidies to e-cars and renewables curtailed in 2019	Very positive

[a] Bilateral Coordination Mechanism.

[b] FLEG = Forest Law Enforcement and Governance; FLEGT covers the same for trade (T).

[c] DWF = distant water fleet, fishing in EEZs (exclusive economic zones, under murky contracts).

[d] IUU = illegal, unreported and unregulated fisheries.

Can China Align to a FTA Sustainable Development Chapter?

Another approach to a meaningful debate about 'green' policy convergence between China and the EU is a reference to 'sustainable development chapters' in EU FTAs. Briefly, I shall first ask whether China could agree with most of the provisions of this chapter in the EPA between Japan and the EU (chapter 16). Second, the recently agreed draft text of the CAI can be compared with (some) similar relevant provisions in EPA's chapter 16.

Chapter 16 of EPA is probably the most ambitious sustainability chapter in any FTA. It is therefore perhaps too ambitious for a country like China which is still catching up in 'greening'. Nevertheless, based on extensive material in Pelkmans (2021a, including the Annex), the perhaps surprising conclusion is that China and the EU are convergent to a very large extent on this basis.[27] The 'green pillar' of this EPA chapter comprises thirty-seven explicit provisions (other than consultations and dispute settlement, as China and the EU have no FTA). The large majority of these provisions should present no problem for China. One among several reasons is that bilateral FTAs in fact rely on many multilateral obligations in MEAs; Table 5.1 has already shown that the EU and China are fully convergent and go far beyond the MEAs specified in FTAs. In other instances, the analysis relies on common statements by the EU and China or clear policy statements by Chinese leaders or in State Council publications. This does not mean there are no concerns, as Table 5.2 shows. These include some issues in fisheries, and the NDC of China under the Paris Agreement, for example, especially about the undiminished role of coal. Other queries exist about transparency (not usually a quality of Chinese governance) and environmental impact assessment. It should be realised that this near-convergence has already gone this far *without* FTA negotiations in the first place.

Secondly, a new practical 'test' of green policy convergence can be conducted now that the draft CAI treaty, the Comprehensive Agreement on Investment between the EU and China, has been signed.[28] However, one has to be much more careful here, not only because this investment draft treaty is nowhere near the same as a FTA, but also because this is the very first time China has explicitly committed on aspects of green

[27] The analysis is not a rigorously legal one, but rather a taxonomy of provisions.

[28] See https://policy.trade.ec.europa.eu/eu-trade-relationships-country-and-region/countries-and-regions/china/eu-china-agreement/milestones-and-documents_en of 22 January 2021.

policy convergence on a bilateral basis. Section IV of the CAI deals with 'investment and sustainable development'. Apart from some general provisions,[29] what matters are the second and fourth sub-sections. The green pillar is in sub-section 2. After recognising the right to regulate but consistently with multilateral commitments, Art. 2 introduces three non-regression clauses, just like in FTAs, as well as non-discrimination between investors. The 'high level of protection' is confirmed. A Dialogue and cooperation article is inserted, not too dissimilar to the one in FTAs, though less specific. Art. 4 is about the commitment to effectively implement MEAs to which China (and the EU) is a party. In the EPA this provision is far more detailed but nevertheless similar. Art. 5 is on 'favouring' green growth, again similar but less detailed than in FTAs (where it is usually on 'trade and investment'); a sub-provision is added on environmental impact assessment, such as exchanging good practices. The sub-section ends with Art. 6 on climate change, stipulating that Parties 'shall' implement the Paris Agreement and its NDC, whilst also promoting and facilitating investment of relevance (with specifications of certain tools such as low-carbon technologies, etc.) as well as a call to cooperate in international fora as appropriate. One might engage in a refined legal analysis but here is not the right place, nor is it the proper focus. The CAI 'green' text is far shorter and covers less than an EU FTA. Unlike EPA, for example, there is nothing on biological diversity, or on sustainable forestry, or on sustainable fishing; nor is there any text on science as a leading guide for 'green' regulation and/or the precautionary approach. Sub-section 4 is on a 'Mechanism to address differences'. In case consultations do not work, there will be a Panel of experts as in the EU–South Korea labour case. Since the language is the same, such a Panel might be thought to be likely one day. However, the cardinal difference with the Korea case is that it is difficult to imagine that the (green) CAI text will give rise to non-compliance of a hard commitment (as was the case with Korea, on ILO core conventions). It seems to confirm that China believes in the cooperative method, much more than in a legal approach.

[29] See Hu and Pelkmans (2021, box 6) for more detail; for a general, largely legal analysis of the CAI, see Hu (2021). In sub-section 1 (context and objectives), many multilateral Declarations are recalled and a commitment to develop investment in such a way as to contribute to the objective of sustainable development. Art. 2 seeks to promote CSR and responsible business conduct.

Answering the Second Research Question

The second research question is whether one can observe a process of green *policy* convergence between the EU and China over the period 1995 and 2020. A feature one cannot but take into account is the initial deterioration of green indicators and the initially hesitant and very selective approach to green EU–China cooperation and to green policy-making in China. Although the policy analysis in China and requested cooperation from the EU was clearly ahead of actual policy interventions and major investments, let alone firm enforcement, the initially severe inconsistencies between policy exchanges and the facts on the ground render it very difficult to sketch patterns of convergence, until rather recently.

Two methods of verifying EU–China green policy convergence over this long period of time have therefore been used. First, a condensed summary of the status of eight Chinese key green policy areas in 2018, 2019 or 2020 as the case may be. Second, an exercise *as if* China would conclude a FTA with the EU with a sustainable development chapter, as in the EPA with Japan.

The summary of eight key Chinese green policy areas shows that – after following a U-shaped curve – green policy-making in China is to a considerable extent still undoing the damage of the past, whereas in other respects it is already in the process of approaching convergence with the EU (and possibly ahead in renewables and e-vehicles). Where targets for 2030 exist, the process of convergence looks promising. A truly problematic feature of China's 'green' policy-making is coal – unless the newly initiated Emission Trading System (ETS) Chinese-style will yield a high enough price for carbon but that will take a few years.

On the exercise of checking whether China could sign a sustainable development chapter as is found in the EPA between Japan and the EU (a high-standard FTA), the answer is broadly affirmative. China turns out to be convergent with EU objectives and priorities in the large majority of the thirty-seven green items in the chapter; a few remain uncertain and would have to be tested, whereas transparency issues may well be less than satisfactory. A first reality test of this exercise has recently been agreed between the EU and China as section IV of the draft CAI treaty. The 'green' substance of Section IV is largely aspirational or prudent, and does not incorporate anywhere near the scope and details of the 'green' aspects of EPA. What is found reflects a trade-off between a similar procedure (Panel of Experts) as in the EU–Korea FTA and a weak or 'soft' formulation of substance. It reflects China's deep preference to cooperate, not to get bogged down in legal frictions.

Answering the Third Research Question: The EU's Pursuit and Effectiveness of Convergence

The basic idea of this chapter is that one can observe a decades-long, complicated if not tortuous process of convergence between the EU and China in climate and environment, guided and supported by intense and multi-variate bilateral exchanges, Dialogues, consultation, practical projects, stimulation of green investments in China (via CDM), programmes and direct local collaboration in the implementation of policy inside China. It is shown that the EU has been active, if not very active, ever since the first Commission paper on EU–China relations in 1995, in assisting the development of China when still a developing country, and in promoting in many ways the direction and intensity of green policy-making directly or indirectly relevant to trade and investment.

The process of convergence has been influenced by the EU, no doubt, but there have been many other actors as well as international agencies that have been helpful in this respect. It is therefore impossible to verify the degree of effectiveness of the EU's promotion of sustainable development in EU–China trade policy in the wider sense with any rigour. Nevertheless, the chapter points to an abundance of EU–China activities and regular support from the EU–China Summit level over two decades. These common activities have widened considerably in scope and have deepened. In several specific policy or expertise issues, the EU has actually supported China directly, be it via local collaboration (e.g. emission trading), or China has adopted EU regulatory requirements (e.g. car emissions requirements).

Given the slowly improving green policy convergence between the EU and China, one is confronted with a *great green paradox*: the simultaneous occurrence of increasing green *policy convergence* with the factual and sometimes large *discrepancies in green indicators*. This 'great green paradox' sows confusion and discomfort among stakeholders and the wider public. At the same time, the paradox was far less extreme in 2020 than (say) a decade before. Indeed, selective quotes about China's green predicament can be thoroughly misleading. The strategic issue is whether China can deliver further convincing progress causing green indicators to move in the right direction, so that the paradox melts away.

The third research question has two parts. One is whether the EU has systematically pursued green policy cooperation with China (and via EU trade policy where appropriate). The chapter shows clearly that the answer is yes. This cooperation has deepened and widened over time, and was also practised multilaterally or plurilaterally. The second part of the research question asks whether this systematic effort by the EU has been effective in supporting a process of convergence. As noted, many other actors – both domestic in China and internationally – have been involved and this makes it impossible to verify causality, except in some specific instances where China requested specific support for immediate policy purposes (e.g. car emission standards; operational support for the ETS China-style; sustainable timber certification; early support of renewables technology). All that one can say is that the mutual preparedness, the high frequency of all kinds of interactions and the eagerness to go for joint funding point to a strong interest to work together and improve green policies.

References

Asian Development Bank (2018), Managing water resources for sustainable socio-economic development, a country water assessment for the P.R. of China, December, www.adb.org/sites/default/files/institutional-document/473576/country-water-assessment-prc.pdf

China State Council (2018), Three years action plan for blue sky defense, June, www.iea.org/policies/8508-three-year-action-plan-for-cleaner-air-also-called-the-blue-sky-war

European Commission (2015), Trade for all: Towards a more responsible trade and investment policy, https://eur-lex.europa.eu/legal-content/GA/TXT/?uri=CELEX%3A52015DC0497

Hu, W. (2021), The EU–China comprehensive agreement on investment, *CEPS Policy Insights* No. PI2021–07, May, www.ceps.eu

Hu, W. & J. Pelkmans (2021), EU's cooperative approach with China for sustainable development, final report (as delivery 6.1), April, https://respect.eui.eu/

Jin, Y., H. Anderson & S. Zhang (2016), Air pollution control policies in China: a retrospective and prospects, *International Journal of Environmental Research and Public Health*, 13(12), 1219. https://doi.org/10.3390%2Fijerph13121219

Johnson, T. M., Li, J., Jiang, Z., & Taylor, R. P. (1996). *China: Issues and Options in Greenhouse Gas Emissions Control*, Washington, DC: World Bank.

Linster, M. & C. Yang (2018) *China's progress towards Green Growth: an international perspective*, Paris, OECD Green Growth Papers No. 2018/05, www.oecd.org/env/country-reviews/PR-China-Green-Growth-Progress-Report-2018.pdf

OECD (2019), *OECD Economic Surveys China*, Paris: OECD.

Pelkmans, J. (2021a), Nudging China to go green, how EU trade and cooperation policies stimulated China, paper for RESPECT, www.respect.eui.eu

Pelkmans, J. (2021b), Linking 'values' to EU trade policy – a good idea?, *European Law Journal*, 26, pp. 391–400.

Snyder, F., ed. (2009), *The European Union and China, 1949–2008*, basic documents and commentary, Oxford: Hart Publishing.

World Bank (1997), *Clear Water, Blue Skies, China's Environment in the New Century*, Washington, DC: World Bank.

Yale Environment Center & World Economic Forum (2019), Environmental Performance Index 2019, https://epi.yale.edu/

6

The Role of Domestic Factors in the EU's Governance of Labour Standards through Trade

FRANKLIN MADUKO, TIMEA PÁL, AND LÁSZLÓ BRUSZT

Introduction

How and under what conditions can the European Union promote non-trade-related policy objectives (NTPOs) such as labour standards among its less developed trade partners? Is this merely a matter of using the right type of conditionality and assistance in the specific field? Or does it involve a more encompassing approach that requires adjusting trade and non-trade-related policy objectives to diverse local conditions? We address these questions through an analysis of the extent and manners in which domestic factors in developing countries condition the ability of the EU to promote labour standards through trade.[1]

Over recent years, EU efforts to promote labour standards among its trade partners have intensified. The inclusion of labour provisions in EU trade agreements has become increasingly common, as demonstrated by the Trade and Sustainable Development (TSD) chapter that has become an integral part of EU free trade agreements (FTAs) (Harrison et al. 2019). Expansion of trade and investments, especially since the emergence of global value chains (GVCs) in the 1990s, have also led to an intensification of market-based mechanisms for diffusion of labour standards, illustrated by the increasing prevalence of private transnational regulation (Locke 2013). Studies of the promotion of labour standards through formal trade policy or actual trade integration have so far focused primarily on the external features of international public and market-based private governance. A key debate, for example, has been around the relative effectiveness of the use of economic incentives and

[1] Labour standards, in our analysis, refer to both fundamental labour rights, such as freedom of assembly and collective bargaining, elimination of forced and child labour, non-discrimination; and working condition regulations, such as minimum wage, overtime restrictions, occupational health and safety.

sanctions, assistance and dialogue, and/or engagement of labour organizations by public or private external governance actors (Hafner-Burton 2005; Kim 2012; Postnikov and Bastiaens 2014; Oehri 2015; Amengual and Distelhorst 2020; Pike 2020). More recently, however, an increasing numbers of studies acknowledge the role of political and economic factors from developing countries in the implementation of these external governance approaches. These point towards the relevance of the exposure of domestic firms to global competition, institutional capacities and the industrial strategies of governments and business organizations, the independence and influence of labour organizations, and the labour standards of key export destinations (Greenhill et al. 2009; Bruszt and McDermott 2014; Amengual and Chirot 2016, Bair et al. 2020, Short et al. 2020).

Building on these studies, we set up an integrated analytical framework to examine the role of the interests and capacity of major stakeholders from developing countries – state, exporting firms and labour organizations – to facilitate or hinder the implementation of international and market-based governance approaches by the EU. We then test the explanatory power of this framework through a combination of quantitative and qualitative analysis. By combining large-scale regression analysis to identify and assess the relative strength of associations between labour standards and domestic factors, on one hand, and comparative studies of processes of change in the domestic contexts of Moldova and Morocco, on the other, we shed more light on the ways in which key actors from developing countries respond to EU labour governance based on the institutions and structures in which they are embedded. The main contribution of our study is to expand our understanding of the relative importance and mediating role of domestic factors identified in past studies. We also highlight the relevance of the sectoral structure of trade integration and the differentiated ability of individual EU member states to trigger changes in developing economies.

Our quantitative study shows the role played by economic mechanisms in domestic responses to external regulatory norms. Exporting to countries with more demanding labour standards has a positive effect, as does exporting in sectors with greater complexity and requiring higher skills. We also find support for the positive effects of strengthening civil society organizations (CSOs) and the upgrading of state capacity. Our case studies help us to establish links between these factors and action on the ground by key economic actors: the state, business and labour. We can identify a vicious circle of the low road of integration into regional markets, with exports going primarily to countries with lower labour standards from sectors of lower technological complexity requiring primarily unskilled labour. In this setting, incumbents base their export strategy on maintaining their competitiveness on the basis of cheap labour. State capacity to design policies of industrial upgrading are weak and the state apparatus is open to the pressure on domestic business to resist improvements in labour standards that could increase labour costs. External assistance to unions or non-governmental organizations (NGOs), or state administration have very little positive effect. However, we can also point to a potentially more positive virtuous circle among these factors and actors. Export to countries with more demanding labour standards and with goods of higher complexity might alter the incentives of the state and business, both domestic and external firms in the production chain. If the state has stronger administrative capacity and it can design and implement upgrading programmes, the probability of a developmental alliance supporting improvements in labour standards among domestic actors also increases.

The structure of the chapter is as follows. We first review some of the insights regarding the role of domestic factors emerging from the literatures on the promotion of labour standards through trade. We then present an analytical framework that highlights how the state, business and labour organizations from developing countries are expected to facilitate (or hinder) the implementation of EU governance mechanisms. The following two sections consist of the regression and comparative analysis respectively, that serve for drawing some general conclusions at the end of the chapter.

Promoting Labour Standards through Trade

A growing body of studies examines the link between labour standards and trade, focusing primarily on how political and private actors from major advanced economies can promote labour standards in developing economies. This field of study is largely divided between the literature that examines the promotion of labour standards through the inclusion of labour provisions in formal trade agreements and deployment of accompanying instruments to ensure implementation (e.g. Hafner-Burton 2005; Kim 2012; Postnikov and Bastiaens 2014; Oehri 2015); and those that analyse the diffusion of labour standards through market integration, particularly through GVCs and the accompanying private governance initiatives (Greenhill et al. 2009; Distelhorst et al. 2015; Short et al. 2020). Over recent years, an increasing number of studies from the literature have shifted attention from the exclusive focus on international or transnational aspects of these governance approaches to greater consideration of the role of domestic factors across the different developing countries where these external arrangements have been implemented.

In the literature on *labour provisions in trade agreements*, studies that focus on the implementation of TSD chapters in the EU's FTA agreements across various national settings reveal the relevance of domestic interests and political institutions. In their paper on the potential of EU–Asia FTAs to promote social norms, Garcia and Masselot (2015) note the lack of commitment or outright resistance among some trade partner governments to EU governance of labour standards through international agreements. In an examination of the EU–Colombia agreement, Brando, Lein and Marx (2016) highlight the significant influence exerted by the Ministry of Trade in the implementation process, as well as the lack of capacity of NGOs and of trade unions to promote workers' interests in the civil societal mechanisms of the agreement. Focusing on the case of Peru, Orbie and Van den Putte (2016) raise concerns regarding the ability of trade unions and state labour inspectorates to ensure adequate implementation of reforms adopted to meet EU requirements. In a comparative study of the operationalization of the TSD framework across the Caribbean, South Korea and Moldova, Harrison and colleagues (2019) reveal additional constraints from a lack of prioritization of labour standards by CSOs and antagonistic state–society relations. More research is needed to understand the mediating role of domestic interests and institutions across developing countries in general (Postnikov and Bastiaens 2014).

In the literature on *market-based governance of labour standards*, a group of empirical studies emphasizes the role of incentives set by social sustainability expectations of public and private entities from major exports markets in raising standards among trade partners. Greenhill, Mosley and Prakash (2009) show that exporting to countries with rigorous collective labour rights leads to more stringent laws in the countries of origin. Cao, Greenhill and Prakash (2013) find a similar association between importing and exporting country standards in the realm of human rights. Malesky and Mosley (2021) show that when opportunities arise to export to the United States, Vietnamese firms are more willing to invest in improving their own labour practices, including skills and better working conditions. On the other hand, Adolph, Quince and Prakash (2017) find that as African countries expand their exports into China, they start to reflect the latter's lower labour standards. Other studies have placed greater emphasis on the relevance of political institutions and interests. In a study of the implications of the expansion of trade for collective labour rights in Costa Rica, for example, Mosley (2008) underlines the importance of trade unions and their ties to left-leaning political parties. Schrank (2009, 2013) argues that policymakers and bureaucrats from the Dominican Republic were able to meet external demands from the United States to improve labour standards by reinforcing their state labour inspectorate.

The literature on private transnational regulation also calls attention to the important role of developing country governments and labour organizations that may hinder or support alternative arrangements (e.g. Locke et al. 2013; Distelhorst et al. 2015). In their work on the apparel sector in Bangladesh, for example, Bair, Anner and Blasi (2020) document the ways in which the state and suppliers, concerned about rising operational costs and continued cost pressures by lead firms, undermine an ambitious private initiative to address health and safety concerns in the aftermath of the Rana Plaza tragedy. Amengual and Chirot (2016) also find that improvements in labour standards in the garment sector in Indonesia through the Better Work programme are largely contingent on the support of the Ministry of Manpower and Transmigration. They attribute state support to political mobilization by trade unions, thus reiterating the important role that labour organizations can play even in developing countries, where freedom of association and the independence of trade unions is often limited. Short, Toffel and Huggill (2020) also find that firms are more likely to improve practices in response to private governance initiatives in national contexts with denser NGO networks and a relatively free press, that pose a greater risk of harmful practices being exposed.

These studies provide some important insights into which economic and political factors might be relevant for the ability of the EU to promote labour standards in developing economies. Our contribution is to integrate these perspectives under a common framework that allows us to assess their relative importance in a more systematic manner. We also extend our analysis to the sectoral composition of trade to better capture the influence of economic pressures on the abilities of domestic actors to respond to EU requirements for labour standards. Our policy proposals are built on combining the exploration of the different domestic factors that shape the incentives of key players, with the insights from the literature dealing with the way various economic integration strategies can shape the incentives and the capacities of domestic actors (Bruszt and McDermott 2014; Bruszt and Langbein 2020). According to the latter, trade policies that include assistance that alters the capacities of domestic actors to profit from increased trade can also change their expectations about the costs and benefits of improved labour standards.

Linking Domestic Factors to EU Labour Governance Approaches

This section focuses on our hypotheses regarding the role of domestic factors from developing countries in the effectiveness of the EU to promote labour standards through either international or market-based governance. Informed by past studies, we focus on the role of the state, businesses and labour organizations that, as interested parties affected by changes in labour standards, might further or block change promoted by EU actors. While international trade policies, on the one hand, and market integration – particularly through GVCs – on the other, obviously overlap, they correspond to different labour governance approaches and have different policy implications. Notwithstanding some efforts to engage social partners and CSOs, EU governance through international trade agreements is more formal and political in character, focusing predominantly on the governments of trade partners. Market-based governance of labour standards, on the other hand, operates primarily at the firm and sector level, although it can also affect governments, in terms of their national relevance. As such, these two alternative mechanisms set different opportunities and constraints for incumbents from developing countries to interfere with their implementation and mediate their impact.

State-Led Processes of Change

Governments of developing countries are generally expected to respond primarily to formal requirements stipulated at the international level. The significance of state efforts to conform with such expectations is often presumed to vary primarily in the magnitude of the incentives and assistance provided (e.g. Schimmelfennig and Scholtz 2008). Neighbouring countries, for example, were offered the possibility of full market integration and access to substantial assistance as part of the European Neighbourhood Policy (ENP), that exceed the benefits offered to most other developing country trade partners. The extent of reforms adopted by developing country governments is, nonetheless, expected to vary across national contexts due to other factors as well. Even within the ENP, governments of individual countries have sought different levels of alignment with the EU based largely on geopolitical considerations and economic development strategies (e.g. Börzel and Lebanidze 2015). Governments that actively pursue export-oriented economic development will most likely make greater efforts to meet the requirements of both public and private actors from the EU in order to ensure market access. This process is expected to affect labour reforms primarily at the formal level, as legal reforms are generally easier to adopt and can serve as visible trademarks for governmental efforts to meet EU requirements.

The implementation of these reforms, however, will be contingent on the economic competitiveness strategy and strength of state capacity, which influence the political will and ability of the government to enforce reforms. As we have seen in the case of the Dominican Republic, improvements in labour practices were possible due to the existence of a state labour inspectorate that combined worker protection with economic efficiency (Schrank 2009, 2013). This in turn was possible due to a public administration system that relied on meritocratic recruitment, higher wages and the fostering of an organizational culture (Piore and Schrank 2008). The capacity of the state to facilitate industrial upgrading towards higher value-added activities, where cost pressures are generally lower, can also facilitate improvements in labour standards (Gereffi and Lee 2016; Marques and Eberlein 2020). In the absence of such capacities, however, economic pressures exerted through international markets, particularly through some GVCs, can greatly constrain the domestic inclination to raise labour standards. In the case of Bangladesh, dependence of the national economy on textile and apparel exports has fuelled government resistance to domestic and external pressures to improve labour standards (Bair et al. 2020). This is because suppliers from low-skilled labour-intensive sectors such as the garment sector are often exposed to particularly strong cost and competition pressures (e.g. Anner 2020). Such pressures are generally attenuated in the more technologically complex sectors such as electronics and automotive, where the ratios of mid-to-high skilled production is generally higher and prospects for workers are better (Barrientos et al. 2011). Governments of developing countries are thus also often exposed to market-based economic and social pressures, with influence on the implementation of national labour regulation.

Hypothesis 1: The extent and type of labour standard improvements facilitated by the state will be contingent on a combination of (a) overall interest in greater economic integration with the EU, (b) state administrative capacity for regulatory enforcement and/or industrial policy, and (c) the national economy's dependence on low-skilled labour-intensive exports.

Business-Driven Processes of Change

Exporting businesses are expected to respond predominantly to market-based incentives and pressures, with differences across developing economies regarding the key destinations and sectoral composition of exports.

Firms seeking to export to large markets with strict standards – particularly the EU – are at the core of studies on upward regulatory convergence (Vogel and Kagan 2004; Bradford 2012). While the California or Brussels effect generally works for product standards that can be easily monitored, the emergence of private regulation overcomes some of the disadvantages that process standards such as labour standards face (Greenhill et al. 2009). CSOs and lead firms from developed economies with high standards can monitor and coerce exporting firms and their governments to improve labour standards (Peterson et al. 2016; Amengual and Distelhorst 2020). Consumers and firms from developed economies are also often willing to pay more for products manufactured ethically (Hainmueller and Hiscox 2015; Distelhorst and Locke 2018). This is echoed by findings that exporting to advanced economies can also entail higher markups (Malesky and Mosley 2018).

While the EU is often understood as a homogeneous entity in these contexts – thus the 'Brussels effect' (Bradford 2012) – we highlight the important differences that exist across individual member states in terms of both stringency of labour regulations and economic prosperity. Notwithstanding continuous efforts towards convergence, such divisions are still particularly important between old and new member states (Meardi 2013). New member states might not meet a minimum threshold that is often necessary to trigger changes in practices that are as culturally and institutionally embedded as those related to fundamental labour rights (Cao et al. 2013). We therefore consider exports to individual member states rather than the EU at large, and expect to find differences in firm-level adjustments in developing countries that export primarily to old EU member states relative to those that sell predominantly to new member states.

The effectiveness of market-based mechanisms is also expected to vary across sectors due to differences in economic pressures exerted through the GVCs of varying technological sophistication. The success of private regulation is often hindered by significant cost and competition pressures (Amengual and Kuruvilla 2020; Bair et al. 2020). The intensity of such pressures tends to vary across sectors due to differences in technological and skill complexity, organizational structure and governance of GVCs (Gereffi et al. 2005; Barrientos et al. 2011). In the textile and apparel sector, for example, where low-skilled labour-intensive production is more prevalent and competition is more global, lead firms tend to pay diminishing prices to suppliers while also imposing short lead times and high order volatility (Anner 2020). The intensity of such pressures might be mitigated to some extent by financial and technical assistance from the state and/or business associations to facilitate industrial upgrading (Gereffi and Lee 2016). Economic pressures on supplier firms are presumably weaker in technologically more sophisticated GVCs, such as automotive industries, where production often requires more skilled workers, major lead firms rely on regional suppliers and relations are more durable (Sturgeon et al. 2008).

Social and economic pressures on exporting firms might also affect state regulation and, as such, influence EU governance at the international level as well, especially when businesses are politically influential. The EU has, after all, actively supported the engagement of social partners and CSOs in the implementation of trade agreements through institutionalized dialogue (e.g. Ashraf and van Seters 2020). Export-oriented producers might support labour reforms at the formal level to satisfy the EU and pressure groups from the EU that their labour standard requirements are met. At the implementation level, however, the influence of export-oriented businesses on regulatory policies in developing countries is generally in the opposite direction, especially when the role of low-skilled labour-intensive sectors is significant.

Hypothesis 2: Export-oriented firms are more inclined to improve practices when exporting to (a) technologically more sophisticated products and/or (b) end markets with higher labour standards, especially when they benefit from state or business association assistance.

Labour-Driven Improvements

Labour organizations – trade unions or NGOs involved in labour issues – can facilitate improvements in labour standards through either international or market-based mechanisms. Their influence is expected to be contingent on their organizational strength and political influence. The former refers primarily to the independence and representativeness of trade unions. The latter can be increased by the social dialogue and new civil societal mechanisms instituted by the EU, but also through connections to political parties.

At the international level, trade unions and NGOs can provide essential information to the EU about major labour concerns and contribute to possible solutions through its civil society. But as these mechanisms are still relatively new, we expect labour organizations to exert their influence primarily through pressure on their national governments that can reinforce EU requirements to improve worker protections. Their contribution, empowered by social dialogue institutions at the national level, could be essential to promote greater protection with respect to working conditions, complementing the primary focus of EU labour provision on fundamental labour rights. Considering the significant gap that often exists between formal regulations and practices on the ground, labour organizations could exert greater pressure on the state or complement state capacity to improve enforcement.

Labour organizations can also facilitate the effectiveness of private regulatory initiatives by providing essential information and engaging in international campaigns. Traditionally, their direct involvement in the regulatory efforts of lead firms in global value chains have been relatively limited. Labour organizations have, however, facilitated changes through contestation of existing practices that lead firms were then forced to address (Amengual and Chirot 2016) and have sometimes used private arrangements to substitute for weak state enforcement (Locke et al. 2013). Finally, labour organizations could also contribute to improvements by facilitating industrial upgrading or ensuring that the gains are shared with workers in export-oriented firms and/or sectors (Gereffi and Lee 2016).

Hypothesis 3: Labour organizations, when organizationally strong and influential, can facilitate improvements in labour standards through both governance mechanisms.

Regression Analysis

In this section, we examine the explanatory power of some of the hypotheses. We do so through a regression analysis of the association between labour standards and several domestic variables across developing countries. Our key variables of interest are state capacity (H1b), a measure of labour standards in key export markets (H2a) and CSO freedom (H3). Textiles and apparel, and technologically more sophisticated exports are proxies for economic constraints on state and business-led improvements in labour standards (H1c and H2b).

Data and Econometric Model

We estimate the relationship between labour standards and our key variables of interest using an unbalanced panel of forty-five countries over the period 1990–2014. These include developing economies from Africa, Eastern Europe, Central Asia, the Middle East, Latin America and the Caribbean that have trade agreements in force with the EU. Among these countries, twelve have become part of the ENP since 2004.[2] Countries with labour provisions in their EU trade agreements are identified by looking at the specific details of the agreements (see Pal et al. 2021 for details).

As our dependent variable is an ordinal variable, we estimate an ordered probit regression model, as specified in Equation (6.1).

$$\begin{aligned} y_{it} = {} & \beta_0 + \beta_1 BTC_{it} + \beta_2 EST_{it} + \beta_4 ETI_{it} + \gamma_3 ENP\&TA_{it} \\ & + \gamma_1 Injud_{it} + \gamma_2 CSO_{it} + \gamma_4 Control_{it} + e_{it} \end{aligned} \tag{6.1}$$

where y_{it} is the worker's right index of country i in time t. This variable was taken from the Cingranelli–Richards (CIRI) Human Rights database (Cingranelli, et al. 2014) and ranges from 0 to 2. It measures mainly the extent to which workers enjoy internationally recognized labour rights and minimum standards regarding working conditions. A score of 0 reflects that workers' rights were severely restricted; a score of 1 indicates that workers' rights were somewhat restricted; and a score of 2 indicates that workers' rights were fully protected during the year in question.

BTC_{it} is the bilateral trade context (BTC) index proposed in Greenhill et al. (2009) that is the weighted average of workers' rights among a country's export partners. Specifically, for each country and in each year in our data, we construct the share of exports to each of the country's export partners, and we use these shares as weights in taking averages of workers' rights for the country's export partners. The measurement equation takes the form below:

[2] These are: Algeria, Armenia, Azerbaijan, Egypt, Georgia, Israel, Jordan, Lebanon, Moldova, Morocco, Tunisia and Ukraine.

$$BTC_{it} = \sum_{\substack{j=1 \\ j \neq i}}^{N} \frac{y_{jt} \times Exp_{ijt}}{Tot\ Exports_{it}}$$

where i denotes a country in our data, j is the export partner of country i, t is the year and N is the number of countries that country i exports to. Exp_{ijt} is the total exports from country i to country j in year t. $Tot\ Exports_{it}$ is the total exports of country i in year t, and y_{jt} measures workers' rights in the export destination. The export data used in this index was taken from the World Integrated Trade Solution (WITS) database. Clearly, countries with larger export shares to destinations with stronger workers' rights will have higher values in the BTC index, and vice versa. This index is part of the variables that help us test for hypothesis 2. Specifically, it enables us to test whether a country's workers' rights depends, amongst other things, on the workers' rights in its main export destinations.

EST_{it} is the ratio of net export of textile/apparels products in total exports in a country in period t, and ETI_{it} is the ratio of net exports of technology-intensive products in total exports in period t.[3] Technology-intensive classification is based on the work by Lall (2000). The product-export-destination data comes from the UN Comtrade database. These variables proxy for the cost and competitiveness pressures exerted through GVCs on the ability of governments and domestic businesses to conform with EU expectations to raise labour standards, that are relevant for hypotheses 1 and 2. We thus expect a negative relationship of EST_{it} and a positive relationship of ETI_{it} with workers' rights, respectively.

CSO_{it} is an index of freedoms in civil society which was taken from the variety of democracy (VDEM) database (Coppedge et al. 2019). Higher values indicate a higher level of freedom in civil society, while lower values imply more repression. The variable proxies for the strength of labour organizations and we expect a positive relationship between CSO freedom and labour standards (H3).

$Injud_{it}$ is a variable which represents the level of judicial independence in each country. This is used as a proxy for state capacity (H1b) to capture the ability of the state to enforce labour reforms adopted to meet EU requirements. This variable was taken from the CIRI database and it ranges from 0 to 2, where higher values represent a more independent

[3] We measure these variables using the equations $EST_{it} = \frac{Total\ net\ export\ of\ textile_{it}}{Total\ Exports_{it}}$ and $ETI_{it} = \frac{Total\ net\ export\ of\ Technology\ Intensive\ Products_{it}}{Total\ Exports}$.

judiciary. We also expect a positive relationship between this variable and labour standards.

$ENP\&TA_{it}$ is a control variable which ranges from 0 to 2 and captures the intensity of international labour governance efforts by the EU. It takes the value 0 if country *i* does not have any EU trade agreements with labour provisions in force in period *t*, 1 if it has an EU trade agreement (TA) with labour provisions in force in period *t*, and 2 if the country joined the ENP. Since labour provisions in EU trade agreements improve workers' rights (Pal et al. 2021), controlling for this variable isolates the effect of domestic factors on labour standards from the effect attributed to EU trade agreements with labour provisions.

We also include a number of other control variables such as foreign direct investment (FDI) inflows, political constraints, GDP (aggregate and per capita) and GDP growth rate. The FDI inflows is the amount of new inflows of foreign direct investments to GDP ratio in a country each year. This controls for the effect of foreign direct investments on labour standards and helps to isolate the effect of foreign-owned production from the technology-intensive production of exports or export destinations. The political constraint variable, taken from the Quality of Government (QoG) database, measures the ease of changing government policy given that one political actor has strong preferences for such policy change. The GDP serves as a measure of national income and income growth and captures the fact that different levels of economic prosperity can have different effects on labour standards.

Results

We present our ordered probit model results in Table 6.1 and the marginal effects in Table 6.2. These results confirm the existence of statistically significant associations between labour standards, on the one hand, and our key domestic variables, on the other, in the expected directions.

The estimates in Table 6.1 indicate a positive relationship between BTC and workers' rights across all specifications. This implies that higher labour standards among countries where a country exports a larger proportion of its foreign sales is associated with an improvement in the country's labour standards, consistent with findings by Greenhill et al. (2009).

We also find that a higher share of technology-intensive production in total exports is positively associated with better workers' rights, while a greater share of textile and apparel in exports is associated with a decline in workers' rights. This is consistent with initial expectations that

Table 6.1 *Effects of domestic factors on labour standards*

Variables	(1) Workers' rights	(2) Workers' rights	(3) Workers' rights	(4) Workers' rights
BTC	0.591***	0.591***	0.583**	0.616**
	(0.218)	(0.224)	(0.236)	(0.241)
Share net tech exports	0.243	0.233	0.475*	0.518**
	(0.168)	(0.185)	(0.248)	(0.252)
Share net textile exports	-2.117**	-2.116**	-1.811*	-1.989**
	(0.924)	(0.950)	(0.976)	(0.973)
ENP&TA		0.209*	0.195	0.231*
		(0.122)	(0.128)	(0.138)
Judicial independence			0.330***	0.359***
			(0.118)	(0.119)
Political constraints			-0.0486	-0.121
			(0.406)	(0.408)
CSO freedom			0.297***	0.299***
			(0.113)	(0.115)
FDI inflows/GDP ratio				2.250*
				(1.344)
Log GDP				-0.540
				(0.884)
Log GDP pc				0.173
				(0.725)
GDP growth				0.0114
				(0.0157)
Observations	823	823	738	738
Country FE	Yes	Yes	Yes	Yes
Year FE	Yes	Yes	Yes	Yes

Robust standard errors in parentheses *** $p < 0.01$, ** $p < 0.05$, * $p < 0.1$

economic integration through low-skilled labour-intensive sectors, like textile and apparel, will be more likely to hinder domestic efforts to meet EU labour standard requirements. Prospects are much more favourable in technologically more sophisticated sectors.

The freedom of civil society organization index (CSO freedom) is positively associated with workers' rights. This implies that policies that strengthen the freedom of civil society will be instrumental in ensuring that labour standards are upheld. This positive influence can be exerted, at least in part, through the engagement of CSOs with the international or transnational labour governance approaches of the EU. Similarly, with respect to judicial independence, there is a statistically significant positive association between labour standards and state enforcement capacity in developing countries that could also facilitate the implementation of the EU's governance efforts to achieve more progress.

We control for a number of variables, including the *ENP&TA* variable that is positively associated with our dependent variable, confirming that having an EU trade agreement with labour provisions or joining the ENP leads to better outcomes in labour standards. This is consistent with previous findings in the literature (Postnikov and Bastiaens 2014; Pal et al. 2021).

We conduct some robustness checks to test whether our results are sensitive to deviations from model specifications and variables redefinitions. First, we estimate a fixed-effect regression model similar to Equation 6.1. Since the dependent variable is ordinal, fixed-effect regression does not take into account the ceiling and floor restrictions on models that include ordinal variables (Winship and Mare 1984) and may result in biased estimates; however, it offers ease of interpretation. In the second sensitivity checks, we use net exports of technology-intensive products, and textiles and apparel products to the EU, instead of the total net exports of these products. We find results from both sensitivity checks to be largely consistent with our baseline results.

Since our dependent variable is ordinal (ranging from 0 to 2), interpretation and quantification of the relationships identified in Table 6.1 are improved through the computation of marginal effects. Specifically, the marginal effects are the partial effects of our explanatory variables of interest on the probability of observing a value of workers' rights = 0, workers' rights = 1 and workers' rights = 2. In Table 6.2 we present the marginal effects corresponding to column (4) of Table 6.1.[4] These

[4] The results in Table 6.2 are expressed in terms of one standard deviation from the mean of the domestic factors.

Table 6.2 *Marginal effects of domestic factors on labour standards*

	Domestic factors				
	Bilateral trade context (BTC)	Net share high-tech exports	Net share textile and apparel exports	CSO freedom	Judicial independence
	(1)	(2)	(3)	(4)	(5)
Workers' rights = 0	−5.8	−8.1	6.9	−8.3	−7.2
Workers' rights = 1	4.8	6.4	−5.5	6.6	5.8
Workers' rights = 2	1.2	1.7	−1.4	1.7	1.5
Observations	738	738	738	738	738

confirm that our independent variables of interest exert a substantial influence on the probability of demonstrating higher labour standards.

The estimates in column (1) of Table 6.2 imply that an increase by one standard deviation from the mean of the workers' rights index of a country's key export destination is associated with being 5.8 per cent less likely to have a workers' rights score of 0, 4.6 per cent more likely to be have a score of 1, and 1.2 per cent more likely to have a score of 2. This suggests that labour standards in a country are very sensitive to the labour standards of the country's trading partners.

In column (2) of Table 6.2, we find that one standard deviation from the mean of the ratio of net export of high-technology products to total exports will be associated with being 8.1 per cent less likely to have a workers' rights score of 0, 6.4 per cent of being more likely to have a score of 1, and 1.7 per cent of being more likely to have a score of 2. In column (3), as expected, we find the opposite results. A one standard deviation from the mean of the net export of textiles and apparel products in total exports is associated with being 6.9 per cent more likely to have a workers' right score of 0, 5.5 per cent less likely to have a score of 1, and 1.4 per cent less likely to have a score of 3. This suggest that policies which promote production and exports of technology-intensive products as against textiles and apparel will increase the likelihood of stronger workers' rights.

In column (4), we find that a one standard deviation from the mean of CSO freedom is associated with being 8.3 per cent less likely to have a workers' rights score of 0, 6.6 per cent more likely to have a score of 1, and 1.7 per cent more likely to have a score of 2. In column (5), we find that a one standard deviation from the mean of judicial independence is associated with being 7.2 per cent less likely to have a workers' rights score of 0, 5.8 per cent more likely to have a score of 1, and 1.5 per cent more likely to have a score of 2. Clearly, this implies a strong sensitivity of workers' rights to both CSO freedom and state capacity (proxied by judicial independence) within a country.

We now explore whether these domestic factors exert part of their influence on labour standards through the increased effectiveness of the EU's international governance approach, captured in our study through the *ENP&TA* variable. To this end, we interact *ENP&TA* with judicial independence, CSO freedom and BTC – as the variables of greatest policy relevance – to determine the magnitude of their positive influence on labour standards across countries without labour provisions in their EU trade agreements, those with labour provisions in their trade agreements and ENP countries. By comparing the coefficients across these groups of countries, we can draw some conclusions on the extent to which their positive influence has been interconnected with the international labour governance approach of the EU.

We present the results from these specifications in columns (1) and (2) of Table 6.3. In column (1), we find that among countries when they have neither a EU trade agreement (with labour provisions) or ENP agreements, judicial independence is strongly positively associated with labour standards. This pattern also exists in countries with EU trade agreements, however, the magnitude of this relationship is weaker. Finally, the estimates show that, among ENP countries, judicial independence is uncorrelated with labour standards. We find a similar pattern of results in column (2) of Table 6.3. The particularly low coefficient levels among the ENP countries can be attributed in part to the fact that both judicial independence and CSO freedoms have been very low with very slight within-country variation among the eastern and southern ENP countries. Overall, these results suggest that irrespective of joining an EU trade agreement with labour provisions or ENP, policies that improve judicial independence and CSO freedom can foster improvements in labour

Table 6.3 *Interaction effects*

Variables	(1) Workers' rights	(2) Workers' rights	(3) Workers' rights
BTC	0.620**	0.677***	
	(0.244)	(0.242)	
Share net tech exports	0.475*	0.394	0.520**
	(0.257)	(0.256)	(0.257)
Share net textile exports	−1.636	−1.720*	−2.004**
	(1.016)	(0.964)	(0.994)
ENP&TA	0.549***	0.360**	−0.372
	(0.164)	(0.158)	(0.531)
ENP&TA = 0 × Jud. independence	0.695***		
	(0.158)		
ENP&TA = 1 × Jud. independence	0.332**		
	(0.147)		
ENP&TA = 2 × Jud. independence	−0.359		
	(0.261)		
ENP&TA = 0 × CSO freedom		0.525***	
		(0.136)	
ENP&TA = 1 × CSO freedom		0.341**	
		(0.137)	
ENP&TA = 2 × CSO freedom		−0.0412	
		(0.182)	
ENP&TA = 0 × BTC			0.562**
			(0.247)
ENP&TA = 1 × BTC			0.883***
			(0.329)
ENP&TA = 2 × BTC			1.217**
			(0.588)
Judicial independence		0.383***	0.355***
		(0.121)	(0.121)
CSO freedom	0.226*		0.298***
	(0.118)		(0.115)
Controls	yes	yes	yes
Observations	738	738	738

Table 6.3 (*cont.*)

Variables	(1) Workers' rights	(2) Workers' rights	(3) Workers' rights
Country FE	Yes	Yes	Yes
Year FE	Yes	Yes	Yes

Notes: Robust standard errors in parentheses where *, ** and *** denotes 1%, 5% and 10% significance levels respectively.

standards. It also suggests an absence of complementarity, at least during the 1990–2014 period, between CSOs and state capacity on the one hand, and EU international labour governance efforts on the other, to bring about improvements in labour standards. These might come about, however, as the EU makes more investments in raising the domestic capacities in these societies where state institutions and the strength of CSOs have been traditionally low.

The positive association of increasing magnitude between ENP/TA and BTC, however, does reveal a synergistic effect between the EU's international labour governance approach and market-based governance of labour standards, as the positive influence on labour standards is the strongest when both the EU and private entities from key EU states set the most intense expectations regarding social sustainability among developing country trade partners.

Enabling and Constraining Factors in Moldova and Morocco

In this section, we use the cases of Moldova and Morocco to expand our understanding of the processes that underpin associations identified in the regression analysis and further examine the validity of the hypotheses. More specifically, we explore how integration into labour- versus technology-intensive value chains influences the willingness and ability of governments and businesses to meet EU expectations regarding labour standards (H1 and H2). We investigate the processes through which the stringency of labour standards in major export markets affects standards within their contexts (H2). Finally, we examine the role of state capacity and labour organizations in promoting labour standards through the EU's international or market-based governance approaches (H1 and

H3). The primary source of data that we rely on consists of approximately thirty-one semi-structured interviews we conducted over the course of 2019 in Chişinău (MD1–17), Rabat and Casablanca (MA1–14), where we met with representatives of the ministries of labour and the economy, state labour inspectorates, employers' associations and private businesses, trade unions, ILO country offices and EU delegations. These are complemented by review of secondary reports prepared by various international, EU and national organizations.

Comparative Strategy

Moldova and Morocco constitute ideal cases for a comparative analysis of the role of domestic factors in the ability of the EU to promote labour standards among trade partners. Over recent decades, the two economies have become integrated into similar EU labour governance systems, at both international and market levels, but differ considerably across several political, economic and social features. Notwithstanding important limitations, both countries have experienced some incremental improvements in labour standards over recent decades (Pal et al. 2021).

At the international level, their relations with the EU have been governed through the ENP that reinforced commitments to international and EU labour standards stipulated in their formal agreements, and deployed additional incentives and assistance to promote reforms (EC 2004, 2005, 2013). Moldova and Morocco have also become increasingly integrated with the EU market, particularly in the textiles and apparel, electronics and machinery sectors, with implications for their exposure to market pressures and private governance initiatives from the EU. In 2018, approximately 65 per cent of their total exports were destined for the EU, representing about 16 per cent of their national economies (WITS database).[5] Textiles and clothing were of greater relevance in the past, but have continued to expand in absolute values and still represents around 15 per cent of their total exports. Over recent years, both Moldova and Morocco have made considerable progress in expanding exports of machinery and electronics products, reaching 20 per cent of their total exports in 2018.

The national contexts in which these relatively similar EU labour governance approaches have been implemented, however, differ

[5] WITS (World Integrated Trade Solutions) database, https://wits.worldbank.org/

significantly. There are three major differences that are particularly relevant for this study. Firstly, while the Moldovan government has demonstrated great commitment towards alignment with the EU by signing a Deep and Comprehensive Free Trade Agreement (DCFTA) in 2014, the Moroccan government has been more reluctant in this regard and suspended negotiations. Secondly, while the EU constitutes the most important export destination for both countries, a significant part of Moldovan exports are destined for Romania and other new member states, while a large part of Moroccan exports go to France and Spain, where worker protections are very high (Cingranelli et al. 2014). A third important difference pertains to the strength of labour unions in the two countries. Workers and unions from Moldova benefit from more freedoms and protections than in Morocco (ITUC 2020). Trade union density has been much higher at approximately 50 per cent in the mid-2000s in Moldova relative to a mere 6 per cent in Morocco (USDS 2004a, 2004b). Finally, while in Moldova workers are represented by the unified National Trade Union Confederation of Moldova (CNSM), in Morocco there have been five nationally representative unions with different political inclinations.

Based on the analytical framework presented here, these differences are expected to have implications for the ability of the EU to promote labour standards in Moldova and Morocco, respectively. While the DCFTA, exporting to EU member states with higher labour standards and stronger labour unions are all presumed to facilitate improvements, including in the textiles and apparel sector, the lack of such improvements is expected to hinder conformance with EU expectations. The remainder of this section analyses how disparities in these regards across Moldova and Morocco have led to the emergence of divergent pathways of improvements in the two contexts, each with its own advantages and disadvantages.

National Reforms with Weak Implementation in Moldova

In Moldova, the state has undertaken ambitious reforms, with trade union support, to demonstrate conformance with DCFTA requirements, but the low-cost-competition strategy pursued by the state and businesses have undermined enforcement. Business-led improvements in actual practices have been connected primarily to the expansion of the technology-intensive sector rather than incentives set by key export markets.

Since the launch of the ENP in 2004, the *Moldovan government* has made continuous efforts to meet EU labour standard expectations, resulting in reforms of fundamental labour rights and working condition regulations (Pal et al. 2021). This tendency has intensified over recent years, as negotiations for a DCFTA were launched in 2012 and convergence with EU regulations were prioritized. The agreement signed in 2014 included specific references to EU directives to guide further alignment efforts (Annex III). By 2019, Moldova had transposed into its national legislation seven out of eight labour law acts, five out of six non-discrimination directives and nineteen out of twenty-five Occupational Safety and Health (OSH) acts (MD10 and 11). These reforms did entail increased protections for workers, especially in areas such as non-discrimination and OSH. Implementation, however, has been undermined by a combination of weak political commitment to strengthen labour regulation that might diminish the competitiveness of the export-oriented economy, and a lack of adequate state capacity to ensure enforcement even in areas that were relatively compatible with this strategy. The state labour administrative system – the Ministry of Health, Labour and Social Protection (MHLSP) and State Labour Inspectorate (SLI) – have benefited from some assistance from the EU as part of the ENP, but the material and administrative resources remained too low and posed increasing challenges as the economy and regulations grew more complex (MD5–6, 10–11). The number of inspectors in fact declined from 121 in 2002 to 109 in 2015 (USDS 2004–2019a; MD6). Even in the OSH area that is more compatible with EU product standards, the SLI and business associations lacked the capacity to ensure adequate implementation (MD5–6, 16).

In the context of greater trade integration with the EU and Commonwealth of Independent States (CIS) countries, national regulation in Moldova has been further hindered by reliance on a competition strategy based on low costs and regulation. The investment promotion strategy, formulated by the Ministry of Economy and the state agency Invest Moldova, continued to emphasize the availability of a relatively cheap and well-educated labour force (MD2, 316). The main strategic plan – the National Development Strategy Moldova 2020 – adopted by the government in 2012, has prioritized the reduction of regulatory burdens on businesses to boost entrepreneurship and competitiveness (MD2, 5–6). This strategy led to a further decline in state labour administrative capacity as regulatory reforms adopted in 2017 to achieve this goal resulted in the loss of the SLI's authority to conduct unannounced visits and enforce OSH regulations (MD8, 10). The number of labour inspectors declined to a mere fifty-nine by 2018 (MD5–6). The MHLSP also lost the entire staff of its department for labour relations and social protections (MD10).

This competition strategy based on low labour costs and regulation has been related to the position of *Moldovan producers* in European value chains and the significant economic pressures they have been exposed to. Export-oriented manufacturing from Moldova has benefited from a relocation of more cost-sensitive parts of production from Romania as the latter experienced a rise in wages and became a member of the EU. With Romania and other Eastern European economies capturing the predominant part (54 per cent) of Moldovan exports over the years (WITS database), the incentives for domestic businesses to meet external social sustainability expectations have been relatively weak. Pressures to retain low production costs have, moreover, continued to be very strong from both Western and Eastern European firms (MD14–15). State support to move from lower to higher value-added activities has been limited thus far. The state did launch some programmes, for example the Industrial Cluster Strategy, but these generally lacked both the necessary coordination capacity and financial resources for successful implementation (MD2). The state has nevertheless facilitated the expansion of the machinery and electronics sectors, through fiscal incentives and other benefits provided to foreign investors, especially in export processing zones (EPZs). While a large part of activities still consist of relatively low-skilled operations in this sector, working conditions, particularly the level of wages, are generally superior than in the rest of the economy (MD11, 13, 16). The textile and apparel sectors have also experienced some industrial upgrading, but the predominant – approximately 80 per cent – of production still takes place in 'Cut and Make' or Lohnarbeit regime, where domestic value added is limited and pressures to keep labour costs low are significant (MD7, 14–15).

In this context, the export-oriented business community has used its political influence to reinforce the low-cost and low-regulation strategy of the state. This influence was in part exerted through the main tripartite institution National Commission for Consultation and Collective Bargaining (NCCCB) where, notwithstanding EU intentions to promote social inclusion, the objective of economic competitiveness has often been prioritized over worker protections. While businesses have largely supported state-led efforts towards alignment with EU norms at the formal level, they would sometimes use these as opportunities to introduce more flexible provisions. In the case of Council Directive 98/59/EC on collective redundancies, for example, reasons for dismissing workers were expanded, and the obligation to consult trade unions before doing so was abolished (MD12; ITUC 2018). But businesses would also exert their influence through alternative and sometimes even less transparent channels (USDS 2016a; ITUC 2018). At the revision of the national labour code of Moldova in 2017, the government favoured a draft proposal prepared by the Economic Council to the Prime Minister – a consultation platform supported by EU development agencies, where business representation has been more prominent – over the one prepared in the more balanced tripartite NCCCB (MD12, 14). There is also a sense that associations representing actors from foreign companies have used their wide access to the government to push for decreasing labour inspections over recent years (ITUC 2015, 2018).

The national *trade union* confederation CNSM did facilitate some improvements in labour standards through its support of state efforts to meet EU labour standards expectations. The CNSM has been very active in the framework of the NCCCB to represent worker interests in the harmonization process, but its influence on final decisions has been mixed due to the prioritization of economic competitiveness by the state and businesses (MD11–13). At the implementation level, noteworthy developments included the establishment of the state's labour inspectorate and the conclusion of a cooperation agreement with the SLI in 2012 to improve implementation of national regulation. CNSM monitoring prioritized the areas of union rights, as concerns regarding the resistance of multinational enterprises (MNEs) to unionization were prevalent, but also in the realm of labour relations and OSH. While the unions lacked the authority to impose sanctions or push for changes, they often engaged in joint problem solving to address areas of concern (MD10–11). They also invested in measuring equipment to increase the credibility and leverage in the OSH area (MD12). These efforts, however, have been insufficient to compensate fully for weak and declining state capacity.

Market-Driven Upgrading of Labour Standards in Morocco

In Morocco, on other hand, improvements have been connected primarily to the market-based governance mechanism of leading EU firms, facilitated by domestic business associations and state initiatives, without a major overhaul of national regulation.

The government of Morocco has also adopted some reforms to ensure harmonization with international labour standards to which it committed in ENP action plans (CE 2005, 2013). With negotiations over the DCFTA paused, however, regulatory convergence with EU labour directives has been more modest. The state labour administrative system has also benefited from some assistance from the EU through the ENP. But as in Moldova, state capacity to ensure enforcement of labour reforms remained low, with the state labour inspectorate affected by insufficient human, financial and technical resources (USDS 2019b). The number of labour inspectors also declined from 496 in 2004 to 398 in 2018 (USDS 2004b, 2018b). This has been particularly problematic in Morocco, as inspectors are also required to serve as mediators in labour disputes. Of greater importance for working conditions in the case of Morocco have been state policies directed towards speeding up the development pace of industrial sectors, such as the Industrial Acceleration Plan (IAP) (MD3, 5). The plan attached great significance to labour issues as well, including improvements in skills and transition from the informal to the formal sector, with the aim of better responding to Moroccan and foreign enterprises' requirements in this regard (MA3–5).

With *Moroccan companies* exporting primarily to France and Spain (51 per cent of total exports in 2018), where labour regulations are more stringent and consumer expectations regarding social sustainability are stronger, lead firms played an important role in encouraging changes in domestic practices. Two of the leading EU companies that purchase a significant part of Moroccan production – Spanish firm Inditex that buys approximately 50 per cent of textiles and apparel products, and French company Renault Group that produces 80 per cent of vehicles, constitute some of the largest companies within their sectors that have international framework agreements (IFAs) in place with global unions, suggesting a more serious commitment to promoting labour standards among their suppliers. The social sustainability requirements of Inditex and other major EU companies, for example, incentivized the Moroccan Textile and Garment Industry Association (AMITH) to launch its own social governance initiative in 2003, known as Fibre Citoyenne (MA13). This consisted of an industry code of conduct and related label to be issued to factories that passed a social audit. Instrumental to its development was the IFA concluded between Inditex and the International Textile, Garment and Leather Worker Federation (ITGLWF) in 2007, now part of IndustriALL, through which Inditex pledged to source only from suppliers with this certification (Miller 2011). Similarly, in the automotive sector, the IFA concluded between the Renault Group and international trade union IndustriALL facilitated cooperation among international and French labour unions with Moroccan unions, leading to some progress in collective bargaining over wages (MA10). The importance of lead firm governance measures in this sector is revealed by the fact that, according to AMITH representatives, inspections of labour standards in the Moroccan textile and apparel sector are performed primarily by private auditors (MA13).

In addition to their labour practices and requirements, leading companies from Spain and France in these sectors were at times also instrumental at promoting social upgrading through other aspects of their business practices. In the case of the textiles and apparel sector, for example, buyer companies have increasingly demanded full-package production over time and provided some technical assistance to major suppliers to achieve it (MA13). Changes in domestic business practices to meet these expectations have also been greatly facilitated by state industrial policies, most notably the IAP, in collaboration with AMITH. The IAP and AMITH played an important role in upgrading technical expertise in the Moroccan textiles and apparel sector, including building design capabilities (MA13). The Ministry of Industry has played a significant role in this upgrading process with the provision of financial assistance through programmes such as the Locomotive programme set up to promote cluster collaboration among SMEs. The assistance also entailed significant investments in training programmes to upgrade skills, through organizations such as the Casa Moda Academy, founded through a public–private partnership with AMITH, the Ecole Supérieure des Industries du Textile et Habillement (ESITH) that also entails a close collaboration with the business association, as well as the technical labs of AMITH. By 2019, approximately 30 per cent of production was full package and an increasing number of Moroccan companies have become involved in fashion design (MA13). Industrial upgrading in the sector has been associated with improvements in working conditions for the more regular and skilled employees in the sectors, but had some negative impacts on the more vulnerable groups of irregular and less skilled employees (Rossi 2013).

Similarly, in the automotive sector, the state and business associations have played an important role in expanding and improving the supplier base for lead companies, particularly the Directorate of Automotive Industries of the Ministry of Industry, tasked with developing and implementing IAP programmes to support investment and training, and the sectoral business association AMICA, which acts as an interface between ministerial departments and members (MA4). A manifestation of their cooperative support includes the establishment and operation of the Automotive Industry Training Institute, where essential training has been provided at four centres; that falls under the authority of the Ministry of Industry but three centres are managed directly by AMICA and one by Renault (MA5). As in Moldova, working conditions in the machinery manufacturing sector are generally superior than in other industries, especially with respect to the level of wages (MA8–11).

The role of *trade unions* in influencing the effectiveness of EU labour governance efforts has been more limited in Morocco than in Moldova. In the context of lower representation, organizational and political fragmentation, their influence on policy outcomes through tripartite consultation has been more modest. Trade unions would often withdraw from tripartite social dialogue to protest the inadequate consideration of their concerns (MA10–11). At the implementation level, one of the Moroccan trade unions also launched their own monitoring efforts in 2010, establishing a national observatory of employees' rights, with the task of collecting data on cases of infringements of trade union freedoms and labour laws, but its subsequent activities have remained very modest and it is no longer in existence (CE 2011; MA12). According to trade unions, their ability to effect changes has also been hindered by restrictions on their entry to export-processing zones, where a significant part of export-oriented manufacturing takes place (ITUC 2015); MA9–10). The ability of Moroccan unions to compensate for weak state enforcement capacity has therefore been even more limited than in Moldova.

Conclusions

In this study we have considered two approaches through which the EU can promote NTPOs such as labour standards among its trade partners: international and market-based governance. Going beyond a predominant focus on the features of these external governance approaches, we used a combination of qualitative and quantitative analysis to understand how domestic factors across developing countries condition their effectiveness. The analyses underpin the view that EU efforts to promote NTPOs through trade need to rely on greater consideration of how trade policies and integration influence the willingness and ability of key stakeholders – the state, businesses and labour organizations – to respond to normative requirements that often accompany them.

Economic factors, in the form of EU member state destination and sectoral composition of exports, condition the incentives and ability of governments and businesses to improve labour standards. A shift away from textiles and apparel to more technologically sophisticated sectors generally entails an improvement in working conditions. Continued reliance on textile and apparel products, however, retains competition and cost pressures, which undermine the effectiveness of EU labour governance efforts. Exports to economically more advanced EU member states with high labour standards accentuate the effectiveness of market-based governance, especially when business associations are strong, as they increase the incentives and in some cases capacity of domestic businesses to improve workers' skills and working conditions. Political factors – state strategies and capacity, independence and strength of labour organizations – are also influential, with potential for positive implications for both EU governance approaches. In addition to the enforcement capacity of the state labour administration, we highlight the relevance of developmental capacity, which can facilitate improvements in working conditions through industrial upgrading. While the freedom and strength of labour organizations is associated with more positive outcomes, and illustrates how they can compensate for weak state enforcement capacity, we find that their limited political influence and business resistance to unionization still set limitations to their ability to reinforce EU labour governance efforts. Finally, we find that improvements are more likely when EU governance through formal policies is reinforced by market-based labour governance.

From the point of view of workers' protection, our findings confirm that international and market-based labour governance mechanisms have their distinct advantages and disadvantages. While market-based governance mechanisms can facilitate improvements in working conditions, these are often limited to a segment of workers (the most skilled with regular contracts) in export-oriented sectors. International labour governance triggers reforms at the national level and often extends to fundamental labour rights, but these often manifest primarily at the formal level.

At a broader policy level, our findings support the call for treating NTPOs as parts of externally supported developmental programmes that aim to improve the conditions of domestic gains from increased trade. Such an integrated approach requires linking the enforcement of external trade and non-trade-related rules to improving the capacity of domestic public and private actors to benefit from increased trade. Isolated or fragmented policies that target CSO, a state's administrative capacity or tripartite institutions alone have little effect if they are separated from assistance that can increase domestic benefits from trade. The latter requires improving the capacities of domestic public and private actors to design and implement policies that can improve the composition of exports and lead to industrial upgrading. EU efforts to strengthen labour standards across all member states and mitigate economic pressures by leading firms on their suppliers could also facilitate more socially sustainable practices among developing countries.

References

Adolph, C., Quince, V., & Prakash, A. (2017). "The Shanghai effect: Do exports to China affect labor practices in Africa?" *World Development* 89, 1–18.

Amengual, M., & Chirot, L. (2016). "Reinforcing the state: Transnational and state labour regulation in Indonesia." *ILR Review* 69(5), 1056–1080.

Amengual, M., & Distelhorst, G. (2020). "Cooperation and punishment in regulating labor standards: Evidence from the Gap Inc supply chain." https://dx.doi.org/10.2139/ssrn.3466936

Amengual, M., & Kuruvilla, S. (2020). "Editorial essay: Introduction to a special issue on improving private regulation of labor in global supply chains: Theory and evidence." *ILR Review* 73(4), 809–816. https://doi.org/10.1177/0019793920927693

Anner, M. (2020). "Squeezing workers' rights in global supply chains: Purchasing practices in the Bangladesh garment export sector in comparative perspective." *Review of International Political Economy* 27(2), 320–347.

Ashraf, N., & van Seters, Jeske (2020). "Making it count: Civil society engagement in EU trade agreements." ECDPM Discussion Paper No. 276.

Bair, J., Anner, M., & Blasi, J. (2020). "The political economy of private and public regulation in post-Rana Plaza Bangladesh." *ILR Review* 73(4), 969–994. https://doi.org/10.1177/0019793920925424

Barrientos, S., Gereffi, G., & Rossi, A. (2011). "Economic and social upgrading in global production networks: A new paradigm for a changing world." *International Labour Review* 150(3–4), 319–340.

Börzel, T., & Lebanidze, B. (2015). "European Neighbourhood Policy at the crossroads: Evaluating the past to shape the future." Working Paper Series No. 12, July.

Bradford, A. (2012). "The Brussels effect." *Northwestern University Law Review* 107(1), n.p.

Brando, N., Lein, B., & Marx, A. (2016). "The protection of labour rights in trade agreements: The case of the EU–Colombia Agreement." *Journal of World Trade* 50(4), 587–610.

Bruszt, L., and Langbein, J. (2020). "Manufacturing development: How transnational market integration shapes opportunities and capacities for development in Europe's three peripheries." *Review of International Political Economy* 27(5), 996–1019.

Bruszt, L., & McDermott, G. (2014). *Leveling the Playing Field: Transnational Regulatory Integration and Development*. Oxford: Oxford University Press.

Cao, X., Greenhill, B., & Prakash, A. (2013). "Where is the tipping point? Bilateral trade and the diffusion of human rights." *British Journal of Political Science* 43 (1), 133–156.

Cingranelli, D. L., Richards, D. L., & Clay, C. K. (2014). "The CIRI Human Rights Dataset." current version copyrights:2014, Dataset version: 2014.04.14, www.humanrightsdata.com/

Commission Européennes (CE) (2005–2015). "Rapport de Suivi Maroc." Document de Travail des Services de la Commission, Bruxelles.

Coppedge, M., Gerring, J., Knutsen, C. H., Krusell, J., Medzihorsky, J., Pernes, J., . . . & Wilson, S. L. (2019). "The methodology of 'varieties of democracy' (V-Dem)." *Bulletin of Sociological Methodology/Bulletin de Méthodologie Sociologique* 143(1), 107–133.

Distelhorst, G., & Locke, R. M. (2018). "Does compliance pay? Social standards and firm-level trade." *American Journal of Political Science* 62(3), 695–711.

Distelhorst, G., Locke, R. M., Pal, T., & Samel, H. M. (2015). "Production goes global, standards stay local: Private regulation in the global electronics industry." *Regulation & Governance* 9(3), 224–242.

European Commission (EC) (2004–2019). "ENP Progress Report on Moldova." Commission Staff Working Paper, Brussels.

Garcia, M., & Masselot, A. (2015). "EU–Asia Free Trade Agreements as tools for social norm/legislation transfer?" *Asia Europe Journal* 13, 241–252.

Gereffi, G., Humphrey, J., & Sturgeon, T. (2005). "The governance of global value chains." *Review of International Political Economy* 12(1), 78–104.

Gereffi, G., & Lee, J. (2016). "Economic and social upgrading in global value chains and industrial clusters: Why governance matters." *Journal of Business Ethics* 133(1), 25–38.

Greenhill, B., Mosley, L., & Prakash, A. (2009). "Trade-based diffusion of labor rights: A panel study, 1986–2002." *American Political Science Review* 103(4), 669–690.

Hafner-Burton, E. (2005). "Trading human rights: How preferential trade agreements influence government repression." *International Organization* 59(3), 593–629.

Hainmueller, J., & Hiscox, M. J. (2015). "The socially conscious consumer? Field experimental tests of consumer support for fair labor standards." MIT Political Science Department Research Paper No. 2012-15, https://ssrn.com/abstract=2062435

Harrison, J., Barbu, M., Campling, L., Richardson, B., & Smith, A. (2019). "Governing labour standards through free trade agreements: Limits of the European Union's trade and sustainable development chapters." *JCMS: Journal of Common Market Studies* 57(2), 260–277.

International Trade Union Confederation (ITUC) (20142020). "ITUC Global Rights Index. The world's worst countries for workers." International Trade Union Confederation (ITUC) publication.

Kim, L. (2012). "Ex ante due diligence: Formation of PTAs and protection of labour rights." *International Studies Quarterly* 56, 704–719.

Lall, S. (2000). "The technological structure and performance of developing country manufactured exports, 1985–98." *Oxford Development Studies* 28(3), 337–369.

Locke, R. M. (2013). *The Promise and Limits of Private Power: Promoting Labor Standards in a Global Economy*. Cambridge Studies in Comparative Politics. Cambridge: Cambridge University Press.

Locke, R. M., Rissing, B. A., & Pal, T. (2013). "Complements or substitutes? Private codes, state regulation and the enforcement of labour standards in global supply chains." *British Journal of Industrial Relations* 51(3), 519–552.

Malesky, E. J., & Mosley, L. (2018). "Chains of love? Global production and the firm-level diffusion of labor standards." *American Journal of Political Science* 62 (3), 712–728.

Malesky, E. J., & Mosley, L. (2021). "Labor upgrading and export market opportunities: Evidence from Vietnam." *Economics & Politics* 33(3), 483–513.

Marques, J. C., & Eberlein, B. (2020). "Grounding transnational business governance: A political-strategic perspective on government responses in the Global South." *Regulation & Governance* 15(4), 1209–1229.

Marx, A., Brecht L., & Brando, N. (2016). "The protection of labour rights in trade agreements: The case of the EU–Columbia agreement." *Journal of World Trade* 50(4), 587–610.

Meardi, G. (2013). *Social Failures of EU Enlargement: A Case of Workers Voting with Their Feet*. New York: Routledge.

Miller, D. (2011). "Global social relations and corporate social responsibility in outsourced apparel supply chains: The Inditex Global Framework Agreement." In K. Papadakis (Ed.), *Shaping Global Industrial Relations* (pp. 179–200). Basingstoke; New York: Palgrave Macmillan; ILO.

Mosley, L. (2008). "Workers' rights in open economies: Global production and domestic institutions in the developing world." *Comparative Political Studies* 41 (4–5), 674–714.

Oehri, M. (2015). "Comparing US and EU labour governance 'near and far' – Hierarchy vs network?" *Journal of European Public Policy* 22(5), 731–749.

Orbie, J., & Van den Putte, L. (2016). "Labour rights in Peru and the EU trade agreement: Compliance with the commitments under the sustainable development chapter." ÖFSE Working Paper No. 58.

Pál, T., Maduko, F., & Bruszt, L. (2021), "Promoting Labour Standards through the European Neighbourhood Policy." Robert Schuman Centre for Advanced Studies Research Paper No. RSC 2021/78, http://dx.doi.org/10.2139/ssrn.3972281

Peterson, T. M., Murdie, A., & Asal, V. (2016). "Human rights, NGO shaming and the exports of abusive states." *British Journal of Political Science* 48(3), 767–786.

Pike, K. (2020). "Voice in supply chains: Does the Better Work program lead to improvements in labor standards compliance?" *ILR Review* 73(4), 913–938.

Piore, M. J., & Schrank, A. (2008). "Toward managed flexibility: The revival of labour inspection in the Latin world." *International Labour Review* 147(1), 1–23.

Postnikov, E., & Bastiaens, I. (2014). "Does dialogue work? The effectiveness of labor standards in EU preferential trade agreements." *Journal of European Public Policy* 21(6), 923–940.

Rossi, A. (2013). "Does economic upgrading lead to social upgrading in global production networks? Evidence from Morocco." *World Development* 46, 223–233.

Schimmelfennig, F., & Scholtz, H. (2008). "EU democracy promotion in the European neighbourhood: Political conditionality, economic development and transnational exchange." *European Union Politics* 9(2), 187–215.

Schrank, A. (2009). "Professionalization and probity in a patrimonial state: Labor inspectors in the Dominican Republic." *Latin American Politics and Society* 51 (2), 91–115.

Schrank, A. (2013). "From disguised protectionism to rewarding regulation: The impact of trade-related labour standards in the Dominican Republic." *Regulation and Governance* 7, 299–320.

Short, J. L, Toel, M. W., & Hugill, A. R. (2020). "Improving working conditions in global supply chains: The role of institutional environments and monitoring program design." *Industrial and Labor Relations Review* 73(4), 873–912.

Sturgeon, T., Van Biesebroeck, J., & Gereffi, G. (2008). "Value chains, networks and clusters: Reframing the global automotive industry." *Journal of Economic Geography* 8(3), 297–321.

U.S. Department of State (USDS) (2004–2019(a)). "Country Report on Human Rights Practices – Moldova." Bureau of Democracy, Human Rights and Labor, Washington.

U.S. Department of State (USDS) (2004–2019(b)). "Country Report on Human Rights Practices – Morocco." Bureau of Democracy, Human Rights and Labor, Washington.

Vogel, D., & Kagan, R. A. (Eds.) (2004). *Dynamics of Regulatory Change: How Globalization Affects National Regulatory Policies* (Vol. 1). Berkeley: University of California Press.

Winship, C., & Mare, R. D. (1984). "Regression models with ordinal variables." *American Sociological Review* 49(4), 512–525.

7

EU Trade Agreements and Non-Trade Policy Objectives

ALESSANDRO FERRARI, MATTEO FIORINI, JOSEPH FRANCOIS, BERNARD HOEKMAN, LISA LECHNER, MIRIAM MANCHIN, AND FILIPPO SANTI

Introduction

Article 2 of the Treaty on European Union (TEU) states that the EU is founded on a set of fundamental values, including rule of law and respect for human rights. Article 21 (TEU) calls on the Union to work for a higher degree of cooperation in all fields of international relations to consolidate and support democracy, rule of law, human rights, and foster the sustainable, economic, social, and environmental development of developing countries. These principles apply to the EU's common commercial policy. Article 207 of the Treaty on the functioning of the EU states that EU trade policy must be consistent with the principles laid out in Article 21 TEU. Thus, the EU's common commercial policy is one instrument to attain these objectives. A reflection of this role is the inclusion of trade and development chapters in EU preferential trade agreements (PTAs). These chapters complement general provisions on human rights and rule of law in EU trade agreements by defining specific commitments that partner countries make with respect to labor and environmental standards. The inclusion of such chapters reflects a desire to use trade to protect and project EU values, as well as ensure that partner countries do not lower social and environmental norms in an effort to attract investment into tradable industries that can benefit from preferential access to the EU market.

Research on the effects (effectiveness) of including non-trade provisions (NTPs) in PTAs is largely inconclusive. The EU has not undertaken a comprehensive assessment of the strategy of linking (conditioning) access to the EU market on the pursuit of non-trade policy objectives (NTPOs). Does the inclusion of NTPs in EU PTAs have a systematic positive effect on non-trade outcomes in partner countries? This is the question that motivates the discussion that follows. Using a simple conceptual framework that distinguishes between a direct channel linking trade policy to non-trade outcomes and an indirect one that operates through trade flows, we combine information on sustainable development indicators (non-trade outcomes), the content of EU PTAs, and bilateral trade flows between the EU and partner countries to analyze the relationship between bilateral trade flows, the coverage of NTPs in EU PTAs and the performance of EU partner countries on several non-trade outcome variables.

We contribute to the literature on the effects of NTPs in PTAs by using synthetic control methods (SCM) to study the causal effect of NTPs in EU PTAs on the realization of non-trade outcomes in partner countries. Studies of trade liberalization and trade policy have made limited use of SCM.[1] This chapter is to the best of our knowledge the first application of SCM to study the impact of NTPs in PTAs on non-trade outcomes.

The descriptive analysis reveals statistically significant correlations between NTPs and different non-trade outcomes (both negative and positive). While this suggests that PTAs with NTPs may have discernible effects, and that such effects are not necessarily positive (consistent with the often-expressed concern that partner countries may lower standards to bolster trade), the SCM application fails to find any robust evidence of a causal effect of including NTPs in EU PTAs on indicators of non-trade outcomes.

The chapter is organized as follows. The next section introduces a simple conceptual framework and summarizes findings from the existing literature on the relationships between trade policy, trade performance, and non-trade outcomes. The following section provides an initial empirical assessment of the potential linkages between EU trade policy and three non-trade outcomes in EU partner countries: civil rights protection,

[1] Billmeier and Nannicini (2013) use SCM to assess the effect of trade liberalization on growth, proxied by per capita GDP; Hannan (2017) estimates the effect of trade agreements on trade among Latin American countries; Adarov (2018) analyzes the effect of the Eurasian Custom Union on trade, comparing SCM results with gravity predictions; Olper et al. (2018) study the causal effect of trade liberalization on child mortality; Aytug et al. (2017) estimate the impact of the Turkey–EU customs union on Turkey's exports to the EU; and Hosny (2012) investigates the causal effect of participation in the Pan-Arab FTA on Algeria's trade performance. Many of these studies find substantial heterogeneity in the impact of trade agreements/policy on the outcome of interest. Such heterogeneity is often impossible to detect using standard econometric techniques.

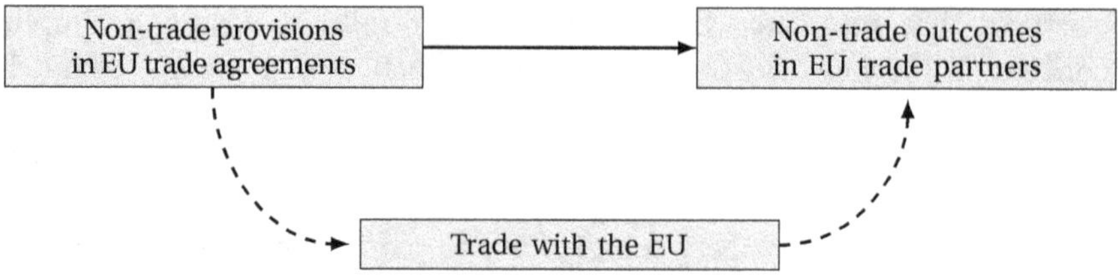

Figure 7.1 Impact channels of trade policy on non-trade outcomes

environmental protection, and protection of labor rights. We then report the results of the SCM exercise to estimate the causal effect of inclusion of NTPs in EU trade agreements on non-trade outcomes in EU partner countries. The final section concludes.

Conceptual Framework and Existing Literature

What is the effect of NTPs in EU trade agreements on non-trade outcomes in partner countries? Take for instance environmental protection as an example of a non-trade issue. What happens to environmental protection in countries that sign a trade agreement with the EU that includes a provision on that specific non-trade issue? Before answering these questions empirically using a SCM exercise, it is useful to identify the main theoretical channels that can cause NTPs in trade agreements to have an impact on the related non-trade outcomes. First, a NTP can affect the related non-trade outcomes simply because it includes prescriptions (with a certain degree of conditionality and/or enforcement) on those outcomes or on domestic policies targeting them. Secondly, in so far as the relevant non-trade outcomes can be affected by the trade performance of signatory parties, the NTP in the trade agreement can have an effect on non-trade outcomes through its impact on trade flows. Figure 7.1 offers a graphical representation of the direct and indirect channels captured by the solid and dashed lines respectively.

The literature on these relationships is growing across disciplines, including political science, law, and economics. Overall, research results are highly heterogeneous as regards empirical evidence for each of the relationships displayed in Figure 7.1: the role of NTPs in trade agreements in affecting non-trade outcomes (the solid line); the impact of NTPs on bilateral trade effects (the dashed line on the left-hand side of the figure); and the impact of trade on non-trade outcomes in EU partner countries (the dashed line on the right-hand side of the figure). Assessing the causal nature of these relationships confronts serious difficulties, including weaknesses in available data and endogeneity issues.

Some studies focus on whether and how inclusion of non-trade issues in trade policy affects the performance of partner countries with respect to relevant non-trade policy outcomes (the solid line in Figure 7.1). Overall, trade agreements cover many different non-trade dimensions which have traditionally been aggregated in three sets of issue areas: civil and political rights, economic and social rights, and environmental protection.[2] Scholars have tended to examine these three issue areas, and the rights that fall under these headings, on a stand-alone, issue-specific basis as opposed to cross- or multi-issue analysis (see for instance Hafner-Burton, 2009; Kim, 2012; Spilker and Böhmelt, 2013; Postnikov, 2014). Among this body of research, McLaughlin Mitchell and Hensel (2007) find that environmental standards are more effective if they are binding in their nature. Hafner-Burton (2009) shows that strong human rights clauses in trade agreements lead to compliance. This has been revisited by Spilker and Böhmelt (2013), who show that the positive effect decreases if one accounts for the selection process of human rights clauses in PTAs. To the best of our knowledge, a direct comparison of all three issue areas in the context of trade agreements has not been undertaken.

Turning to the two dimensions of the indirect channel (the two dashed lines in Figure 7.1), there is a large literature on the effects of PTAs, their depth, and other features of their design on trade performance (see Rose, 2004; Baier and Bergstrand, 2007; Büthe and Milner, 2008, 2014; Mansfield and Reinhardt, 2008; Antràs and Staiger, 2012; Orefice and Rocha, 2014; Baier et al., 2014; Dür et al., 2014; Osnago et al., 2017; Miroudot and Rigo, 2019; Laget et al., 2020). These studies usually focus more on trade-related issues, including investment, services, intellectual property rights, and

[2] Civil and political rights cover many areas and vary across studies. They may include human dignity, the right to political participation, the right to free movement, women's and children's rights, protection of minorities, and rule of law. Economic and social rights encompass the right to work, rights at work, the right to education, the right to development, and the right to health. Rights at work span the right of collective bargaining, the elimination of all forms of forced and compulsory labor, the effective abolition of child labor, the elimination of discrimination in respect of employment and occupation, minimum wages, and the right to leisure. Environmental protection encompasses care for natural resources (water, soil, forests), reducing waste and air pollution, and protection of wildlife and game.

trade facilitation provisions, rather than human rights, labor rights, and environmental protection provisions, which are the focus of this chapter. The relationship between non-trade issues and trade is discussed by Limão (2007). That paper develops a theoretical framework where PTAs with NTPs act as a stumbling block to global free trade. Brandi et al. (2020) instead find that environment-related provisions help to reduce dirty exports from trade partners, although this depends on the initial level of environmental protection there. Other studies analyzing this relationship include Kohl et al. (2016) and Brown et al. (2013).[3]

Existing evidence on the effect of trade on non-trade outcomes (Hafner-Burton, 2005, 2009) suggests that trade may play an important role in shaping domestic policy towards human and civil rights protection in trading partners. Chyzh (2016) notes that the effect of trade on human and civil rights depends on the distance in the trade network from countries with high standards: the larger the distance, the greater the trade pressures on human and civil rights protection. This pressure decreases the more the trade with countries with high standards is intermediated by third parties. Kis-Katos and Sparrow (2011, 2015) look at how child labor and poverty are affected by the additional trade generated by tariff reductions in Indonesia. In both cases, sectors that are most impacted by tariff cuts experience the greatest improvements in the relevant non-trade outcome indicator, partly mediated by improvements in labor standards. Other studies include Greenhill et al. (2009) on trade and labor rights; Juhn et al. (2013); Sauré and Zoabi (2014) on trade and gender; and Copeland (2013), McAusland and Millimet (2013), and Halicioglu and Ketenci (2016) on trade and the environment.

Non-Trade Outcomes, EU Trade Policy, and Trade

In this section we provide descriptive evidence on selected non-trade outcomes in EU partner countries, trade with the EU, and EU trade policy, as well as on the key relationships between these variables. Throughout the analysis we focus on three non-trade outcomes: civil

[3] Two recent papers focusing on the effects of NTPs in PTAs on FDI also have differing findings. Kox and Rojas-Romagosa (2020) investigate the effect of provisions targeting civil, political, economic, and social rights as well as environmental protection on inward FDI. None of these NTPs prove to be detrimental for bilateral investment, though only civil and political rights provisions positively and significantly affect investment. Ubaldo and Gasiorek (2020) obtain opposite results using greenfield FDI data.

rights, environmental protection, and labor rights. These issues figure prominently in EU trade agreements: provisions on each are included in more than 50 per cent of EU trade agreements (Lechner, 2018).

Data

We combine information from three sources: datasets on non-trade outcomes, the coverage of non-trade issues in trade agreements, and bilateral trade flows. The dataset on non-trade outcomes (NTPOID_v2 dataset) contains data along economic, political, environmental, and social dimensions, with a large number of variables. The dataset was constructed by merging and consolidating several sources.[4] The timespan of the resulting dataset is from 1946 to 2018, with country coverage ranging between 195 and 247 jurisdictions. For most variables, the panel structure is fairly unbalanced, resulting in heterogeneous coverage across non-trade outcomes. From this dataset, we construct aggregate indexes built using principal component analysis.[5]

The second dataset contains information on the inclusion of non-trade issues in trade agreements. This covers all non-trade issues which are included in 665 preferential trade agreements signed between 1945 and 2018 (Lechner, 2018). They include provisions on civil and political rights, economic and social rights, environmental protection, and security matters. The EU is a signatory to 90 of these 665 PTAs. Finally, bilateral trade data are sourced from the UN COMTRADE database.

Descriptives

We start by looking at the distribution (across EU partner countries and/ or over time) of our key variables of interest: performance in non-trade outcomes, trade with the EU, and non-trade issues in trade agreements with the EU. Figure 7.2 depicts changes in non-trade outcomes over time in partner countries. More specifically, the maps show changes between the first year in our sample (1995) and the last year in which data are

[4] In particular, the Database of Political Institutions 2017 Codebook (DPI), 2018 Environmental Performance Index Report (EPI), International Political Economy Data Resource Version 3.0 (IPE), Structural Policy Indicators Database for Economic Research (SPIDER), 2018 Quality of Government dataset (QoG)) and the World Bank's World Development Indicators (WDI).

[5] See further details on the construction of these summary indexes in Manchin (2021).

Panel A: Civil rights protection

Panel B: Environmental protection

Panel C: Labor rights protection

Figure 7.2 Change in non-trade outcome indicators since 1995
Notes: Percentage variation in civil rights, environmental, and labor rights protection occurring between 1995 and the last year available.

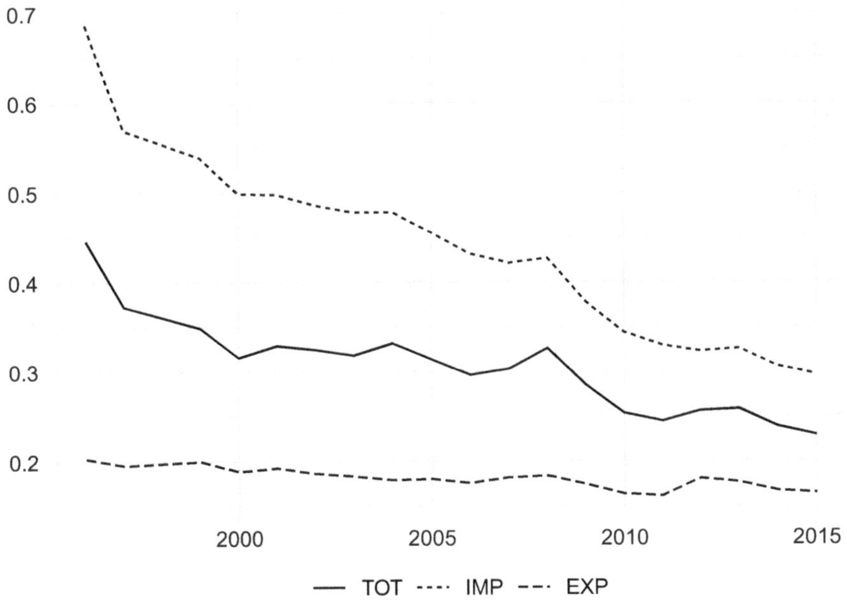

Figure 7.3 EU share of partners' trade
Notes: Trade flows used to compute these shares are expressed in constant US$.
Source: UN-Comtrade.

available.[6] The maps reveal that for several developing countries in Africa, Asia, and South America, there was significant improvement in environmental protection, while the trend appears to be less positive in terms of labor rights and civil rights protection. These trends are consistent with the literature (Flanigan, 2006; Mosley and Uno, 2007; Donnelly, 2013; Li and Jennings, 2017). All in all, EU trade partners do not register unidirectional improvement in non-trade outcomes. Reversals and deterioration in non-trade indicator performance is frequently observed across countries and issue areas.

Figure 7.3 looks at the evolution of trade flows between the EU and the rest of the world. More specifically, it plots the average share of trade

[6] The sample period is constrained by data availability. To provide a consistent overview of the data used in the synthetic control exercise presented in the next section, we limit our sample to the period between 1995 and the last year in which the information for each non-trade outcome is available (2012, 2011, and 2015 for civil rights, environmental, and labor rights protection respectively).

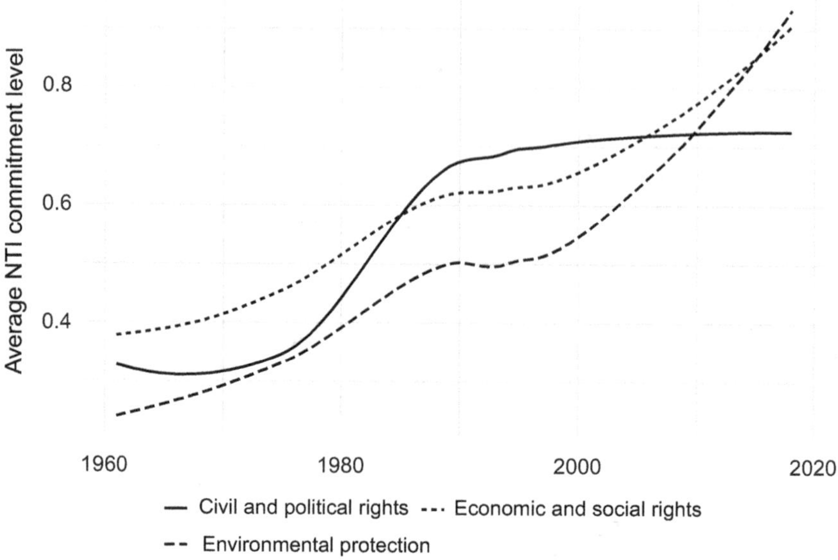

Figure 7.4 Non-trade issue coverage in EU PTAs (average, 1995–2015)
Notes: Average commitment across EU partner countries on non-trade-related issues in EU trade agreements, 1995–2015.
Source: Lechner (2018).

flows (total trade, exports, and imports) across non-EU countries accounted for by EU Member States. It reveals a clear decreasing trend in the average share of imports from EU countries. A similar, although much less pronounced negative trend characterizes the evolution of share of exports to the EU. On average, across all potential partner countries, the EU has become a relatively less important trade partner over time.

Strong positive trends instead characterize the evolution of non-trade provisions in EU trade agreements, covering an increasingly broad range of issue areas. Figure 7.4 reports the evolution of the inclusion of civil rights, environmental protection, and labor rights issues in EU PTAs over time.[7] There is a clear trend in gradual expansion of the coverage of

[7] Using latent trait analysis (Rasch, 1980), we aggregate the data-points per issue area to one index on civil and political rights, one index on economic and social rights, and one index on environmental protection. We standardize the measures to range from 0 to 1. Also note that all EU PTAs are included in this descriptive analysis, irrespective of their inclusion in the SCM exercise.

these three non-trade issue areas in EU PTAs, with the average level of commitments on civil and political rights plateauing after 2000.

This simple descriptive assessment reveals that non-trade outcome indicators are not systematically improving in EU trade partners. On the contrary, aggregate indicators of civil rights and labor rights protection suggest a deterioration in non-trade policy areas (Figure 7.2). Over the time period considered, trade with the EU becomes relatively less important on average for many of the EU's trade agreement partner countries, reflecting more rapid growth in trade with the rest of the world (Figure 7.3), while the content of EU trade policy is increasingly focused on non-trade issues (Figure 7.4). To assess the potential relationships between these trends and determine whether non-trade outcome performance co-moves with trade and with the content of EU trade policy, we start with standard regression analysis. Focusing on our three non-trade outcome variables of interest (i.e. civil rights protection, environmental protection, labor rights protection), we estimate the empirical relationship between bilateral trade intensity and EU PTAs including relevant NTPs and non-trade outcomes. We present results in Table 7.1 for regressions where the three non-trade outcomes of interest are the dependent variables. For each outcome of interest we fit a simple fixed-effect regression taking the form:

$$\mathrm{NTO}_{it} = \beta \mathrm{Provision}_{it} + \gamma \mathrm{Openness}_{it} + \eta_i + \tau_t + \epsilon_{it} \tag{7.1}$$

The dummy $\mathrm{Provision}_{it}$ takes value one for all years following the signature of the first agreement signed by country i with the EU that includes relevant NTPs;[8] $\mathrm{Openness}_{it}$ is the ratio of total trade (Import + Export) as a share of a country's GDP measuring the trade openness of the country; specifications include time and country fixed effects (η_i and ϕ_t respectively).

Given our focus on NTPs in EU trade agreements, we also control for trade with the EU, to see if, given openness, more intensive trade with the EU is associated with non-trade outcomes. Hence we control for trade intensity with the EU, using respectively a measure of the share of trade with the EU in total trade (denoted as 'Intensity: EU trade'), the share of imports from EU on total imports (Intensity: IMP from EU), and the share of exports toward the EU on total exports (Intensity: EXP to EU). One might expect that a country for which access to EU markets is more

[8] Due to the time coverage of our sample, we only consider agreements signed after 1995.

Table 7.1 *EU PTAs and non-trade outcomes*

Panel A	Civil rights protection			
Provision	0.262**	0.262**	0.267**	0.00988
	(0.0865)	(0.0863)	(0.0863)	(0.111)
Openness	−0.0465**	−0.0461**	−0.0437**	−0.0431**
	(0.0143)	(0.0142)	(0.0155)	(0.0155)
Intensity: EU trade	−0.0295			
	(0.179)			
Intensity: IMP from EU		−0.0237		
		(0.175)		
Intensity: EXP to EU			−0.149	−0.387
			(0.251)	(0.262)
Provision × Intensity: EXP to EU				1.423***
				(0.426)
Obs.	2992	2992	2992	2992
Adj. R^2	0.772	0.772	0.772	0.772
Panel B	**Environmental protection**			
Provision	−0.0913**	−0.0900**	−0.0848**	−0.0824*
	(0.0282)	(0.0285)	(0.0287)	(0.0340)
Openness	−0.00575	−0.00502	−0.00188	−0.00188
	(0.00390)	(0.00377)	(0.00386)	(0.00386)
Intensity: EU trade	−0.0344			
	(0.0517)			
Intensity: IMP from EU		−0.0654		
		(0.0518)		
Intensity: EXP to EU			−0.212**	−0.210**
			(0.0704)	(0.0717)
Provision × Intensity: EXP to EU				−0.0139
				(0.0746)
Obs.	3591	3591	3591	3591
Adj. R^2	0.962	0.962	0.962	0.962
Panel C	**Labor rights protection**			
Provision	−0.0559*	−0.0557*	−0.0492+	0.0896**
	(0.0274)	(0.0274)	(0.0274)	(0.0342)
Openness	−0.0102**	−0.00951**	−0.00512	−0.00453
	(0.00345)	(0.00337)	(0.00328)	(0.00325)

Table 7.1 (*cont.*)

Intensity: EU trade	−0.0473			
	(0.0435)			
Intensity: IMP from EU		−0.0398		
		(0.0425)		
Intensity: EXP to EU			−0.302***	−0.0967
			(0.0638)	(0.0665)
Provision × Intensity: EXP to EU				−1.043***
				(0.155)
Obs.	4,288	4,288	4,288	4,288
Adj. R^2	0.951	0.951	0.951	0.951

Notes: $^+ p < 0.10$, $^* p < 0.05$, $^{**} p < 0.01$, $^{***} p < 0.001$. Robust standard errors in parentheses. All regressions include country and time fixed effects. Openness to trade refers to the country's trade over GDP. The dummy Provision takes value 0 until the first agreement containing the provision of interest is signed. It takes value 1 thereafter.

important (i.e. with a higher share of EU exports in total exports) would respect and fulfill the provisions included in the EU trade agreement to a greater extent, and hence would have better non-trade outcome performance related to the provisions. To investigate this, we present interaction effects for the share of exports to the EU and the relevant NTPs in a final specification. Estimation results are reported in Table 7.1.

Results suggest that improvements in civil rights protection are associated with inclusion of NTPs in a country's PTA with the EU, while the opposite is found for environmental and labor rights protection. Furthermore, the results indicate that more open countries tend to have worse non-trade outcomes.

The share of exports is negative for all three non-trade issue areas, and statistically significant for labor and environmental protection. Thus, the more important the EU is as an export destination for countries in our sample, the worse these countries perform in terms of civil rights, environmental, and labor rights protection. Total trade and EU import shares are never statistically significant. Moreover, results based on the specification presented in the fourth column indicate that the interaction effects are sometimes significant, although with differing signs. In the case of civil rights, we find that higher reliance on EU market access together with provisions in trade agreements is associated with improved civil rights protection. The opposite is found for labor rights.

These results suggest that potentially there is a negative relationship between openness/more exports to the EU and non-trade outcomes. More generally, the results suggest that the relationship between NTPs in EU PTAs and non-trade outcomes is heterogeneous. While the findings are consistent with the descriptive trends observed in the non-trade indicators of interest, we cannot interpret them in terms of the causal effects of non-trade provisions on non-trade outcomes. In fact, a relatively good or bad performance on a specific non-trade outcome might determine the incentives of a partner country, and ultimately its negotiating position, with respect to the relevant non-trade provision. This and similar selection issues motivate serious endogeneity concerns in the context of panel regression models such as the one estimated above.

In conjunction with the diverging results emerging from existing studies, our regression results reinforce the importance of determining the causal linkages between the different variables. In the rest of the chapter we focus on the effect of NTPs on non-trade outcomes using a synthetic control methodology to establish causality.

The Causal Effect of Non-Trade Provisions in EU PTAs

Synthetic control methods offer a means of assessing the causal effect of NTPs in EU PTAs on the realization of non-trade outcomes in partner countries. SCM (Abadie and Gardeazabal, 2003; Abadie et al., 2010; Athey and Imbens, 2017) addresses the problem confronting non-experimental quantitative analyses that lack a truly comparable control group and thus undermine robust inference (establishment of causal effects). As is well known, when the selection of control units is subject to some degree of arbitrariness, the identification of any effect may reflect the characteristics of the control sample and bias the counterfactual estimates (Cunningham, 2021). The SCM overcomes such limitation by pooling all potential control units to create a synthetic counterfactual. Control units are aggregated using an optimization process that minimizes the pre-treatment deviation from the treated unit. In this way, the synthetic counterfactual is able to give a reliable picture of the outcome's trend that would be experienced by the treated unit in the absence of the external shock that is the object of the analysis (conditional on the matching being modeled correctly).

Applied to the problem of interest in this chapter, the SCM enables evaluation of the effectiveness of EU trade strategy by comparing the performance of each country signing a PTA with the EU that includes a relevant NTP (the treated unit) with an alternative synthetic scenario where no such agreement has been ratified. Thus, we apply the SCM by taking as outcome variable the country-level performance on a specific non-trade outcome, defining the treatment as the event of signing a PTA with the EU that includes a relevant NTP. A country that signs such a PTA is identified as a treated unit and the year of signature flags the treatment. For each treated unit, we define the set of control units (the "Donor Pool") as the set of countries that signed (at least) one trade agreement as close in time as possible to the treatment period and that did not sign any PTA including the relevant NTP, nor any PTA with the EU in a sufficiently long time span around the treatment period. All the suitable control units are pooled to build the synthetic counterfactual.[9]

With respect to the descriptive analysis presented in the previous section, the requirements of SCM force us to limit the coverage of our empirical sample in two respects. First, we need to identify those countries that signed an agreement with the EU, with the provision of interest, and for which the commitment to such provision could actually trigger a policy change. For this reason, we look for treated units among the set of low- and middle-income non-EU countries. We exclude all countries whose socioeconomic conditions are similar to the EU, under the simplifying assumption that they could enforce similar standards with respect to the non-trade outcomes of interest.[10] Secondly, SCM requires that both the treated country and all the countries included in the donor pool are observed for a sufficiently long period before and after the treatment (i.e. we need to have data for a pre-treatment matching period and for a post-treatment follow-up period). For this reason, we only consider EU agreements signed over the period 1999–2008, with the

[9] Since the EU tends to sign similar trade agreements with multiple countries within very short time spans, we relax the temporal matching between a treated unit and its donor pool, to reduce instances of ending up with an empty donor pool.

[10] We follow the World Bank Income classification to define and exclude high-income countries. As a result, partners such as Canada, the USA, New Zealand, and Australia are excluded from the analysis.

matching and follow-up periods exceeding these limits by up to five and four years respectively, depending on the treatment year.[11]

Once the donor pool is defined, the Synthetic Counterfactual is the result of a convex combination of a set of selected control units. The weights attached to each control unit are defined according to a set of "matching variables", which are considered to be predictors of the post-treatment outcome, and are defined to minimize the distance between the treated and the synthetic counterfactual. Formally speaking, taking X as a matrix of pre-treatment matching variables, the weighting scheme has to minimize $\sum_{m=1}^{k} v_m \left(X_{tr,m} - \sum_{dp=1}^{n} \omega_{dp}^{*} X_{dp,m} \right)^2$, where n indexes the control units in the donor pool, v is a non-negative weight reflecting the importance of a matching variable when measuring the total distance between the synthetic and treated unit, and ω_{dp}^{*} is the non-negative weight assigned to each country in the donor pool. The weights v_k can therefore be seen as a rough measure of the predictive power of a matching variable with respect to the post-treatment outcome level. The fact that ω_{dp}^{*} can be null implies that not all the suitable countries in the donor pool will necessarily be considered by the SCM algorithm.[12] For the purpose of our analysis, we consider real GDP, per capita GDP, and population (expressed both in levels and growth rates) as matching variables. Following Athey and Imbens (2017) and Kaul et al. (2015), we additionally include three out of the five possible lags of the outcome variable of interest as additional predictors.

We use the results of the SCM exercise in a difference-in-difference (DID) analysis in which, for each outcome of interest, we pool all treated units and the related synthetic counterfactuals. In practical terms, a DID can be seen as a generalization of the SCM to the case of multiple treated

[11] More precisely, given a treatment to occur in year t, control units are defined as the countries that signed a trade agreement without the provision of interest and not with the EU in any year $t_0 \subset [1999 - 2008]$, and that did not sign any trade agreement in the time span $[t_0 - 5, t_0 + 4]$. We impose two additional limitations: first, we require that control units did not sign agreements with the USA, Canada, Australia, and New Zealand for the period $[t_0 - 5, t_0 + 4]$. And second, for each non-trade outcome of interest, we exclude all potential control units that signed an agreement with any trading partner in the previous ten years containing the related provision.

[12] Cunningham (2020) provides a brief and intuitive description of the methodology, the relationship between matching and post-treatment outcome, and the relationship between the covariates' matching weighting scheme and the donor pool one.

and multiple control units, where the size of the two sub-samples allows us to infer the average effect of a treatment/event on a given outcome of interest (see Angrist and Pischke, 2008).

Starting from the individual outcomes collected via SCM, we fit a "standard" econometric regression of the form

$$Y_{it} = \alpha + \gamma \text{Treated}_i + \lambda \text{Treatment Period}_t \\ + \delta \text{Treated}_i \times \text{Treatment Period}_t + \epsilon_{it}$$

Treated_i is a dummy taking the value 1 for all treated units and 0 for all synthetic counterfactuals; the binary variable $\text{Treatment Period}_t$ takes the value 1 in the post-treatment period, and the interaction $\text{Treated}_i \times \text{Treatment Period}_t$ captures the effect of the treatment on the treated countries. If the control and the treatment group are indeed comparable, then the coefficient δ identifies the effect of having signed an agreement, controlling for the potential initial differences among treated units and their counterfactuals.[13]

The results reported in Table 7.2 reveal no evidence of a causal effect of NTPs on non-trade-related outcomes on average.[14] The inclusion of NTPs in EU trade agreements does not appear (on average) to be an effective tool for promoting EU values among trading partners.

The absence of a positive average effect of inclusion of NTPs in EU PTAs may conceal heterogeneous responses across EU trade partners that prevent the identification of any average effect of a given NTP on the associated non-trade outcome indicator(s). Figure 7.5 illustrates this possibility. It reports results for three non-trade issues for three EU trade partners. The cases were selected to be representative of each possible treatment outcome: worsening non-trade outcome performance, lack of any effect, and improvement in the respective non-trade outcome.[15]

[13] Similar to SCM, which represent a recent application of DID to cases where the number of treated units is too low to permit inference, DID relies on the assumption that the control units are representative of the trend that treated units would have experienced in the absence of any treatment. The fact that our control units are the synthetic counterfactuals identified via SCM gives us some confidence that this parallel trend assumption holds.

[14] Some caution has to be exercised when interpreting the results on civil rights protection. The dependent variable in this case was constructed from ordinal index variables. Although the constructed index is continuous, some information is lost due to the cardinal nature of the underlying variables, potentially leading to a somewhat less precise matching process in the synthetic control approach.

[15] We only report results for three countries that meet these conditions. Results for all countries for which a pool of control units has been identified are available upon request.

Table 7.2 *Aggregate results – difference in difference estimator*

	Civil rights protection	*Environmental protection*	*Labor rights protection*
Treated	0.0827	0.00133	−0.00645
	(0.0690)	(0.00197)	(0.00695)
Treatment period	0.0627	0.00619	0.00860
	(0.333)	(0.00474)	(0.0583)
Treated × Treatment period	−0.120	0.00677	−0.0437
	(0.249)	(0.00800)	(0.0547)
Constant	−0.655	−0.171	−1.208*
	(0.523)	(0.226)	(0.421)
Obs.	120	200	200
Mean	0.0524491	0.1088617	0.0050542
Standard deviation	2.156357	2.579003	1.389452

Notes: * $p < 0.05$, ** $p < 0.01$, *** $p < 0.001$. Robust standard errors in parentheses. The variable Treated × Treatment Period identifies the effect of EU's NTP policy on the selected aggregate policy outcome.

The absence of a systematic visual pattern in Figure 7.5 suggests at least two considerations. First, consistent with the aggregate results from Table 7.2, the evidence compiled from the SCM analysis for selected countries points to extensive heterogeneity in the observed relationships between NTPs and non-trade outcomes. The existence of both negative and positive responses suggests that the effectiveness of the EU strategy of linking trade agreements to NTPOs should be evaluated case by case, as it is likely to depend on partner-specific characteristics and not simply on whether a given type of NTP is included in a PTA. The case of Chile is illustrative: Labor rights seem to improve after signature of the PTA, which was one of the first EU agreements to include substantive clauses on labor rights. Second, the broad scope of the NTPs included in EU agreements appear to be associated with partner countries concentrating efforts in some policy domains and not (or less) in others. This is illustrated in the plots for Egypt and Mexico, for which performance on non-trade outcome indicators following the signature of a PTA with the EU that includes the same NTP diverges substantially. This is observed for civil rights and environmental protection in the case of Egypt, and civil and labor rights protection in the case of Mexico.

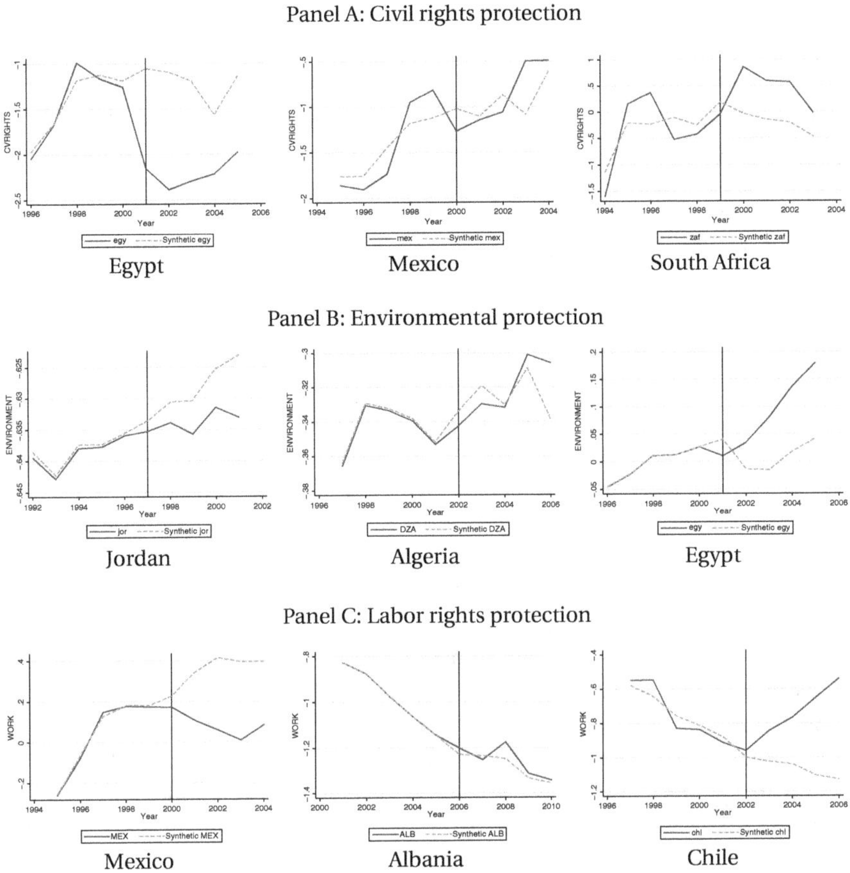

Figure 7.5 Heterogeneous effects of NTPs across EU partner countries
Notes: We report two distinct robustness tests for the results shown in Figure 7.5 in the Appendix (Figures B7.1 and B7.2).

Conclusion

A central feature of EU external policy is a strategy that uses trade as an instrument to pursue non-trade objectives, specifically a range of European values pertaining to human rights, rule of law, democracy, other civil and social rights, and protection of the environment. Whether this strategy is effective in improving the targeted non-trade outcomes is a central feature of the RESPECT research project. There are many potential channels through which NTPOs can be realized. Trade (and associated FDI flows) may indirectly impact non-trade outcomes, either positively or negatively, depending on the actions of both the firms involved and the policies of EU partner countries. The probability and magnitude of potential positive effects may be enhanced by inclusion of NTPs in EU PTAs committing EU partner countries to pursue actions in relevant areas of domestic policy. PTAs may further enhance the prospects of improving non-trade outcome indicators if they are complemented by flanking measures such as technical and financial assistance. However, the inclusion of NTPs in EU PTAs may also have detrimental effects insofar as it induces potential partner countries to refrain from participating in PTAs, reducing their ability to expand exports to the EU, and thus limiting the potential positive effects of trade on non-trade outcomes.

The analysis in this chapter focuses on the role of NTPs in EU PTAs and looks at a subset of the possible linkages between trade, PTAs, and non-trade outcome variables associated with the European values that are central to the European treaties. Specifically, the focus is on the potential impact of NTPs on the associated non-trade outcomes in EU partner countries and on the indirect relationship between NTPs, trade, and non-trade outcomes. Standard regression analysis of these two potential channels between NTPs and non-trade outcomes results in statistically significant coefficient estimates that suggest some NTPs are positively correlated and others are negatively correlated with the respective non-trade outcome indicators. These findings appear to lend some support to both "march to the top" and "race to the bottom" hypotheses that feature prominently in the literature on trade and non-trade issues. However, the application of synthetic control methods indicates that the regression results are not robust. The SCM-based analysis does not support the conclusion that inclusion of NTPs in EU trade agreements has caused either a positive or negative effect on non-trade outcomes in EU trading partners. NTPs have no discernible effect. The absence of a positive (or negative) average effect of inclusion of NTPs in EU PTAs might conceal heterogeneous responses across EU trade partners to NTPs. Country-specific SCM analysis provides some evidence of such heterogeneity, suggesting that analysis of the potential effects of NTPs in PTAs should focus on the country level as opposed to cross-country analysis of panel data.

References

Abadie, Alberto, and Javier Gardeazabal, 2003, "The economic costs of conflict: A case study of the Basque Country," *American Economic Review*, 93 (1), 113–132.

Abadie, Alberto, Alexis Diamond, and Jens Hainmueller, 2010, "Synthetic control methods for comparative case studies: Estimating the effect of California tobacco control program," *Journal of the American Statistical Association*, 105 (490), 493–505.

Adarov, Amat, 2018, "Eurasian economic integration: Impact evaluation using the gravity model and the synthetic control methods," Technical Report, wiiw Working Paper.

Angrist, Joshua D., and Jörn-Steffen Pischke, 2008, *Mostly Harmless Econometrics: An Empiricist's Companion*, Princeton University Press.

Antràs, Pol, and Robert W. Staiger, 2012, "Offshoring and the role of trade agreements," *American Economic Review*, 102 (7), 3140–3183.

Athey, Susan, and Guido W. Imbens, 2017, "The state of applied econometrics: causality and policy evaluation," *Journal of Economic Perspectives*, 31 (2), 3–32.

Aytug, Huseyin, Merve Mavucs Kutuk, Arif Oduncu, and Subidey Togan, 2017, "Twenty years of the EU–Turkey customs union: A synthetic control method analysis," *JCMS: Journal of Common Market Studies*, 55 (3), 419–431.

Baier, Scott L., and Jeffrey H. Bergstrand, "Do free trade agreements actually increase members' international trade?," *Journal of International Economics*, 2007, 71 (1), 72–95.

Baier, Scott L., Jeffrey H. Bergstrand, and Michael Feng, 2014, "Economic integration agreements and the margins of international trade," *Journal of International Economics*, 93 (2), 339–350.

Billmeier, Andreas, and Tommaso Nannicini, 2013, "Assessing economic liberalization episodes: A synthetic control approach," *Review of Economics and Statistics*, 95 (3), 983–1001.

Brandi, Clara, Jakob Schwab, Axel Berger, and Jean-Frédéric Morin, 2020, "Do environmental provisions in trade agreements make exports from developing countries greener?," *World Development*, 129, 104899.

Brown, Drusilla K., Alan V. Deardorff, and Robert M. Stern, 2013, "Labor Standards and Human Rights: Implications for International Trade and Investment," in Zdenek Drabek and Petros C. Mavroidis (eds.), *Regulations of Foreign Investment: Challenges to International Harmonization*, World Scientific Studies in International Economics, World Scientific Publishing Company, pp. 153–195.

Büthe, Tim, and Helen V. Milner, 2008, "The politics of foreign direct investment into developing countries: Increasing FDI through international trade agreements?," *American Journal of Political Science*, 52 (4), 741–62.

Büthe, Tim, and Helen V. Milner, 2014, "Foreign direct investment and institutional diversity in trade agreements: Credibility, commitment, and economic flows in the developing world, 1971–2007," *World Politics*, 66 (1), 88–122.

Chyzh, Olga, 2016, "Dangerous liaisons: An endogenous model of international trade and human rights," *Journal of Peace Research*, 53 (3), 409–423.

Copeland, Brian R., 2013, *Trade and the Environment*, Palgrave Macmillan UK.

Cunningham, Scott, 2021, *Causal Inference: The Mix Tape*, Yale University Press.

Donnelly, Jack, 2013, *Universal Human Rights in Theory and Practice*, Cornell University Press.

Dür, Andreas, Leonardo Baccini, and Manfred Elsig, 2014, "The design of international trade agreements: Introducing a new dataset," *Review of International Organizations*, 9 (3), 353–375.

Flanigan, Robert J., 2006, *Globalization and Labor Conditions: Working Conditions and Worker Rights in a Global Economy*, Oxford University Press.

Greenhill, Brian, Layna Mosley, and Aseem Prakash, 2009, "Trade-based diffusion of labor rights: A panel study, 1986–2002," *American Political Science Review*, 103(4), 669–690.

Hafner-Burton, Emilie M., 2005, "Trading human rights: How preferential trade agreements influence government repression," *International Organization*, 59 (3), 593–629.

Hafner-Burton, Emilie M., 2009, *Forced to Be Good: Why Trade Agreements Boost Human Rights*, Cornell University Press.

Halicioglu, Ferda, and Natalya Ketenci, 2016, "The impact of international trade on environmental quality: The case of transition countries," *Energy*, 109, 1130–1138.

Hannan, Swarnali Ahmed, 2017, *The Impact of Trade Agreements in Latin America Using the Synthetic Control Method*, International Monetary Fund.

Hosny, Amr Sadek, 2012, "Algeria's trade with GAFTA countries: A synthetic control approach," *Transition Studies Review*, 19 (1), 35–42.

Juhn, Chinhui, Gergely Ujhelyi, and Carolina Villegas-Sanchez, 2013, "Trade liberalization and gender inequality," *American Economic Review*, May 103 (3), 269–273.

Kaul, Ashok, Stefan Klößner, Gregor Pfeifer, and Manuel Schieler, 2015, "Synthetic control methods: Never use all pre-intervention outcomes together with covariates." IDEAS: Munich Personal RePEc Archive, https://ideas.repec.org/p/pra/mprapa/83790.html

Kim, Moonhawk, 2012, "Ex ante due diligence: Formation of PTAs and protection of labor rights," *International Studies Quarterly*, 56 (4), 704–719.

Kis-Katos, Krisztina, and Robert Sparrow, 2011, "Child labor and trade liberalization in Indonesia," *Journal of Human Resources*, 46 (4), 722–749.

Kis-Katos, Krisztina, and Robert Sparrow, 2015, "Poverty, labor markets and trade liberalization in Indonesia," *Journal of Development Economics*, 117, 94–106.

Kohl, Tristan, Steven Brakman, and Harry Garretsen, 2016, "Do trade agreements stimulate international trade differently? Evidence from 296 trade agreements," *The World Economy*, 39 (1), 97–131.

Kox, Henk L. M., and Hugo Rojas-Romagosa, 2020, "How trade and investment agreements affect bilateral foreign direct investment: Results from a structural gravity model," *The World Economy*, 43(12), 3103–3406.

Laget, E., A. Osnago, N. Rocha, and M. Ruta, 2020, "Deep trade agreements and global value chains," *Review of Industrial Organization*, 57 (2), 379–410.

Lechner, Lisa Maria, 2018, "The European Union's inclusion of non-trade issues in preferential trade agreements," RESPECT mimeo.

Li, Zijian, and Aaron Jennings, 2017, "Worldwide regulations of standard values of pesticides for human health risk control: A review," *International Journal of Environmental Research and Public Health*, 14(7), 826.

Limão, Nuno, 2007, "Are preferential trade agreements with non-trade objectives a stumbling block for multilateral liberalization?," *Review of Economic Studies*, 74 (3), 821–855.

Manchin, Miriam, 2021, "Description of version 2 of the panel dataset on non-trade policy outcome indicators," EUI RSCAS Working Paper.

Mansfield, Edward D., and Eric Reinhardt, 2008, "International institutions and the volatility of international trade," *International Organization*, 62 (4), 621–52.

McAusland, Carol, and Daniel L. Millimet, 2013, "Do national borders matter? Intranational trade, international trade, and the environment," *Journal of Environmental Economics and Management*, 65 (3), 411–437.

McLaughlin Mitchell, Sara, and Paul R. Hensel, 2007, "International institutions and compliance with agreements," *American Journal of Political Science*, 51 (4), 721–737.

Miroudot, Sébastien, and Davide Rigo, 2019, "Preferential trade agreements and multinational production," RSCAS Working Papers, 2019/14.

Mosley, Layna, and Saika Uno, 2007, "Racing to the bottom or climbing to the top? Economic globalization and collective labor rights," *Comparative Political Studies*, 40 (8), 923–948.

Olper, Alessandro, Daniele Curzi, and Johan Swinnen, 2018, "Trade liberalization and child mortality: A synthetic control method," *World Development*, 110, 394–410.

Orefice, Gianluca, and Nadia Rocha, 2014, "Deep integration and production networks: An empirical analysis," *The World Economy*, 37 (1), 106–136.

Osnago, Alberto, Nadia Rocha, and Michele Ruta, 2017, "Do deep trade agreements boost vertical FDI?," *World Bank Economic Review*, 30 (1), 119–125.

Postnikov, Evgeny, 2014, "The design of social standards in EU and US preferential trade agreements," in David Deese (ed.), *Handbook of the International Political Economy of Trade*, Edward Elgar, pp. 531–549.

Rasch, Georg, 1980, *Probabilistic Models for Some Intelligence and Attainment Tests*, University of Chicago Press.

Rose, Andrew K., 2004, "Do we really know that the WTO increases trade?," *American Economic Review*, 94 (1), 98–114.

Sauré, Philip, and Hosny Zoabi, 2014, "International trade, the gender wage gap and female labor force participation," *Journal of Development Economics*, 111, 17–33.

Spilker, Gabriele, and Tobias Böhmelt, 2013, "The impact of preferential trade agreements on governmental repression revisited," *Review of International Organizations*, 8 (3), 343–361.

Ubaldo, Mattia Di, and Michael Gasiorek, 2020, "Non-trade provisions in trade agreements and FDI," Working Paper Series 2120, Department of Economics, University of Sussex Business School, December.

APPENDICES

Appendix A

EU Partners and NTI Included in Trade Agreements

Table A7.1 *List of EU partners that signed at least one PTA with the EU*

Country	Environmental **protection**	Labor **protection**	Civil **rights**	Country	Environmental **protection**	Labor **protection**	Civil **rights**
ABW	1970	1970	1970	LIE	1972	1972	1972
AIA	1970	1970	1970	LSO	2016	2016	2016
ALB	2006	2006	2006	MAR	1969	1976	1969
AND	1989		1989	MDA	2014	2014	2014
ARM	2013	2013	2013	MEX	2000	2000	2000
ATF	1970	1970	1970	MKD	2001	2001	2001
ATG	2008	2008	2008	MNE	2007	2007	2007
BDI	2016	2016	2016	MOZ	2016	2016	2016
BHS	2008	2008	2008	MSR	1970	1970	1970
BIH	2008	2008	2008	MYT	1970	1970	1970
BLZ	2008	2008	2008	NAM	2016	2016	2016
BRB	2008	2008	2008	NCL	1970	1970	1970
BWA	2016	2016	2016	NIC	2012	2012	2012
CAN	2016	2016	2016	NOR	1973	1973	1973
CHE	1972	1972	1972	PAN	2012	2012	2012
CHL	2002	2002	2002	PCN	1970	1970	1970
CIV	2008	2008	2008	PER	2012	2012	2012
COL	2012	2012	2012	PNG	2009	2009	2009
CRI	2012	2012	2012	PYF	1970	1970	1970
CYM	1970	1970	1970	RWA	2016	2016	2016
DMA	2008	2008	2008	SGP	2016	2016	2016
DOM	2008	2008	2008	SGS	1970	1970	1970

Table A7.1 (*cont.*)

Country	Environmental	Labor	Civil	Country	Environmental	Labor	Civil
DZA	1976	1976	1976	SHN	1970	1970	1970
EGY	1972	2001	1972	SLV	2012	2012	2012
FJI	2009	2009	2009	SMR	1991	1991	
FLK	1970	1970	1970	SPM	1970	1970	1970
FRO	1991		1991	SRB	1980	1980	1980
GEO	2014	2014	2014	SUR	2008	2008	2008
GRD	2008	2008	2008	SWZ	2016	2016	2016
GRL	1970	1970	1970	SYR	1977		1977
GTM	2012	2012	2012	TCA	1970	1970	1970
GUY	2008	2008	2008	TTO	2008	2008	2008
HND	2012	2012	2012	TUN	1969	1995	1969
IOT	1970	1970	1970	TUR	1995	1995	1995
ISR	1975	1975	1975	TZA	2016	2016	2016
JAM	2008	2008	2008	UGA	2016	2016	2016
JOR	1977	1997	1977	UKR	2014	2014	2014
JPN	2018	2018	2018	VCT	2008	2008	2008
KEN	2016	2016	2016	VGB	1970	1970	1970
KNA	2008	2008	2008	VNM	2016	2016	2016
KOR	2010	2010	2010	WLF	1970	1970	1970
LBN	1972	2002	1972	ZAF	1999	1999	1999
LCA	2008	2008	2008				

Appendix B

Main Robustness Checks to the Main Results of the Synthetic Control

When it comes to claiming a causal relationship within a synthetic control approach, displaying a good pre-treatment match and a clearly divergent post-treatment follow-up is not sufficient. In the past fifteen years, the literature has suggested that results should be supported by a sound robustness test. Below, we report the graphical representation of two of them. The first test reported consists of a simplified version of the visual representation of the root mean squared error (RMSPE) test proposed by Abadie and Gardeazabal (2003). Practically speaking, the RMSPE test consists of iteratively replacing the treated unit with each and every comparable unit in the donor pool, computing the RMSPE ratio between the pre- and post-treatment period of each unit, and then computing a sort of p-value of the distribution of such ratio. The rationale of this RMSPE test can be summarized as follows: assuming the treatment of interest to be the only determinant of a significant change in the outcome of interest between a given treated unit and its synthetic counterfactual, the treated unit should be the one displaying the most extreme value of the computed RMSPE ratio. In the same spirit, we perform a simple *in-space* placebo, which similarly captures the "extremeness" of the treated unit by simply plotting the result of the iterative SCM (Figure B7.1): if signing a given agreement including a certain provision has a causal impact on the related outcome of interest, then the line associated with the actually treated unit should stand out from the bulk placebo units. The second and final test ensures the robustness of the synthetic counterfactual to the inclusion of particularly relevant control units. Similarly to the in-space placebo, the *leave-one-out* test reconstructs many synthetic counterfactuals as the number of units in the donor pool, removing iteratively one of those units from it in any round. If the entire synthetic counterfactual is driven by the characteristics of a specific individual control, its omission should result in a drastically different trend. The results from this test are shown in Figure B7.2.

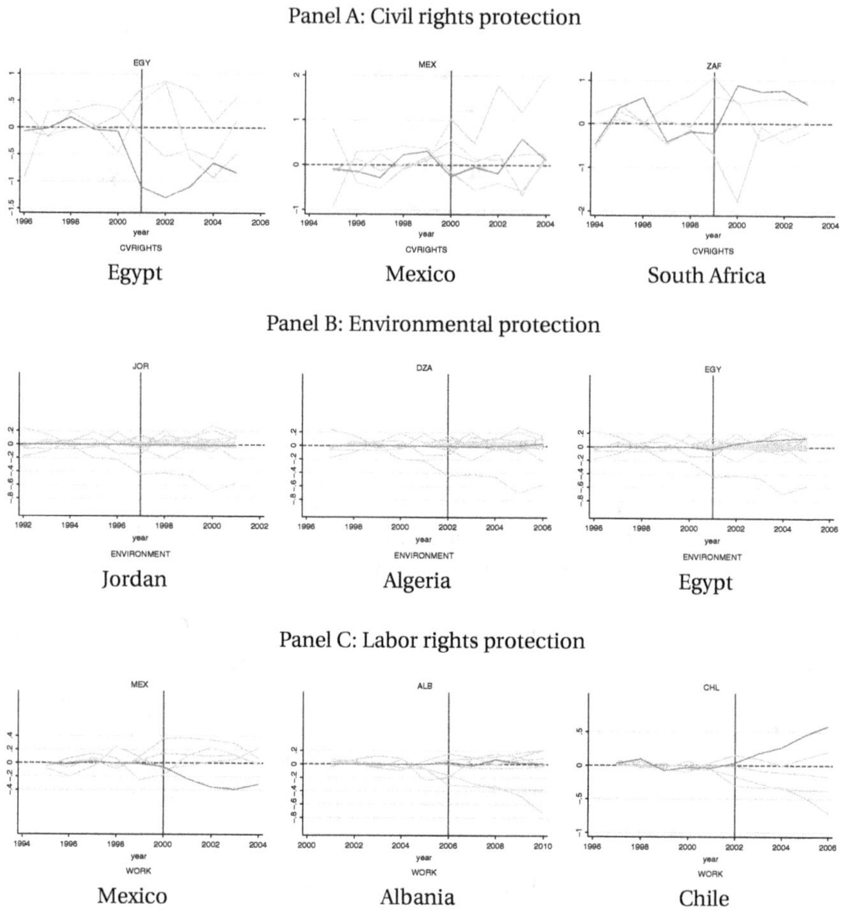

Figure B7.1 In-space placebo for selected countries and NTPs

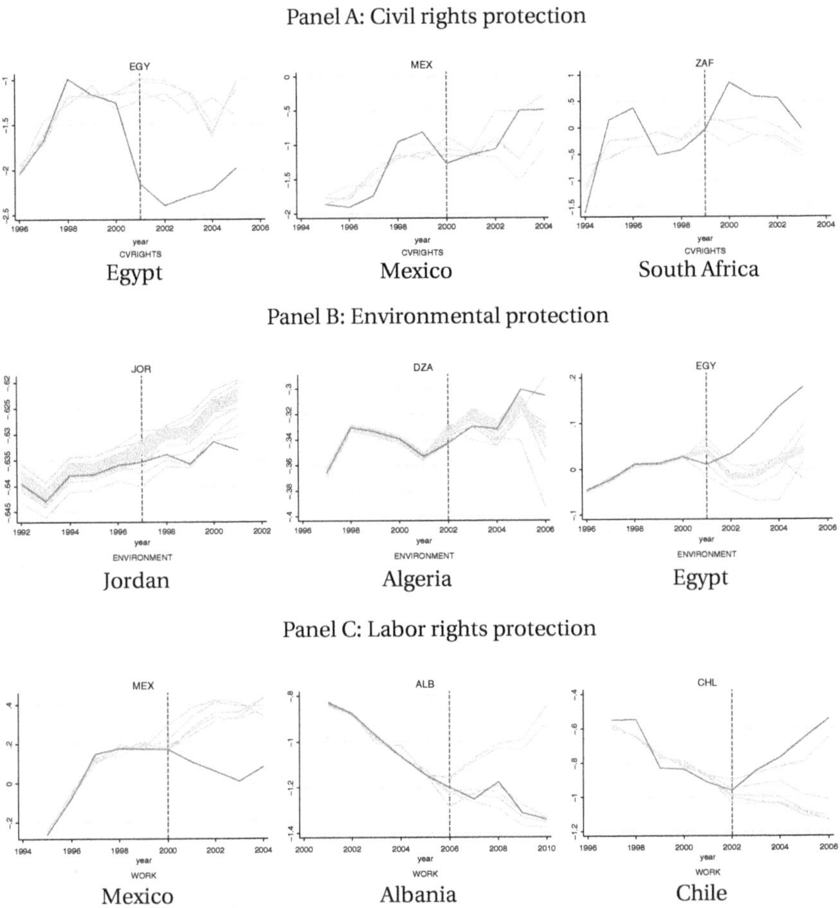

Figure B7.2 Leave-one-out test for selected countries and NTPs

8

Trade, the G20 and the EU

Soft Power for Greater Policy Coherence?

BERNARD HOEKMAN AND RORDEN WILKINSON

Introduction

Rising resort to unilateral trade measures by the United States, as-yet-unresolved trade conflict between the United States and China, and the disruption to employment trade flows arising from the COVID-19 pandemic have put the global trading system under considerable pressure. Although these trade tensions capture most public attention, many other trade challenges confront governments. Technical innovation is changing the structure and composition of international trade, reflected in global value-chain-based production, a rising share of services and associated "digitalization" of the economy. These dynamics give rise to new policy concerns and spillovers such as localization requirements for data storage, security, and privacy policies. National regulatory requirements are moving center stage, driven by concerns in the business community about the trade-impeding (cost-raising) effects of differences in applicable regulatory norms and standards, licensing requirements, and certification and compliance assessment procedures for products and production processes used by suppliers of goods and services. Similar issues arise as regards the relationship between the Sustainable Development Goals and the multilateral trading system and demands for aligning trade rules and work programs to recognize the social and environmental dimensions of trade.

We are grateful to San Bilal, Peter Holmes, Massimo de Luca, Jacques Pelkmans, and participants in a 20–21 January 2020 RESPECT project workshop at the Centre for European Policy Studies in Brussels for helpful comments and suggestions. The project leading to this study received funding from the European Union's Horizon 2020 research and innovation program under grant agreement No. 770680 (RESPECT).

The G20 is a unique forum bringing together the leaders of the major economies of the world with a focus on cooperation to address global spillovers.[1] While the composition of the group is idiosyncratic and difficult to rationalize, it includes all the major trading nations. Of relevance from an EU perspective is that Europe accounts for one-quarter of its membership. The presidents of the European Commission and Council represent the EU along with the leaders of France, Germany, and Italy. The United Kingdom is a member. Spain attends as a permanent invitee. The leaders of the "big four" trade powers that must agree on any initiative to address trade tensions (China, the EU, Japan, and the United States), however organized, meet regularly under G20 auspices. The more the G20 operates as a forum these players use to move towards an accommodation in trade matters, the more relevant it will be in sustaining an open, rules-based global trading system.

Europe (the EU plus the United Kingdom) has a major stake in the trade system and is also represented strongly in the G20, providing a basis to exercise greater leadership in the G20 to address trade tensions and revitalize the World Trade Organization (WTO). Continued pursuit of trade agreements and the launch of plurilateral initiatives in the WTO demonstrate that many countries retain an interest in trade cooperation, and there is an increasing focus on WTO reform to enhance the operation of the organization. The 2021 revision to the EU trade policy strategy highlights the importance that the EU attaches to WTO reform to better enable the organization to assist members in dealing with international policy spillovers. New initiatives should build on the experience obtained in negotiations on trade and investment facilitation, e-commerce, and efforts to reduce global overcapacity in steel production to generate support for preparing a broader work program to generate concrete WTO reform proposals for consideration by the WTO membership.

There is much the EU might do through the G20 with like-minded members to bolster multilateral trade cooperation. The challenge is to

[1] The G20 comprises Australia, Canada, Saudi Arabia, the United States, India, Russia, South Africa, Turkey, Argentina, Brazil, Mexico, France, Germany, Italy, the United Kingdom, China, Indonesia, Japan, South Korea, and the European Union. There are also a few permanent guest invitees. At the time of writing, these comprised the African Union (AU), Asia Pacific Economic Co-operation (APEC) forum, the Association of Southeast Asian Nations (ASEA), the Financial Stability Board (FSB), the International Labour Organization, the International Monetary Fund, Spain, the New Partnership for Africa's Development (NEPAD), the Organisation for Economic Co-operation and Development (OECD), the World Bank, and the WTO.

recognize and address the factors that have reduced the ability of the WTO to fulfill its intended role as a platform for global trade governance. This chapter offers suggestions on the role the EU and its member states can play in shifting the dial on trade in a more favorable direction. We do this while mindful of the Von der Leyen Commission vision[2] and the fact that the EU has limited hard power. Access to the EU single market is the main "hard" instrument available to the Union, but as a net exporter, the EU has a strong interest in keeping markets open, reducing the credibility of threats to foreclose access to its market to major trading nations – notwithstanding the stated intention of the EU to pursue a more assertive trade policy (European Commission, 2021).

A major advantage of devoting more resources to the G20 is that the forum is not policy- or sector-specific. The G20 spans all of government, with leaders able to take a broader view and overcome silo problems that can – and have – reduced the ability of reaching agreement in the WTO and in trade agreements more generally. Although much attention is given to market access conditionality as an instrument of EU external policy, the EU has considerable soft power as well. It is the world's largest provider of development assistance and has extensive experience in setting regulatory norms that support the operation of its open internal market while maintaining high levels of social, safety, and environmental standards and defending broader European values. The latter may (and, indeed, have) become focal points for non-EU countries independent of trade considerations. These dimensions of external policy figure prominently in G20 deliberations, enhancing the voice of the EU.

The G20 in a Decade of Rising Trade Tensions

The G20 has included a focus on trade since the first summit in 2008 when the Bush administration used the gathering as a vehicle to coordinate responses to the global financial crisis.[3] The 2009 G20 Summit declaration stressed that reinvigorating world trade and investment was an essential element of restoring global growth and that protectionist responses to the crisis would exacerbate the sharp decline

[2] The von der Leyen Commission has characterized itself as being committed to sustainable policies and a guardian of multilateralism. See https://ec.europa.eu/commission/presscorner/detail/en/IP_19_5542.

[3] See Bery (2018) for a wide-ranging assessment of the G20.

in demand in crisis-hit countries. Leaders agreed not to repeat the mistakes of protectionism of previous eras; to refrain from raising new barriers to investment and trade in goods and services; and not to use WTO-inconsistent measures to stimulate exports. They also mandated the WTO and other international organizations to monitor and report publicly on the adherence by G20 members to these undertakings on a quarterly basis (after the immediate crisis had passed these became semi-annual). In addition to commitments to exercise restraint, they took action to increase the availability of trade finance (by at least US$250 billion over two years), called on regulators to use available flexibility when setting new capital requirements for trade finance, and indicated their commitment to an ambitious and balanced conclusion to the Doha Development Agenda (DDA) and to provide the political attention needed to achieve this goal (Drezner, 2014).

Subsequent summits (see Table 8.1) reiterated in large measure promises to refrain from protectionism (through standstill and rollback commitments) and conclude the DDA. The first promise was broken almost immediately. G20 governments made active use not only of all the instruments that are permitted by the WTO – such as antidumping, countervailing duties, and safeguard actions – but also implemented many subsidy programs, supporting exporters through fiscal incentives, export credit schemes, and national industrial policies that affect international competition. As documented by the Global Trade Alert, many of the actions taken by EU member states centered on supporting exporters through programs of national Export–Import banks and development finance institutions.[4] Over time, the disconnect between G20 trade policy promises and practices became impossible to ignore, resulting in the removal of the "no protectionism" pledge in the 2018 G20 leaders' statement.[5]

Analyses of the economic effects of protectionist measures in the post-2008 period have tended to look mostly at tariffs and trade defense actions and neglect policy instruments such as subsidies (Evenett and Fritz, 2015). Between 2009 and 2020, G20 members put in place over

[4] During the 2009–2019 period, Germany ranked third behind China and the United States in terms of number of measures taken that impact on trade flows, mostly reflecting export support measures (trade finance; export credit and guarantees). See www.globaltradealert.org/.

[5] www.consilium.europa.eu/media/37247/buenos_aires_leaders_declaration.pdf.

Table 8.1 *G20 leaders' summits, 2008–2021*

Date	Host country	Host city	Trade ministers' meeting?
14–15 November 2008	United States	Washington, DC	No
2 April 2009	United Kingdom	London	No
24–25 September 2009	United States	Pittsburgh	No
26–27 June 2010	Canada	Toronto	No
11–12 November 2010	South Korea	Seoul	No
3–4 November 2011	France	Cannes	No
18–19 June 2012	Mexico	Los Cabos	Yes
5–6 September 2013	Russia	Saint Petersburg	No
15–16 November 2014	Australia	Brisbane	Yes
15–16 November 2015	Turkey	Serik, Antalya	Yes
4–5 September 2016	China	Hangzhou	Yes
7–8 July 2017	Germany	Hamburg	No
30 Nov.–1 Dec. 2018	Argentina	Buenos Aires	Yes
28–29 June 2019	Japan	Osaka	Yes
21–22 November 2020	Saudi Arabia	Riyadh	Yes
30–31 October 2021	Italy	Rome	Yes

Source: G20 Information Centre (www.g20.utoronto.ca/summits/index.html).

20,000 measures that distorted trade.[6] The use of trade policy instruments was significant and has intensified over time. In 2020 three times as many new trade-distorting measures were observed as liberalizing measures. Trends in use of trade-distorting measures suggest a steady increase over time (Figure 8.1). The numerous trade-distorting measures taken by all G20 members were implemented in a period in which global trade grew at the same anemic rate as global GDP. The 2010–2019 period was the longest spell of slow trade growth that the world experienced for many decades. The reasons for the slowdown are complex, but policy

[6] See www.globaltradealert.org/. The G20 mandated the WTO and other organizations to monitor the no protectionism pledge, which generated regular (joint) reports by the WTO, UN Conference on Trade and Development (UNCTAD), and the OECD. However, these have picked up substantially fewer measures than the Global Trade Alert. In part this may reflect the greater reliance on notifications as opposed to independent collection of information, as well as lack of specificity as to what should be covered and how far to go beyond the policy instruments subject to WTO rules.

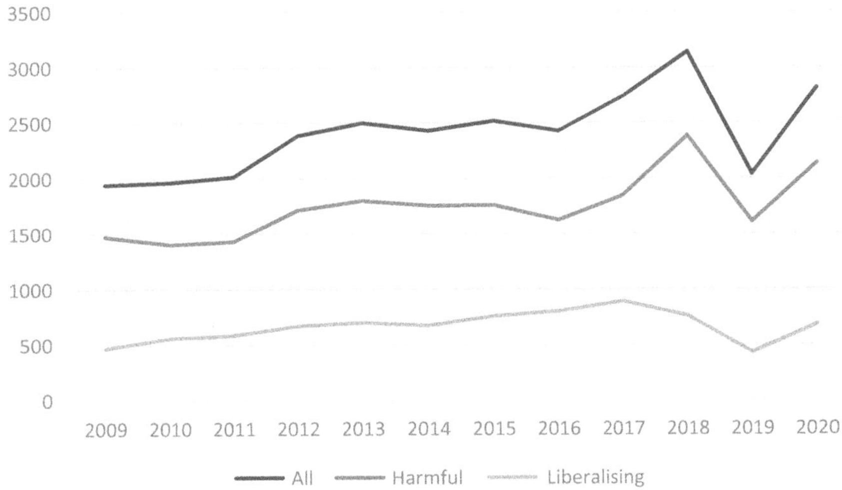

Figure 8.1 Number of trade interventions implemented per year, 2009–2020
Source: Global Trade Alert (www.globaltradealert.org/global_dynamics).

factors have played a role, including the steady escalation in the use of trade-distorting measures following the election of Donald Trump as president of the United States and the launch of a trade war by the United States against China (IMF, 2019).

Trade in the G20

Priorities in the G20 have varied over time, with trade being prominent throughout, but particularly so in 2008–2009, when leaders were concerned to avoid a beggar-thy-neighbor dynamic of the type that arose in the 1930s. Growth and employment have, not surprisingly, generally been at the top of the G20 agenda. In most G20 meetings, the focus of attention has been on macroeconomic and financial policy, with the initial G20 summits dealing with measures to address both the causes and consequences of the crisis, including efforts to bolster financial regulation to improve financial stability and tax collection. Early G20 summits included a focus on the eurozone debt crisis, including EU decisions to pursue fiscal discipline/austerity, which pitted the EU against the United States and emerging-economy G20 members, which supported more expansionary policy stances. Over time, new items were added to the G20 agenda, reflecting national priorities of relevance to the group as a whole. Examples include the refugee crisis (Turkey) and implementation of the 2030 Agenda for Sustainable Development and the Paris Agreement on climate change (including a push to conclude the WTO talks on an agreement to reduce tariffs on environmental goods).[7]

Collective commitments not to resort to protectionism when addressing the crisis were a staple of G20 summit declarations until 2018. They were not very effective, however, as illustrated by the launch of a trade war against China by the United States in 2017 and the parallel campaign by the United States against the WTO Appellate Body and the operation of the WTO more generally.[8] G20 members also did not deliver on the commitment to conclude the DDA. Six years after the initial G20 crisis summits, the DDA effectively was abandoned at the 2015 Nairobi WTO Ministerial conference – a development consolidated two years later in Buenos Aires (Hannah et al., 2018). The ineffectiveness of the oft-repeated instruction by leaders to their trade ministers to conclude the DDA and to refrain from (not to speak of rolling back) protectionist measures suggests, statements to the contrary notwithstanding, that G20 members were not willing to walk the proverbial talk.

Since its establishment in 1995, the WTO has played a central role in the operation of the global trade regime. Its membership has expanded to 164, taking in an additional 36 countries – including China and Russia; it has presided over the mediation of almost 600 disputes; and it has played an important role in ensuring the transparency of member countries' trade policies. However, disagreements among G20 countries regarding the costs and benefits of committing to additional policy disciplines, most notably between the USA on one side and major emerging economies such as India on the other, blocked progress in core areas of the WTO's traditional market access agenda – import tariffs, agricultural support, and services trade liberalization. The opportunity cost of the DDA failure

[7] To date, WTO negotiations on a critical mass basis to conclude an Environmental Goods Agreement have been able to be concluded. In part, this is because the focus is narrow, centering on reducing tariffs and other discriminatory market access barriers, as opposed to a broader effort that includes technical assistance and a focus on achieving sustainable development linked to attainment of Paris climate change commitments.

[8] The United States undermined the effective functioning of the WTO dispute settlement process through refusal to sanction replacement appointments to the Appellate Body because of perceived derogations from agreed rules and creeping judicial overreach. As of mid-December 2019, only one Appellate Body member was left in function, making it impossible to appeal panel rulings.

was significant not just because of the real global income benefits forgone, but because it meant that the WTO did not play the role it was designed for: to be a forum in which countries discuss and address sources of trade tensions and avoid unilateral recourse to trade measures and trade wars. The absence of the compromise needed to conclude the DDA led WTO members to eschew a focus on new policy issues that impact on the ability of firms and consumers to source and sell the goods and services that drive investment and employment decisions.

Following the 2008–2011 global financial crisis phase of the G20, in implicit recognition that calls by G20 leaders to conclude the DDA were having no effect, it was decided to bring trade ministers into the G20 process. In 2012, under Mexico's Presidency of the G20, a meeting of G20 trade ministers was held as part of the G20 work program. In their 2015 meeting in Antalya, G20 leaders called on their trade ministers to meet on a regular basis and to create a G20 Trade and Investment Working Group (TIWG). G20 working groups are mechanisms for coordination and substantive discussion on issues, informed by analysis, monitoring, and evaluation provided by staff of international organizations. The G20 agenda is overloaded, in part because each country that presides over the annual summit has its own set of priorities, and in part because different interest groups in and outside of government push to have "their" issues tabled in the G20. Subjects that do not have an institutional basis or structure through which to develop initiatives for approval by leaders and to coordinate and monitor follow-up actions have little prospect of being operationalized. In principle, the creation of the TIWG established a focal point for more sustained attention on trade issues. Subjects addressed in the TIWG meetings reflect the preferences and priorities of those G20 members that participate in the group, as well as the organizations represented.

The TIWG allows G20 officials to draw on key international organizations to prepare the ground for discussions and decision-making by leaders on trade matters, including defining a work program and/or action plans and creating mechanisms to hold each other accountable for progress in implementing what is agreed. The TIWG includes representatives of the Organisation for Co-operation and Development (OECD), the UN Conference on Trade and Development (UNCTAD), and the World Bank, as well as the WTO. As a result, it has acted as a coordination device to support collaboration between international organizations active in trade and investment-related areas. TIWG deliberations helped prepare the ground for the launch of plurilateral discussions on e-commerce and investment facilitation in the WTO, illustrating that the G20 has been able to influence the launch of initiatives on subjects that could not be addressed on a multilateral basis in the WTO.

EU Trade Priorities and the G20

The EU has always pursued a multi-pronged trade strategy. Following the entry into force of the WTO in 1995, the EU's trade strategy was strongly multilateral, eschewing its past history of pursuit of bilateral and regional trade agreements. In the mid-2000s, in part reflecting a perception that multilateral negotiations in the framework of the WTO were not sufficiently ambitious, European trade policy was reoriented to include pursuit of deeper preferential trade agreements (PTAs) that encompass nontariff and domestic regulatory policies.[9] As the DDA became deadlocked, the EU focused more on the bilateral-cum-regional track, launching negotiations on a Transatlantic Trade and Investment Partnership (TTIP) with the USA and pursuing Economic Partnership Agreements and deep PTAs with OECD countries such as Canada, Japan, Australia, and New Zealand. Although the Trump administration called the TTIP negotiations to a halt in January 2017 (as of April 2019 the EU considered them to be "obsolete and no longer relevant" – Council of the European Union, 2019, para. 3), deep agreements between the EU and Canada and Japan were concluded successfully and many PTAs negotiations are ongoing at the time of writing.

Notwithstanding the exit of the United Kingdom from the EU, for the last two decades most WTO members emulated the EU in devoting considerably more resources and attention to the negotiation of PTAs than to negotiations in the WTO. From both an efficiency and a global equity perspective, PTAs are second-best solutions when it comes to the development of multilateral rules, given the organization of production and trade into international value chains/networks spanning many regulatory jurisdictions. PTAs do not cover all the countries involved in many (most) global value chains (GVCs), thus limiting the positive impact they can have in reducing the costs of regulatory differences and uncertainty for firms and consumers. PTAs also give rise to the possibility of trade

[9] See https://eur-lex.europa.eu/LexUriServ/LexUriServ.do?uri=COM:2006:0567:FIN:en:PDF

and investment diversion and contribute to further economic and political fragmentation of the multilateral trading system.

The EU's main trade focus in G20 summits has been on the commitment to anti-protectionism and support for multilateralism.[10] A strong supporter of the rules-based multilateral trading system, following the demise of the Doha talks in 2015 and the subsequent failure of WTO members to agree to stronger rules on fishing subsidies at the 2017 ministerial conference in Buenos Aires, the EU became a proponent of plurilateral approaches, supporting the launch of talks on e-commerce, investment facilitation, domestic regulation of services, and an initiative to support participation of micro, small and medium-sized enterprises (MSMEs) in the trading system. The explicit shift to plurilateral approaches was driven in part by the insistence of India and other developing countries that new across-the-board multilateral negotiations could not proceed without first resolving the outstanding Doha issues (Hannah et al., 2018).[11] In contrast to China and the United States, the EU participates in all the plurilateral groups established in 2017–2018.

Over time, as trade tensions and conflicts deepened after 2017, the EU put greater emphasis on defense of multilateralism.[12] The EU has been at the forefront of discussions on WTO reform and deliberations to address US concerns regarding the operation of the WTO Appellate Body, seeking to engage with the United States while in parallel preparing the ground for a coalition of WTO members to cooperate in establishing a (temporary) alternative appellate function after the Appellate Body became non-operational in December 2019.[13] A joint letter from Presidents Juncker and Tusk before the 2016 G20 summit in Hangzhou, China noted that the "G20 must make the case for open trade and investment" and that the "G20 has a particular responsibility to buttress the multilateral trading system ... [and] should therefore

[10] Wouters et al. (2013) discuss the role of the EU in the G20 from a broader perspective.

[11] See, for example, www.hinrichfoundation.com/research/article/wto/plurilaterals-a-way-forward-wto/.

[12] www.euractiv.com/section/economy-jobs/news/eu-says-g20-summit-priorities-to-be-multilateralism-and-wto-reform/.

[13] In January 2020, Australia, Brazil, Chile, China, Colombia, Costa Rica, Guatemala, South Korea, Mexico, New Zealand, Panama, Singapore, Switzerland, and Uruguay agreed they would join the EU, Canada, and Norway in participating in this initiative (www.reuters.com/article/us-trade-wto/eu-china-other-wto-members-agree-temporary-body-to-settle-disputes-idUSKBN1ZN0WM). For a description of the envisaged mechanism see https://trade.ec.europa.eu/doclib/press/index.cfm?id=2053.

provide genuine guidance for the future global trade and investment agenda."[14] Priorities identified in the letter stressed the need to cut overcapacity in the steel and other sectors – including by tackling subsidies and other market-distorting measures – and opening the WTO to new issues such as digital trade, investment or export restrictions. As a "first step towards greater policy coherence" in the area of investment, leaders endorsed the G20 Guiding Principles for Global Investment Policymaking and WTO-consistent plurilateral, regional, and bilateral trade agreements.[15]

Ahead of the 2017 G20 summit in Hamburg, the second time an EU country had hosted the G20, Presidents Juncker and Tusk noted that concerns about job losses and erosion of standards attributed to trade would be at the top of the agenda. Their 2017 joint letter identified three priority areas for action. First, that the G20 adhere to its anti-protectionism pledge and strengthen the WTO by filling gaps in the rulebook, including on e-commerce and subsidies. Second, that G20 members implement domestic policies empowering workers and companies to benefit from open markets and assist them to adjust to change. Third, that G20 governments engage in an "honest, fact-based conversation with citizens" to take stock of the effects of globalization, and the responsibility of businesses to address them and to improve social and environmental standards in global supply chains.[16] Other priorities included making the international monetary and financial system more resilient; demonstrating that ambitious climate action is good for economic growth and jobs; developing common G20 standards for 5G mobile communication networks; promoting free flow of information while respecting applicable legal frameworks for privacy and personal data protection; advancing the global fight against tax avoidance and evasion; continuing the fight against terrorism and terrorist financing; shared responsibility for refugees and migrants; and partnering with Africa for investment, growth, and jobs.[17]

[14] www.consilium.europa.eu/en/press/press-releases/2016/08/30/tusk-juncker-joint-letter-g20/.

[15] www.consilium.europa.eu/en/press/press-releases/2016/09/05/g20-leaders-communique/.

[16] www.consilium.europa.eu/en/press/press-releases/2017/07/05/tusk-juncker-joint-letter-g20/.

[17] To give a flavor of the many areas targeted, the outcome of the summit included the G20 Hamburg Action Plan; Climate and Energy Action Plan for Growth; Taking forward the G20 Action Plan on the 2030 Agenda; Annual Progress Report 2017; G20 Action Plan on Marine Litter; G20 Africa Partnership; G20 Initiative for Rural Youth Employment; High Level Principles on the Liability of Legal Persons for Corruption; High Level Principles on

While trade has been a staple item on the G20 agenda, in our view improving the operation of the multilateral trade regime and addressing the fundamental factors that underlay the DDA failure was given insufficient attention in G20 deliberations. WTO governance and reform appeared on the G20 agenda for the first time in 2019. This contrasts with the EU push on other subjects that resulted in tangible changes to global regulation and governance, such as the drive to address tax competition from tax havens, and the agreement on the Multilateral Convention to Implement Tax Treaty Related Measures to Prevent Base Erosion and Profit Shifting. The Convention was a concrete outcome of an EU push for G20 action against tax avoidance and evasion. The EU made no bones about leading the global effort in this area or that the EU expected "wide and effective implementation of the agreed standards on tax transparency and good governance" and that those "not ready to cooperate should bear the consequences."[18] An equivalent degree of engagement and associated commitment of resources and political capital is needed on the trade agenda.

It is important to recognize that, to some degree, the type of engagement needed has already begun to emerge with EU support. The creation of the TIWG and its work on trade and investment facilitation, and on policy dimensions of digital trade, provides an illustration. Work in the TIWG helped to provide a basis for the launch of plurilateral initiatives on these subjects in the WTO. Another example is the creation under G20 auspices of the Global Forum on Steel Excess Capacity (discussed later in this section). Such initiatives may provide the basis for agreements akin to those on tax evasion if G20 members can overcome free riding (participation) constraints. The subjects addressed by the TIWG that helped lead to plurilateral engagement in the WTO are divided into two types. As discussed in the next section, one is largely about agreeing on good regulatory practices. An example is investment facilitation (Zhan, 2016). The other concerns policies where cooperation entails "conditionality" in the sense that whatever norms/rules/regulatory standards emerge must be applied by any country wishing to benefit from the agreement. Examples

Organizing against Corruption; High Level Principles on Countering Corruption in Customs; High Level Principles on Combating Corruption related to Illegal Trade in Wildlife and Wildlife Products; G20 Initiative #eSkills4Girls; Women Entrepreneurs Finance Initiative; and G20 Resource Efficiency Dialogue. See www.g20germany.de/Webs/G20/EN/G20/Summit_documents/summit_documents_node.html.

18 2017 joint letter from Presidents Juncker and Tusk, at www.consilium.europa.eu/en/press/press-releases/2017/07/05/tusk-juncker-joint-letter-g20/.

include common data privacy norms or agreement to refrain from requiring data localization. Such conditionality ("reciprocity") is a basic element of PTAs as well as unilateral "recognition arrangements" where access to a market is conditional on implementation in the exporting country of regulatory regimes that are equivalent to those of the importer. EU data adequacy determinations are an example of the latter.

Trade tensions are often associated with potentially competition-distorting industrial policies, national tax/subsidy programs, or regulatory policies that are not under the purview of trade ministries. This is an important reason why the G20 can add value to WTO processes. G20 summits can cut across prevailing silos in government to bring together the key actors at national level in ways that sectoral ministers (e.g. trade ministries) cannot. Insofar as the source of cross-border spillovers is associated with national tax/subsidy measures, these will be under the purview of finance ministries – which play a prominent role in G20 deliberations. Many of the potentially competition-distorting policies put in place by governments since 2009 are tax and subsidy related. This makes the G20 a particularly relevant forum to discuss and address the cross-border effects of domestic regulatory measures. More broadly, given differences in national priorities and capacity, sustaining cooperation may require transfers – technical and/or financial assistance. These are instruments that trade ministries do not have and may find difficult to orchestrate when needed to support international agreements. The fact that the major international organizations are part of the G20 process (i.e. participate in the TIWG) is another distinguishing feature. These agencies are not at the table in WTO negotiations and are merely invited guests at the organization's Ministerial Conferences.

To some extent, the G20 has already taken initiatives that cut across silos in government and international organizations to address sources of trade tension. A prominent example is the G20 Global Forum on Steel Excess Capacity,[19] an EU-led initiative established at the 2016 G20 summit in China. The mandate of this forum, facilitated by the OECD, included producing and sharing reliable statistics on production capacity and capacity utilization across major steel producers, and identifying measures to reduce global production.[20] Assessing the role of subsidies in generating

[19] See, e.g., www.g20.utoronto.ca/2018/global-forum-on-steel-excess-capacity-180920.pdf and https://www.steelforum.org/.

[20] The forum allowed participants to identify the underlying causes of steel overcapacity and define concrete actions to address them. See https://trade.ec.europa.eu/doclib/press/index.cfm?id=2077.

overcapacity was part of the forum's terms of reference. The forum provided a platform for the exchange of data on steel capacity and subsidies and related support measures, thus improving the information base and the transparency of the relevant policies implemented by major steel-producing countries. The forum reported to G20 ministers annually during 2017–2019 and met at least three times a year during this period.[21]

As we discuss in the next section, similar (plurilateral) approaches that focus on national policies deemed to generate large negative cross-border spillovers can form the basis for efforts to establish rules of the game for such policies. If pursued under the umbrella of the WTO, such efforts may also help to revitalize multilateral cooperation. Doing so may help foster sustained participation by countries such as China by placing cooperation into a framework that assures an appropriate balance between the sovereign right to pursue national development objectives and minimizing associated cross-border spillovers, accountability for implementation of commitments, assistance in adopting less distortive policies, and access to effective conflict-resolution mechanisms. The "policy space" for pursuit of such approaches was endorsed by many G20 trade ministers in a September statement, which, according to the summary of the chair (Saudi Arabia) made clear that only some G20 members consider the "practice of consensus-based decision making in the WTO, expressly carried over from the GATT [General Agreement on Tariffs and Trade] in the Marrakesh Agreement ... to be a principle of the WTO," making clear a majority were ready and willing to consider plurilateral approaches in – or outside – the WTO. The 2020 G20 deliberations also made explicit that "Many members ... expressed the view that S&DT [special and differential treatment] is a tool to facilitate the achievement of WTO objectives and should be applied on the basis of demonstrable needs" (i.e. rejecting the argument made by India that S&DT is "a principle that is integral to and underpins the WTO").[22]

[21] In October 2019, China decided not to continue participation in the Forum, refusing to join the consensus regarding further specific subsidy- and capacity-reduction targets established by the group, arguing it had done its fair share by "slash[ing] total steel production capacity by more than 150 million tonnes since 2016, or 114 per cent of the global steel capacity cut ... and ... redeploy[ing] 280,000 steel workers, which is more than the combined deployed number of steel workers in the US, the EU and Japan." See www.scmp.com/economy/china-economy/article/3034753/global-steel-forum-scrapped-china-says-it-has-done-more-its.

[22] G20 Trade and Investment Ministerial Meeting Communique, 22 September 2020, p. 12. At www.g20.utoronto.ca/2020/G20SS_Communique_TIMM_EN.pdf.

Bolstering Global Trade Governance

The unwillingness of G20 members to refrain from putting in place competition-distorting policies, roll back protectionist measures (including by concluding the Doha round), and establish a new agenda for trade negotiations once it became clear that the DDA was deadlocked, has come at a significant opportunity cost. Although the launch of plurilateral negotiations under WTO auspices was a broadly positive development, the reasons for the failure to use the WTO as a platform to address rising trade tensions is a matter G20 leaders should do more to reflect on. For too long the focus was on the DDA, even after it had become clear that this would not address many of the emerging sources of trade tension. The DDA would have generated a potential medium-term boost to global welfare but did not encompass many of the policies that increasingly became the source of trade conflicts. The focus was primarily on reductions in tariff bindings (that is, maximum permitted tariffs) and disciplines on agricultural support policies – a sector that accounts for only a small share of global trade. Issues such as subsidies, industrial policies, anticompetitive behavior of state-owned enterprises, digital trade, or policies towards foreign investment were not central to the DDA and discussions in these areas were actively discouraged by several G20 members. Moreover, services, which were initially part of the DDA and represent more than 60 per cent of GDP in many economies, were effectively taken off the WTO table in 2015.[23]

Many national policies can give rise to negative cross-border spillovers. They include policies restricting trade and investment in services (digital trade), policies of a fiscal nature (tax exemptions, subsidies, and related industrial policies), and global governance of trade measures associated with the fight against climate change (for example, trade policy dimensions of any "Green Deal" adopted by the EU). Addressing the cross-border spillovers of such policies calls for a mix of plurilateral cooperation and agreements, and initiatives to reform WTO working practices

[23] Instead, a group of WTO members launched negotiations on a Trade in Services Agreement (TiSA). This group did not include most of the major emerging and developing economies, which also tend not to participate in deep PTAs that include services commitments. The TiSA experience illustrates that plurilateral negotiations that encompass market access policies need a critical mass of participants to internalize most of the benefits. They also suggest a need to include measures to assist countries to improve regulatory frameworks needed to govern more open services markets (Fiorini and Hoekman, 2018).

to enable the organization to provide a supportive framework for new legal frameworks that assure developing countries that they do not stand to lose and can benefit from them. The EU can do good while doing well by combining the pursuit of EU values with measures that enhance the ability of developing countries to use trade to attain the SDGs by better addressing the cross-border spillovers of policies that are not or inadequately covered by WTO rules. This is a necessary condition for sustaining the relevance of the multilateral trading system, which the EU has set as an objective for itself (the mission statement of the incoming Commission; Von der Leyen, 2019). Bridging the trade policy divides between G20 members that emerged in recent years is a basic element of attaining this goal. It requires identifying the policies that generate significant negative systemic externalities and negotiating rules of the road that will attenuate such negative effects. The G20 can be a platform for the major players to engage with each other, and in the process act as a potential bridge to agreements on and in the WTO.

Our premise is that critical mass initiatives, where the benefits extend on a nondiscriminatory basis to all countries, should be feasible if they involve the key players in the G20. In practice, specific initiatives need not necessarily include all G20 member countries. Indeed, imposing that constraint would greatly limit the scope for action given the wide divergences within the G20 as regards desirable actions on the trade front. The critical mass needed to internalize a large share of the total benefits associated with rules for policies, such as industrial policies, is very small, essentially encompassing China, the EU (and United Kingdom), Japan, and the United States. The experience obtained with the Global Forum on Steel Overcapacity illustrates both the potential and the challenge of pursuing small-numbers agreements to help resolve current trade conflicts.

The situation confronting the trading system today has parallels with the 1980s, which saw extensive recourse to trade-distorting measures in response to a rapid rise in exports from East Asian economies. This motivated the launch of a preparatory process by countries that informed the design of the Uruguay Round negotiation agenda (see, e.g., Hoekman and Kostecki, 2009). A similar effort is needed today, aimed at resolving the trade conflicts that are of greatest relevance from a systemic perspective. Two areas are particularly important: (i) rulemaking to address major international spillovers from national industrial policies; and (ii) improving the functioning of the WTO, including more effective approaches to address disparities in capacity and economic development.

Cooperation to Internalize Large Cross-Border Spillovers

Progress on rulemaking to resolve trade conflicts requires agreement between the major trade powers: China, the EU, Japan, and the United States. All four entities have engaged in bilateral discussions, with the EU, Japan, and the United States additionally launching a trilateral process to identify ways to strengthen disciplines on services-related policies, subsidies, state-owned enterprises, and industrial development policies more broadly.[24] The same need pertains to governing the use of trade policies (for example, border carbon adjustments) as an element of programs motivated by climate change, such as the European Green Deal that will be pursued by the Von der Leyen Commission (Von der Leyen, 2019). A necessary condition for meaningful outcomes is that all the major trading powers are involved in the associated deliberations-cum-negotiations. There is no magic bullet: the key players need to agree on rules of the road.

Determining where plurilateral agreements can make a difference and establishing a new road map for the WTO calls for analysis of the size and incidence of the spillover effects of contested policy measures. A common understanding of the magnitude of negative welfare effects generated by policies that are only partly, if at all, subject to multilateral rules is needed to distinguish between those that are of systemic importance and distort competition in a major way and those that do not. This calls for generating information on applied policies (evidence) and analysis of their effects. Analysis is also needed to identify how best to attenuate major spillovers and establish effective incentives to comply with commitments. Relying on efforts to improve WTO members' notifications of trade policies is unlikely to suffice, even if governments were to accept doing so, as the policies that matter most may not be covered by WTO agreements. Engagement by the major players to define the specific policies that are of concern requires dialogue and joint efforts to collect the required information to establish a common knowledge base. This was a key motivation for the formation of the Global Forum on Steel Overcapacity, which illustrates that such efforts are feasible. Initiatives such as the Global Trade Alert also demonstrate that much information is already available. In addition to compiling the necessary information,

[24] See, e.g., Joint Statement on Trilateral Meeting of the Trade Ministers of the United States, Japan, and the European Union, 9 January 2018. At https://ustr.gov/about-us/policy-offices/press-office/press-releases/2019/january/joint-statement-trilateral-meeting.

what is needed is analysis of the effects of the relevant policies so as to determine which generate serious spillovers and should be the focus of negotiation to define the rules of the game.

An important question in this regard for G20 members is to determine the appropriate type of cooperation. Many policy areas can generate negative spillovers for other countries, but they may also have positive effects. Examples are export restrictions, which are detrimental to net importing countries but can benefit other exporters and "green" subsidies (ranging from minimum feed-in prices for electricity generated from renewable resources to subsidies for the development or use of specific technologies) that help to address global climate change even though they may have adverse consequences for competing firms from other countries. Policies constraining digital trade and e-commerce – an area that is of critical important to MSMEs as well as multinational businesses – may not have the goal of restricting trade. Some of these issues are addressed in PTAs; others are not. PTAs reveal the continued interest in extending trade governance to a greater set of policies than is covered by the WTO. PTAs among like-minded countries by definition apply to only a few countries. From a systemic perspective, the challenge is to multilateralize elements of PTAs that deal with issues not covered by the WTO – for example, the Comprehensive and Progressive Trans-Pacific Partnership (CPTPP) provisions on digital trade. The trend towards PTAs makes clear that the global trading system cannot be monolithic. Nor should it be.

There are good rationales for pursuing cooperation on certain types of regulatory, "behind the border" policies on a small group basis. One reason is that a uniform rule for a given policy may be inefficient; another is that even if there is agreement that a given regulatory rule is desirable, not all countries will satisfy the preconditions for implementing it. There are good reasons for small group cooperation, especially on regulatory matters, given the great diversity in circumstances and priorities across the WTO membership. While plurilateral cooperation and "variable geometry" is and will be an inherent feature of the global trading system, the challenge is to do so in a way that supports rather than undercuts the WTO and which recognizes that an exclusive focus on minilateral outcomes (that is, plurilateral agreements and RTAs) is suboptimal systemically as well as in terms of aggregate welfare gains. From the perspective of the trading system, G20 countries should do more to pursue discussions on such issues under the umbrella of the WTO as opposed to limiting these to bilateral or PTA settings. In determining what policy areas to prioritize, the G20 can draw on the TIWG and its affiliated international organizations to assist in both data collection and compilation and the requisite analysis of the cross-border effects of contested national policies.

Rethinking Reciprocity: Towards "Open Plurilateral Agreements"

The WTO offers three alternative mechanisms for members to make trade policy commitments: (i) multilateral agreements under which a country makes a binding commitment to apply a certain policy on a nondiscriminatory basis to all other countries; (ii) PTAs that apply on a discriminatory basis to signatories only; and (iii) "clubs" where members agree on an issue of common interest. The latter need not involve all WTO members. One type of club is a so-called critical mass agreement (CMA); another is a Plurilateral Agreement (PA) under Art. II.3 WTO.[25] Both involve negotiated disciplines that apply only to signatories. They differ in that the benefits of a CMA apply on a nondiscriminatory basis to all countries, including non-participating nations, whereas in a PA they do not. Examples of CMAs include the Information Technology Agreement and agreements on basic telecommunications and financial services (Hoekman and Kostecki, 2009).

In considering different types of trade cooperation under the umbrella of the WTO, G20 countries need to determine whether agreements will require cross-issue linkages to be feasible and whether free-riding constraints apply, and, if so, what constitutes a critical mass of participation that internalizes enough of the benefits within the participating group of countries. The top part of Table 8.2 characterizes the different types of trade agreements – multilateral package deals, PTAs, and CMAs/PAs. All involve reciprocal commitments by signatories on policies that by design impede market access. Multilateral package deals and CMAs that reduce market access barriers are only feasible if most of the associated benefits are internalized by participants. Free-riding concerns will otherwise preclude agreement. This is a problem for trade liberalization because the WTO requires border trade policies to be applied on a most-favored-nation (MFN) basis to all WTO members. This constraint can easily be binding, as shown by negotiations on an Environmental Goods Agreement (EGA) to reduce tariffs on products salient for reducing

[25] The WTO currently has one Plurilateral Agreement: the Agreement on Government Procurement (GPA).

Table 8.2 *Alternative instruments for cooperation*

			Characteristics of cooperation outcome	
Type of cooperation	Main issue	Type of spillover	Nondiscrimination (MFN)	Benefits limited to participants
***Type 1*: Trade agreements** Binding state-to-state treaties with fixed terms and binding, self-enforcing dispute resolution	*Discriminatory policies affecting market access*	"Terms of trade" effects of trade/ industrial policies Pecuniary spillovers	Multi-issue *multilateral agreements* (Uruguay and Doha rounds) Issue-specific *critical mass agreements* (e.g. Information Technology Agreement; GATS Telecom Reference paper; Environmental Goods negotiations)	Reciprocal *preferential trade agreements* (PTAs) Issue-specific, discriminatory *plurilateral agreements* under Art. II WTO (e.g. Government Procurement Agreement)
			Open, nondiscrimination	**Open, conditional application**
***Type 2*:** **Open plurilateral cooperation** Severable, flexible, dynamic, issue-specific	*Regulatory heterogeneity*	Cross-border effects of domestic regulatory policies Non-pecuniary spillovers	*International standard setting* (ISO, Codex Alimentarius, UNECE) *Good regulatory practices* (OECD; APEC) *Open plurilateral agreements* • Digital Economy Partnerships • COVID-19-related public health agreements • New WTO clubs	*Mutual recognition* (conformity assessment agreements) *Regulatory equivalence regimes* (Unilateral: EU data adequacy findings Bilateral: air safety agreements; EU Forest Law Enforcement, Governance and Trade regime *Clubs with trade penalty defaults* (e.g. Agreement on Climate Change, Trade & Sustainability negotiations)

Source: Hoekman and Sabel (2021).

carbon emissions. These have not been concluded because of free-riding concerns. Similar concerns arose in the now aborted negotiations on a Trade in Services Agreement (TiSA). Although the successful Information Technology Agreement (ITA) demonstrates that CMAs can be negotiated, arguably a factor making it more difficult to reach agreement in such negotiations is that the deliberations are limited to market access and do not include a focus on complementary measures such as development assistance and related measures to bolster regulatory capacity. The latter may be important if the focus of attention is on regulatory policies as opposed to market access barriers.

The bottom part of Table 8.2 presents alternative types of cooperation where the main focus is not on removing market access barriers but on agreement to cooperate on domestic regulation. Such agreements can take the form of harmonization (international standardization), adoption of commonly agreed good regulatory practices, and mutual recognition of equivalence of standards or regulatory regimes. Agreement on regulatory standards and regimes may be associated with improving access to markets insofar as regulatory standards must be satisfied as a condition for supplying a product. What and how much can be done will depend on whether free riding is a constraint. It will be for narrow market access liberalization negotiations but may be much less of a factor for regulatory cooperation given that countries can decide not to extend cooperation if local circumstances or social preferences differ too much and exclude countries that do not satisfy the negotiated preconditions for cooperation to occur.

Clubs may extend the benefits of cooperation unconditionally on a nondiscriminatory basis or extend benefits on a conditional basis. Examples of the former include the WTO Trade Facilitation Agreement (TFA), which defines a set of good regulatory practices to facilitate trade that all WTO members have agreed to implement, with countries determining for themselves the timeline for implementation and having the ability to request technical assistance if needed. Other examples are collaborative efforts in fora such as the OECD and the Asia Pacific Economic Cooperation (APEC) forum to define good regulatory practices and agreement by countries to adopt these. They also include international collaboration to develop product and process standards in intergovernmental bodies such as the International Organization on Standardization (ISO). Cooperation involving identification and agreement on good regulatory practices can be applied on an MFN basis as this is insensitive to free-riding considerations: the policies are in the self-interest of countries independent of whether other countries do so.

In practice, regulatory cooperation may need to be conditional on joint action by the parties. Such conditionality will vary in intensity, ranging from low forms such as mutual recognition agreements that require satisfying minimum standards to very high instances such as regulatory equivalence regimes. Countries that do not have adequate regulatory institutions will not be able to benefit from mutual recognition, let alone equivalence arrangements. Furthermore, insofar as commitments pertain to policies that give rise to potentially significant spillovers, agreements need to overcome the free-rider problem – that is, all the major players need to participate. This may preclude cooperation if one of the major trade powers does not participate. Equally, it may facilitate cooperation if the set of players needed to internalize the benefits of cooperation is small, so that not all WTO members need to be part of a deal. For many if not most policies that generate significant spillovers, if all G20 members participate, free riding by other nations is much less likely to be a concern given that their policies are unlikely to create significant external effects. Providing a forum for the large players to engage with each other is a core "comparative advantage" of the G20. In the past, the OECD has played an important role in facilitating dialogue and informing potential rules to address spillovers. Examples of this include what came to be incorporated into the GATT/WTO on product standards, agricultural support, and public procurement (the Government Procurement Agreement). It cannot play such a role today because the large emerging economies (China and India) are not OECD members. They are, however, members of the G20.

Improving the Functioning of the WTO

Plurilateral cooperation is part of the solution to addressing trade tensions, but as important are institutional reforms to reestablish the WTO appellate function, bolster oversight of the operation of WTO bodies, and address concerns of developing countries. Space constraints prevent a detailed discussion of issues and options, which we have elaborated in other work, much of which is consistent with the broad contours of the suggestions for WTO reform that have been laid out by the European Commission in its 2021 annex paper accompanying the new EU trade policy strategy.[26]

[26] See, e.g., Hoekman (2019, 2020) and https://ec.europa.eu/commission/presscorner/detail/en/ip_21_644.

Actions to integrate business and civil society interests better into the operation of the trading system may also help to enhance the relevance of the WTO. Another possible G20 initiative in support of the global trading system would be the promotion of partnerships with business associations, international organizations dealing with trade and investment policies, and civil society (Hannah et al., 2017). At present, there is virtually no scope for such engagement in the WTO which is restricted to central government, state-to-state interaction. The absence of meaningful non-state involvement is no longer appropriate. Companies set standards for quality, and health and safety for both products and processes that occur in their supply chains and increasingly cooperate in private standards-setting activities that have as a goal achievement of inter-operability and minimum standards across supply chains – sometimes in cooperation with nongovernmental organizations (NGOs) and governments. NGOs do the same – there is a plethora of private standards-setting bodies that develop norms and offer certification services to companies that engage in international trade. Regulators frequently have their own mechanisms through which they interact with each other internationally. The WTO must find ways to connect to these networks and communities of practice if it is to retain the political support needed to stay relevant. The EU can help build support for such a move through a G20 initiative that includes all the international organizations that participate in the TIWG.

Such a broadening of engagement with stakeholders and other multilateral agencies can also help address the challenge of recognizing development differences. The traditional approach of less than full reciprocity in trade negotiations and acceptance that developing nations should have more freedom to use trade policies than high-income countries has become increasingly contested and is no longer acceptable to the EU, the United States, and other OECD member nations. What is needed is a shift in focus to negotiating agreements that deliver concrete benefits to developing country firms. That could start with currently ongoing plurilateral negotiations on e-commence, domestic regulation of services, and investment facilitation. These talks provide a focal point for the EU to engage with other G20 countries and encourage those who have stayed out to contribute to these deliberations, and task the TIWG international agencies with identifying potential G20 initiatives to assist firms operating in developing economies to benefit from the trading system.[27]

[27] The joint initiative group on MSMEs provides one potential forum for action.

Concluding Remarks

G20 discussions and declarations on trade have been limited to WTO negotiations and the pledge to refrain from protectionist actions in responding to the 2008 financial crisis and its aftermath. These two dimensions have also tended to be at the core of EU engagement on trade in the G20. Neither track has been particularly effective. Focusing on these areas alone does not go far enough. Instead of bolstering the multilateral trading system (which is a key priority for the EU), there has been an opposite trend, with increasing recourse to unilateral policies. The G20 offers a unique forum for the EU to engage leaders on an action agenda that can help to reverse the negative trends. There are positive developments to build on: notably the plurilateral joint initiatives under the auspices of the WTO and the example of the G20 Global Steel Forum. The EU has been at the forefront of these initiatives. It has also been one of the most active WTO members in engaging in WTO reform discussions.

The foregoing suggests two priorities for the EU leadership. The first is to encourage greater participation in the plurilateral initiatives launched in 2017, as all of the subjects covered are important for all WTO members, especially developing economies. This calls for more than simple advocacy. Providing targeted assistance, both financial and technical, through EU member state development agencies and aid-for-trade provided by the European institutions, working in tandem with the relevant international organizations, can help address participation concerns and constraints. The importance of this was illustrated in the TFA negotiations and applies as much if not more to the policy areas covered by the joint initiative groups. The ability to provide such assistance is a core element of EU soft power. Although aid priorities have shifted in recent years as a result of increasing migration pressures and refugee flows into the EU, this is an area where policy coherence calls for development assistance to accompany trade initiatives.

A necessary condition for both WTO reforms and addressing current trade conflicts and disputes is agreement among the major trade powers. The G20 is the only forum that brings the leaders of these countries together on an annual basis. In recent years, the profile of trade issues has increased in G20 activities, with meetings of trade ministers and the creation of the Trade and Investment Working Group. These developments provide a good basis for the EU to build on with a view to using the G20 forum to bolster trade cooperation. Not all G20 members need be on board. As illustrated by the current plurilateral discussions under

WTO auspices, in which India is not participating, a subset of G20 country participation may be enough to constitute a critical mass. The challenge in the near term is for these talks to result in agreements and to focus attention on additional policy areas that both create systemic spillovers and are important to emerging economies and developing countries. The effort by the EU to mobilize a coalition of WTO members to agree to put in place an ad hoc appeals mechanism while the WTO Appellate Body is not operational illustrates the EU's capacity to lead. While a good stop-gap, what is needed is engagement with the USA and other major users of the dispute settlement system to address the substantive concerns of the United States as part of a broader effort to reform the WTO.

The need for deliberation and good-faith engagement is even more important when it comes to policy areas that are priorities for the EU and where trade is part of the agenda. The most immediate example is the proposed European Green Deal and the intention to use carbon border adjustments to prevent carbon leakage. The approach of New Zealand and like-minded countries to negotiate an open plurilateral agreement is arguably the way forward, one that should be emulated by the EU in pursuing objectives that involve both trade and national "behind-the-border" regulatory policy. The WTO plurilateral talks and the New Zealand-led initiative illustrate that universal participation is not needed for cooperation on some, perhaps many, policy areas.[28] The key players that could not reach agreement on the DDA are all G20 members. Some G20 members are less supportive and less willing to contribute to the global public good of an open trading system than are others (Wolfe, 2015).

The current (geo)political situation is not particularly propitious for joint action on trade matters. EU member states confront major internal challenges, with respect to the functioning of the EU itself and the need to boost economic activity in the wake of the COVID-19 pandemic, as well as external challenges coming from the EU's near neighborhood (including managing refugee flows). US trade policy under the Trump

[28] As of January 2020, the initiative included Costa Rica, Fiji, Iceland, New Zealand, Norway, and Switzerland. The aim is to conclude an open plurilateral Agreement on Climate Change, Trade and Sustainability to promote sustainable development and mutual supportiveness between trade and environmental policies. See www.mfat.govt.nz/en/trade/free-trade-agreements/trade-and-climate/agreement-on-climate-change-trade-and-sustainability-accts-negotiations/.

administration, motivated by concerns about China's economic development strategy, and the defensive trade policy mode pursued by important G20 developing countries such as India and South Africa further complicate prospects for effective cooperation. Sustaining multilateral trade cooperation and an open trade regime requires a willingness to utilize the opportunities that exist for variable geometry arrangements operating under the umbrella of the WTO. Deeper integration will inevitably occur within clubs – what is needed from the perspective of an effective and efficient multilateral trading system is to ensure such variable geometry is not limited to discriminatory PTAs but is pursued with a view to be open to any WTO member. The G20 is an obvious forum through which large trading powers can exercise leadership in dialing down trade tensions by demonstrating a willingness to take initiatives such as those discussed here. A credible commitment to ensure that the clubs are open to all WTO members and are transparent is a necessary condition for such plurilateral cooperation to support the revitalization of the multilateral trading system (Hoekman and Sabel, 2019, 2021).

Leadership is paramount. It is unlikely to come from either the United States or China, even though these two protagonists have a clear interest in negotiating an end to their trade war and putting in place a framework to govern their geo-economic competition. In its 2020 "phase one" agreement with China, the United States showed little concern for compliance with basic WTO rules such as nondiscrimination, reflected in recourse to managed trade.[29] The EU has a strong interest in bolstering the rulebook that applies to competition from Chinese firms and inducing the United States to back away from mercantilism and unilateral trade policy. Pursuing plurilateral deals under the auspices of the WTO is already part of the EU trade strategy: the EU is the only major player to participate in all four of the post-Buenos Aires ministerial WTO plurilateral deliberations and negotiations. Making these initiatives a success is key to ensuring the WTO stays relevant as a mechanism for countries to deal with trade policy challenges in the twenty-first century. But by themselves, even if successful, these initiatives will need to be complemented by new rules of the game for policy areas that give rise to

[29] The "phase 1" deal concluded by China and the United States in January 2020 partially reduced the additional tariffs imposed unilaterally on Chinese exports in return for a promise by China to increase imports from the United States within two years by $200 billion more than in 2017 (see USTR, 2020).

systemic conflict – notably subsidies and, looking forward, the appropriate (legitimate) role of trade policy instruments in programs to reduce carbon footprints.

The record of accomplishment of the G20 on trade is not one that suggests initiatives such as those discussed here will be easy to pursue. But the opportunity costs for the EU – and for trade multilateralism – of not attempting to leverage the G20 and the nascent shift to plurilateral cooperation to agree on common approaches to reduce the spillovers created by subsidy and climate policies may greatly outweigh the time and resource costs associated with trying to do so.

References

Bery, S. 2018. "The G20 Turns Ten: What's Past Is Prologue," Bruegel Policy Contribution No. 10 (November).

Council of the European Union. 2019. "Council Decision (EU) . . . authorizing the opening of negotiations with the United States of America for an agreement on the elimination of tariffs for industrial goods," 6052/19, 9 April. www.consilium.europa.eu/media/39180/st06052-en19.pdf.

Drezner, D. 2014. "The System Worked: Global Economic Governance during the Great Recession," *World Politics*, 66(1): 123–164.

European Commission. 2021. "Trade Policy Review – An Open, Sustainable and Assertive Trade Policy." COM(2021) 66 final. www.eesc.europa.eu/en/our-work/opinions-information-reports/opinions/trade-policy-review-open-sustainable-and-assertive-trade-policy.

Evenett, S. and Fritz, J. 2015. *The Tide Turns? Trade, Protectionism, and Slowing Global Growth*. 18th Global Trade Alert Report. London: CEPR Press.

Fiorini, M. and Hoekman, B. 2018. "Trade Agreements, Regulatory Institutions and Services Liberalization," *Global Policy*. https://doi.org/10.1111/1758-5899.12583.

Hannah, E., Scott, J., and Wilkinson, R. 2017. "Reforming WTO–Civil Society Engagement," *World Trade Review*, 16(3): 427–448.

Hannah, E., Scott, J., and Wilkinson, R. 2018. "The WTO in Buenos Aires: The Outcome and Its Significance for the Future of the Multilateral Trading System," *The World Economy*, 41(10): 2578–2598.

Hoekman, B. 2019. "Urgent and Important: Improving WTO Performance by Revisiting Working Practices," *Journal of World Trade*, 53(3): 373–394.

Hoekman, B. 2020. "WTO Reform Priorities Post-COVID-19," *East Asian Economic Review*, 24(4): 337–348.

Hoekman, B. and Kostecki, M. 2009. *The Political Economy of the World Trading System*. Oxford: Oxford University Press.

Hoekman, B. and Sabel, C. 2019. "Open Plurilateral Agreements, International Regulatory Cooperation and the WTO," *Global Policy*, 10(3): 297–312.

Hoekman, B. and Sabel, C. 2021. "Plurilateral Cooperation as an Alternative to Trade Agreements: Innovating One Domain at a Time," *Global Policy*, 12(S3): 49–60.

International Monetary Fund (IMF). 2019. World Economic Outlook: Global Manufacturing Downturn, Rising Trade Barriers. Washington, DC, October.

USTR. 2020. "Economic and Trade Agreement between the Government of the United States and the Government of the People's Republic of China," 15 January. https://ustr.gov/sites/default/files/files/agreements/phase%20one%20agreement/Economic_And_Trade_Agreement_Between_The_United_States_And_China_Text.pdf.

Von der Leyen, U. 2019. "A Union That Strives for More: My Agenda for Europe," https://commission.europa.eu/system/files/2020-04/political-guidelines-next-commission_en_0.pdf

Wolfe, R., 2015, "First Diagnose, then Treat: What Ails the Doha Round?" *World Trade Review*, 14(1): 7–28.

Wouters J., Van Kerckhoven S., and Odermatt J. (2013) "The EU at the G20 and the G20's Impact on the EU," in B. Van Vooren, S. Blockmans, and J. Wouters (eds.), *The EU's Role in Global Governance: The Legal Dimension*. Oxford: Oxford University Press, 259–270.

Zhan, J. 2016. *G20 Guiding Principles for Global Investment Policymaking: A Facilitator's Perspective*. E15 Initiative. Geneva: International Centre for Trade and Sustainable Development (ICTSD) and World Economic Forum.

9

Enhancement of the European Parliament's Monitoring for Better Coherence between Trade Policy and NTPOs

WOLFGANG WEIẞ

Introduction: Trade Policy and Non-Trade Policy Objectives (NTPOs)

Since the Treaty of Lisbon, trade policy has become an explicit part of the EU's external policy and must be integrated into the general framework of the EU's external policy. The general objectives of EU foreign policy now also apply to the common commercial policy. According to article 207 (1) of the Treaty on the Functioning of the European Union (TFEU), the common commercial policy shall be conducted "within the framework of the principles and objectives of the Union's external action", in accordance with articles 205 TFEU and 21 (3) of the Treaty on the European Union (TEU). This constitutional integration of foreign policy within overall policy principles and objectives is quite unique and exemplary internationally. At the same time, under article 207(3) TFEU, trade policy must be compatible with internal policies and rules. This re-contextualization of trade policy has recently been emphasized by the European Commission in particular in its Communication "Trade for All". There, the Commission states that an

> effective trade policy should … dovetail with the EU's development and broader foreign policies, as well as the external objectives of EU internal policies, so that they mutually reinforce each other … The EU will continue its long-standing commitment to sustainable development in its trade policies, contributing to the newly agreed global sustainable development goals (SDGs) under the 2030 Agenda for Sustainable Development.
>
> (European Commission 2015, p. 3)

The objectives of trade policy thus go beyond the genuinely commercial policy objectives set out in article 206 TFEU (harmonious development of world trade, the gradual removal of restrictions on trade and direct investment and the reduction of customs and other barriers) and comprise founding principles such as respect for democracy and human rights, and fundamental policy objectives such as sustainable development, respect for international law, and a cooperative and just world order (article 21(1) and (2) TEU). The inclusion of, for example, development policy objectives in trade policy – including in trade treaty making – has reached a high level of maturity nowadays, so that trade policy is more consistent with development policy objectives, unlike agricultural policy (Weiß 2017, pp. 337–338). Since the Common Commercial Policy (CCP) is a continuation of the internal market concept – it serves to increase the external trade of EU Member States – it must not contradict internal law and internal objectives. Thus, the CCP as a whole is subject to a requirement of multiple coherence.

The comprehensive commitment of trade policy confirms the pre-Lisbon practice that trade policy is not limited to trade issues.[1] The explicit embedding of the EU's CCP in non-genuine trade policy objectives under the Lisbon Treaty continues with this traditional approach. The broad politicization of trade policy and its conditionality has thus acquired a definitive legal basis (Asteriti 2017, p. 124). Contrary to the comprehensive goal-orientation of trade policy, the determination of the Union's interest in autonomous trade policy by the European Commission, for example in the adoption of anti-dumping measures, has so far usually been based on purely commercial interests. In some cases, this is expressly prescribed by law (see article 9 of the Trade Enforcement Regulation 654/2014),[2] whereas in others, the wording used is much more open so as to include non-commercial interests (see article 21 of the Basic Anti-dumping Regulation 2016/1036).[3] Recently, there have been increasing signs of a cautious change in the decision-making

[1] Opinion procedure 3/15, Opinion of Advocate General Wahl delivered on 8 September 2016, ECLI:EU:C:2016:657, para. 69 ff.

[2] Regulation (EU) No. 654/2014 of the European Parliament and of the Council of 15 May 2014 concerning the exercise of the Union's rights for the application and enforcement of international trade rules and amending Council Regulation (EC) No. 3286/94 laying down Community procedures in the field of the common commercial policy in order to ensure the exercise of the Community's rights under international trade rules, in particular those established under the auspices of the World Trade Organization, OJ L 189, 27 June 2014, p. 56.

[3] Regulation (EU) 2016/1036 of the European Parliament and of the Council of 8 June 2016 on protection against dumped imports from countries not members of the European Union, OJ L 176, 30 June 2016, p. 47 ff.

practice of the Commission. In setting the anti-dumping duties for Chinese solar modules, ecological aspects have at least been addressed. In recent measures imposing definitive anti-dumping duties, the Commission has discussed the negative impact of anti-dumping measures on the fulfilment of climate change objectives but has considered this to be negligible at that time. Other anti-dumping implementing regulations have deliberated about the possible frustration of energy efficiency and environmental objectives by taking defensive measures, but as these effects were only minor, they did not influence the determination of the Union's interest.

As to the substantive effect of the broad policy orientation, it is not yet clear whether the EU's external policy objectives do all engender material impact – that is, whether they guide the substance of trade policy, or whether some of them merely translate into procedural obligations (Cremona 2017, p. 14 ff.).[4] Such procedural obligations could, for example, imply the obligation to extend the Commission's Sustainability Impact Assessments to include consideration of the human rights situation in the treaty partner of the EU (as has been usual practice since 2011)[5] and to establish obligations to provide reasons in this respect, thus enabling judicial control of trade policy. In any case, the requirement that international law be observed is clear (see article 3 (5) TEU), and the objectives are not merely political agendas (Müller-Ibold 2019, p. 150). They influence the interpretation of the EU's competence in trade policy, so that chapters on sustainable development became part

[4] Case C-104/16P, *Council of the European Union* v. *Front populaire pour la libération de la saguia-el-hamra et du rio de oro (Front Polisario)*, Opinion of Advocate General Wathelet delivered on 13 September 2016, ECLI:EU:C:2016:677 deliberates (in paras. 254 and 274) about an obligation flowing from article 21 TEU to examine the human rights situation in the third country before concluding an agreement. The CJEU, Case C-104/16 P, *Council* v. *Front Polisario*, 21 December 2016, ECLI:EU:C:2016:973, did not comment on whether the Council must comprehensively assess all the circumstances for the assessment of the situation and the international law situation before concluding an agreement. Rather, the decision of the GC, Case T-512/12, *Front Polisario* v. *Council of the European Union*, 10 December 2015, ECLI:EU:T:2015:953, was set aside on grounds of disregard (in paras. 223 ff., 247) for the requirements of international law.

[5] Ombudsman O'Reilly has found a breach of good administration by the Commission in relation to the FTA with Vietnam, because the evaluation on this issue in 2009 did not include human rights, for which the Commission failed to provide adequate reasons, contrary to article 21 TEU. See Decision in Case 1409/2014/MHZ of 26 February 2016 on the European Commission's failure to carry out a prior human rights impact assessment of the EU–Vietnam free trade agreement (www.ombudsman.europa.eu/en/decision/en/64308).

of the EU's CCP (Cremona 2018, p. 242 ff.).[6] As a result of the reference to EU objectives in article 216 (1) TFEU, they impact on the interpretation of the EU's external competences generally.[7] Thus, the EU general objectives are reflected in the substance of EU trade agreements;[8] the EU's trade policy increasingly became linked to the pursuit of NTPOs (Bilal and Hoekman 2019, p. 9 ff.; Borchert et al. 2020). The most traditional example for NTPOs reflected in trade agreements is the EU human rights conditionality. Implementing the conclusions of the Luxembourg European Council of June 1991 on human rights[9] and following the introduction of this objective in the Maastricht Treaty, the EU relatively consistently began to include value clauses in agreements from 1992 onwards, in the form of commitments to democratic principles and human rights as the basis and condition for cooperation and the respective agreement (see Bartels 2014, p. 7 ff.; Hoffmeister 1998). These clauses are regularly accompanied by additional provisions laying down the consequences of non-implementation.[10] Some agreements are limited to mere preambular confessions to human rights, such as the most recent Free Trade Agreement with Singapore, whose human rights conditionality only arises through article 16.18 in conjunction with the accompanying Partnership and Cooperation Agreement, article 44 of which permits suspension in case of non-compliance.[11]

The concrete political transposition of the CCP's commitment to respect general EU objectives, in particular the mutual weighing and balancing of these highly diverse and sometimes conflicting objectives, is left to the political process. The political process will, however, find only a rather sketchy and patchy framework in the above-mentioned

[6] Opinion 2/15 of the Court, 16 May 2017, ECLI:EU:C:2017:376, para. 142 ff. See also Opinion procedure 1/17, Opinion of Advocate General Bot delivered on 29 January 2019, ECLI:EU:C:2019:72, paras. 177 ff. and 195; Case C-244/17, *European Commission* v. *Council of the European Union*, Opinion of Advocate General Kokott delivered on 31 May 2018, ECLI:EU:C:2018:364 para. 78.

[7] See Opinion 2/15 of the Court, paras. 239 ff.

[8] Cremona (2017, p. 11) rightly points out that the political impact of the objectives need not necessarily be reflected in specific chapters in the agreements.

[9] See Annex V "Declaration on Human Rights" to the Conclusions of the Council. Therein, the Council declares that respecting human rights is a decisive factor of international relations and a cornerstone of European cooperation. See www.europarl.europa.eu/summits/luxembourg/default_en.htm.

[10] For the different legal techniques used to express the conditionality see Beke et al. (2014, p. 55 ff.).

[11] For a critical assessment insofar see Meissner and McKenzie (2017, p. 832).

TEU provisions as their rather vague formulations of the EU's objectives make room for considerable executive discretion in determining their meaning in a given situation. Trade policy practice is characterized by a wide range of interests that have to be considered and balanced against each other, so that the responsible EU institutions have a wide discretion in determining trade policy. The concrete formulation of the EU's trade policy strategy must therefore weigh up the various objectives according to current problems and needs (see the mandate to the European Council in article 22 TEU and to the Council and the Commission in article 207 (3) TFEU). The institutions have always done so, as can be seen in the development of external trade policy. None of the objectives set out in articles 206 TFEU and 21 TEU has any legally required priority.

Beyond the constitutional obligation, another driver for a stronger inclusion of non-genuine commercial policy objectives in trade policy is the orientation of contemporary trade politics and trade agreements towards the so-called behind-the-border issues of national regulation (Hoekman 2018, p. 243). Since the 1980s, non-tariff barriers to international trade have become core concerns for trade policy. Since tariffs have already been largely dismantled, the focus of multilateral as well as bilateral trade policy has been shifting to the reduction of regulatory barriers. Consequently, and going beyond World Trade Organization (WTO) disciplines, FTAs contain an increasing number of provisions addressing domestic regulatory policies or even regulations, and include chapters on policy areas that have traditionally been primarily the subject of national legislation, such as consumer protection, environmental protection, or product safety. This expansion of trade policy issues thus leads to the fact that the resulting policy objectives influence the orientation of trade policy. Such policy objectives need to be included in trade policy. From an institutional point of view, this orientation also has a significant consequence as it results in a situation where trade policy becomes more intertwined with domestic policies and regulatory policy, and therefore the actors primarily responsible for national legislation – that is, parliaments – advocate for their extended participation in determining trade policy, and rightly so for reasons of transparency, control and political inclusiveness. The interference of trade instruments with traditionally domestic policies increases the need for democratic legitimization of trade policies. Hence, for democratic legitimacy reasons, parliaments must be given more opportunity to participate in determining trade policy (Petersmann 2017, p. 44 ff.; Young and Peterson 2006, pp. 795 and 797), which again will increase transparency and information for the general public.

Parliaments thus become actors of respect for and positive consideration of non-commercial policy objectives in trade policy. This applies not only to national parliaments (Jančić 2017, p. 204 ff.), but also to the European Parliament (EP). The broad political mandate and thus decision-making powers of the EP generally as legislator and treaty consenter, its membership from diverse regional and political contexts, and its Members' accountability towards their manifold constituencies make the EP particularly apt and receptive for also considering and combining diverse political objectives transnationally. From these institutional conditions, the EP is a lively forum and suitable actor for pluralistic deliberation of political issues in which diverse aspects of common interest to the EU can be fed into the policy formation cycle, in particular when compared to the Council that predominantly represents domestic governments and hence a majoritarian political approach that might be more receptive for mere technocratic approaches to determining (trade) politics (Weiß 2018, p. 552). Hence, an institutional design of policy formulation cycles and decision-making in EU trade policy that strives for better coherence of trade concerns with NTPOs must focus on strengthening the influence of the EP and improve its participatory rights in decision-making and its control and monitoring mechanisms. Institutionalism informs us about the relevance of institutional designs and arrangements for policy outcomes. Hence, searching for ways to strengthen the role of an actor for a specific policy outcome requires analysis of this actor's preferences, as expressed in its mandate and composition, as well as the actor's powers and roles in the related policy processes (Milner and Moravcsik 2009). Consequently, proposals for improving the EP's monitoring mechanisms for the benefit of NTPOs in trade policy are derived here from an analysis of weaknesses in the currently foreseen implementation mechanisms; additional insights might be won from a comparative view to domestic parliamentary instruments for impacting trade policy.

The EP and NTPOs

One actor particularly active in making trade policy receptive to and available for non-economic objectives is the EP. The Treaty of Lisbon has strengthened the importance of the EP in the Common Commercial Policy, especially with regard to the conclusion of international agreements, because trade agreements are now subject to a requirement of explicit consent by the EP (article 218 (6) lit. (a) (v) TFEU). The EP uses this newly acquired power to influence the substance of trade agreements. This increase in EP powers strengthens the political dimension of trade policy.

Parliament's newly gained importance in trade policy was also recognized by the Commission early on, as confessed in the Commission's trade strategy "Trade, Growth and World Affairs",[12] presented in November 2010, soon after the entry into force of the Lisbon Treaty. The Commission proposed the new trade policy agenda "within the new institutional framework of the Lisbon Treaty, which should be seen as a major opportunity in that it lends greater transparency and legitimacy to EU trade policy, gives a new voice to the European Parliament in trade matters".[13] Besides this institutional-constitutional reason for the more influential, augmented formal powers that the Parliament soon amended by (partly pre-existing) informal channels of exercising influence on trade politics (Kerremans et al. 2019, pp. 12–14; Meissner 2016), the above-mentioned trade policy interference with domestic legislative affairs contributes, also in the EU institutional set-up, to a stronger role of the EP in advocating non-commercial policy objectives in trade politics. Thus, both the increased powers of the EP in trade policy, formally as well as informally, and the interference of trade policy with internal policies allow the EP to be even more active and effective in feeding NTPOs into trade policy, which is required by both the re-contextualization of trade policy within the general objectives of the EU and the thematic expansion of trade policy. Both developments are mutually reinforcing: The strengthening of parliamentary influence in trade policy was motivated by the effort to increase the democratic input legitimacy of trade policy and, conversely, as regards the substance of trade policy, it also contributes (by implementing the commitment to EU objectives, and by considering regulatory interference) to the increase in the output legitimacy of trade policy.

This theoretical expectation is confirmed by the EP's actual practice. Core demands of the EP repeatedly relate to NTPOs in the context of trade agreements and trade relations more generally. The EP often calls for enhanced respect, intensified disciplines and strengthened enforcement mechanisms, for example with regard to human rights, labour standards and environmental issues (EP 2019). In particular with regard to new-generation trade agreements, the EP also raised demands for strengthening sustainability commitments contained in specific chapters of the EU FTAs. Furthermore, the EP calls for their increased enforceability, and it does so out of an attempt to place sustainable development objectives and

[12] Communication of the European Commission, Trade, Growth and World Affairs – Trade Policy as a Core Component of the EU's 2020 Strategy, COM (2010) 612 final.

[13] See ibid., pp. 4–5.

disciplines on an equal footing with those on trade. Analyses of the EP's influence on trade agreement negotiations demonstrate that the EP, in different ways, contributes to policy formation and influences the substance of a treaty under negotiation, in particular with regard to linkage of trade issues with social, labour, sustainability and environmental issues (Meissner 2016; Ott 2016, p. 1012 ff.; Rosén 2018, pp. 118 and 122 ff.; Schütze 2014, p. 385 ff.; Wessel and Takács 2017, p. 113 ff.), but EP involvement also leads to the defence of sectorial economic interests (Passos 2016, p. 104). With regard to the Comprehensive Economic and Trade Agreement between EU, its Member States and Canada (CETA), for example, the change from the Investor–State Dispute Settlement system (ISDS) provided in the first version of the CETA agreement of 2014 to the novel Investment Court System which is provided for in chapter 8 of the final version of CETA was also caused by demands from the EP which raised concerns over the legitimacy of the traditional arbitral versions of ISDS (see Kerremans et al. 2019, p. 18).

Besides, the EP also backs or calls for the suspension of trade relations or preferences for reason of lack of conformity with NTPOs.[14] Furthermore, the EP fosters the pursuit of NTPOs in the EU's autonomous trade policy by setting sustainability standards in import regulations (as for example in the EU conflict minerals regulation, see Jaremba 2020, p. 172 ff.) or by introducing channels for their consideration in other relevant legislative instruments (such as the Generalized System of Preferences (GSP)+ Scheme in Regulation 978/2012).[15]

The EP's Monitoring in the Negotiation Stage of FTAs with a View to NTPOs

State of Play

The most pivotal instrument for the inclusion and implementation of NTPOs into trade policy are trade agreements. Even though recent

[14] See e.g. EP resolution of 14 March 2019 on the situation in Nicaragua (2019/2615(RSP)), www.europarl.europa.eu/doceo/document/TA-8-2019-0219_EN.html, or with regard to the suspension of some GPA preferences of Cambodia, see European Parliament resolution of 14 March 2019 on the implementation of the GSP Regulation (EU) No. 978/2012 (2018/2107(INI)), para. 16, www.europarl.europa.eu/doceo/document/TA-8-2019-0207_EN.pdf.

[15] Regulation (EU) No. 978/2012 of the European Parliament and of the Council of 25 October 2012 applying a scheme of generalized tariff preferences and repealing Council Regulation (EC) No. 732/2008, OJ L 303, 31.10.2012, pp. 1–82.

research suggests that stakeholders do not consider trade agreements in themselves to be the most effective instruments for the realization of NTPOs (Yildirim et al. 2021, p. 563), trade agreements are nevertheless central to this, because the pertinent commitments enshrined in trade agreements (e.g. in the Trade and Sustainable Development (TSD) chapters, which are part of the EU's new-generation FTAs since the conclusion of the EU FTA with South Korea in 2011) form the basis for relevant obligations and any effective implementation efforts after their conclusion. Hence, it seems that the lack of effective monitoring of the implementation of trade agreements and their provisions on non-genuine trade policy objectives (such as human rights, labour and environment, development commitments) is behind the view that trade agreements themselves are not effective instruments in this respect (Yildirim et al. 2021). Consequently, the EP's monitoring powers regarding trade agreements and their implementation will form the focus of this and part of the next section of this analysis.

Due to the EP's power to constitutively express consent to trade agreements, the EP and the Council of the EU "enjoy the same powers" in a policy field also with regard to the procedure for adopting international agreements, thus in the negotiation phase of trade agreements.[16] During the preparations (i.e. mandating stage) and the negotiations leading to an FTA, the EP also has a right to be informed (article 218 (10) of the TFEU), the details of which have been set out in the Interinstitutional Framework Agreement on relations between the EP and the Commission[17] with a view to accomplish equality between Council and EP also with regard to access to information (Puccio and Harte 2019, p. 395). Hence, the EP demands "immediate, full and accurate" information (Kerremans et al. 2019, p. 14) at all stages of the procedures, and to be given access to the EU negotiation mandates and negotiation texts and documents (EP 2014, para. 46), subject to the appropriate procedures and conditions,[18] as a prerequisite for taking its

[16] Case C-658/11, *European Parliament* v. *Council of the European Union*, 24 June 2014, ECLI:EU:C:2014:2025, para. 56.

[17] Framework Agreement on relations between the European Parliament and the European Commission, OJ L 304, 20.11.2010, pp. 47–62.

[18] The Interinstitutional Agreement of 12 March 2014 between the EP and the Council concerning the forwarding to and handling by the EP of classified information held by the Council on matters other than those in the area of the common foreign and security policy, OJ C 95, 1.4.2014, pp. 1–7, provided details of the EP's access to the adopted negotiating mandates and guidelines (hence being Council documents, to which the EP

final decision with full knowledge of the subject matter. Thus, the right to be informed and the power to approve or deny consent allows the EP to exercise monitoring and control functions over the Commission as the chief negotiator and to play a significant political role from the very beginning of the preparatory process,[19] also in view of introducing NTPOs into the substance of trade agreements. Its main instrument is its resolutions, which set out the EP's position and indicate the conditions for its consent to a treaty. The EP can thereby also respond to the Commission's draft negotiating authorization/mandate and negotiating directives sent to the Council,[20] of which the EP has to be informed (van der Mei 2016, p. 1066 ff.).[21]

The practice of the EP indeed demonstrates that it uses its position as a veto player, its information rights and also its informal methods of trade policy formation (Kerremans et al. 2019, pp. 11–14) effectively to enter into a constant dialogue with the Commission,[22] in particular via its Committee on International Trade (INTA), its monitoring groups (consisting of INTA Members, EP staff and Commission staff, Puccio and Harte 2019, p. 396), but also via its Committee on Development with regard to development-oriented trade policy issues,[23] and to express its political preferences and ideas from the beginning, even prior to the formal start of the negotiations. The EP adopts resolutions regarding future agreements, communicating its red lines before the Council adopts the negotiating directives (Kerremans et al. 2019, p. 11; for an example see EP 2017 regarding the negotiating mandate for negotiations with New Zealand, communicating its position before the Commission tabled its draft). The EP expects the Commission to "take Parliament's views as far as possible into account".[24] At least during the negotiation phase, the Commission is under a duty to explain whether and how the views and comments were incorporated into the texts and if not why not (the

does not have immediate access), but as these texts are now made public, practice has gone even further.

19 See Framework Agreement, OJ L 304, 20.11.2010, Annex III, para. 1.

20 Ibid., para. 23.

21 Case C-263/14, *European Parliament* v. *Council of the European Union*, 14 June 2016, ECLI:EU:C:2016:435, paras. 75 ff.

22 Taking CETA as an example, MEPs were continuously informed by Commission staff about the negotiation rounds; there were 148 parliamentary questions posed to the Commission. See for example Committee on International Trade (2011, 2014); for more detail Kerremans et al. (2019, p. 15).

23 European Commission, EU Report 2019 on Policy Coherence for Development, p. 15.

24 See Framework Agreement, OJ L 304, 20.11.2010, para. 24.

Commission's guidelines indicate such commitment also in the mandating phase, Kerremans et al. 2019, p. 9), which signals that the Commission is not under a legal obligation to follow the EP's wishes.[25] This can be seen as an imbalance of power compared to the Council's position as, first, the Council adopts the Commission's drafts of negotiating mandates and guidelines and hence can change them and, second, the Commission is formally obliged to consult the Trade Policy Committee, hence a Council committee, whereas there is no such formal consultation mechanism – as opposed to mere reporting – provided for with regard to the EP (see article 207 (3) TFEU and Kerremans et al. 2019, p. 9). Nevertheless, the Council is in a position comparable to the EP, as it is the Commission which conducts the negotiations and hence shapes the substance of agreements.

In sum, one can state that the EP, by virtue of its monitoring powers in the preparatory and negotiation phases of EU FTAs, manages to influence the substance of a treaty under negotiation by its resolutions, its public debates, hearings and exchanges with other institutions, by the work of its monitoring groups and its parliamentary diplomacy through delegations. The EP does so in particular with a view to linking trade with social, labour, sustainability and environmental issues (Meissner 2016; Ott 2016, p. 1012 ff.; Rosén 2018, pp. 118 and 122 ff.; Schütze 2014, p. 385 ff.; Wessel and Takács 2017, p. 113 ff.). The EP strives for conditioning market access to the EU's internal market or preferences on trade partners fulfilling NTPO commitments. Combining trade rules with labour and environmental standards initiates important reforms in the partner countries.[26] Therefore, the EP supports the inclusion of strong and enforceable NTPO clauses such as on human rights in all EU trade agreements (Zamfir 2019, p. 11). The human rights situation in a treaty partner is an important factor in the EP's debates about the approval of an agreement (Zamfir 2019, p. 5), so that the EP is in a position to use its consent power to enforce changes in NTPO clauses such as those on human rights to make them more effective, in particular by adding strong monitoring and enforcement mechanisms (such as proposed by Bartels 2014, p. 21); however, the EP does not always use its powers to this effect. An example of this is the EP's resolution on the EU trade agreement with Colombia and Peru, in which the EP called "on the Andean countries to ensure the establishment of a transparent and

[25] Ibid., Annex III, paras. 4 and 5.
[26] European Commission, EU Report 2013 on Policy Coherence for Development, p. 54 ff.

binding road map on human, environmental and labour rights" and suggested to "take into account the Action Plan related to Labour Rights between Colombia and the US". It also made particular reference to enforcement and implementation by domestic legislation and policies, and urged the European Commission to produce a regular report to be presented and assessed by the European Parliament (EP 2012, para. 15). This call neither changed the agreement in any substantial way, nor led to any meaningful improvement of the relevant situation in Colombia as the EP was satisfied with Colombia presenting an action plan on human, labour and environmental rights which did not contain any new commitments (Marx et al. 2016, p. 589 ff.; Van den Putte et al. 2014, p. 7). More recently, however, the EP resolution on the trade negotiations with New Zealand (EP 2017, para. 20 lit. g) expressed the attitude of the EP that an FTA, in order to be truly advantageous for the EU, should include

> in view of CJEU Opinion 2/15 on the EU–Singapore FTA that trade and sustainable development fall within the EU's exclusive competence and that sustainable development forms an integral part of the EU's common commercial policy, a robust and ambitious sustainable development chapter [as] an indispensable part of any potential agreement; provisions for effective tools for dialogue, monitoring and cooperation, including binding and enforceable provisions which are subject to suitable and effective dispute settlement mechanisms, and consider, among various enforcement methods, a sanctions-based mechanism, while enabling social partners and civil society to participate appropriately, as well as close cooperation with experts from relevant multilateral organisations; provisions in the chapter covering the labour and environmental aspects of trade and the relevance of sustainable development in a trade and investment context, encompassing provisions that promote adherence to, and effective implementation of, relevant internationally agreed principles and rules, such as core labour standards, the four ILO priority governance conventions and multilateral environmental agreements, including those related to climate change.

From a comparison of the latter text with the former, one can infer that the EP has strengthened its stance with regard to the NTPO clauses by stipulating clearer commitments and striving for more effective implementation mechanisms already enshrined in the FTAs.

In addition, the EP could use its veto power to demand the inclusion of treaty institutions that could also be used as communicating vessels for NTPOs. As has been done in some agreements (in particular in association agreements and in the Cariforum EPA), parliamentary committees and consultations with civil society in trade agreements could be established as both fora can adequately address, for example, human or labour rights issues that arise during the lifetime of an agreement. The EP also demands that the Commission adopt a more structured and strategic approach to human rights dialogues in future agreements which may provide for ex post monitoring mechanisms that allow for tangible action in case of breach of commitments, such as sanctions (Zamfir 2019, p. 11).

This influential position of the EP also applies to agreements' provisional application, although article 218 (5) of the TFEU attributes the decision-making solely to the Council. Under current political practice (and there are sound constitutional reasons for it, Passos 2016, p. 121), the Council's decisions on provisional application only enter into force after the EP gives its consent (see EP 2014; Framework Agreement 2010, Annex III, para. 7; Passos 2017, pp. 384 and 387–388; van der Loo 2019, p. 222).

Enhancing the EP's Monitoring at the Negotiation Stage

Even though the veto power, information rights and formal and informal mechanisms of the EP's influence on the substance of trade agreements appear quite effective and influential, one could still think of enhancing the EP's influence on trade negotiations when comparing it to the mechanisms used by the US Congress in its monitoring of trade negotiations by the US Trade Representative (USTR). Under the trade promotion authority, the US Congress first of all sets out a detailed rule-based mandate for the negotiations conducted by the USTR that specifies the issues to be tackled in extensive detail (da Conceição-Heldt 2013, p. 27). Compared to that, the red lines set out in the EP's resolutions on the Commission's negotiating mandate merely formulate the agenda of topics to be dealt with in the future agreement and prescribe only rather general negotiating guidelines that leave ample discretion to the negotiator. Hence, more detailed guidance for the Commission might prove a more effective tool in communicating red lines. Furthermore, the US Congress has strengthened its expertise in the monitoring of the negotiations by establishing trade policy advisory committees (some of them are more general policy-oriented, whereas most of them deal with technical and sectoral issues), which allows Congressmen to rely on the knowledge and assessments of organized interest groups, representing economic interests, local governments, think tanks and universities (da Conceição-Heldt 2013, p. 27 ff.). While the EP INTA committee establishes monitoring groups for each trade negotiation to be monitored and has gathered considerable in-house expertise (Coremans and Meissner

2018, p. 567 ff.; Kerremans et al. 2019, p. 12), the EP could use advisory institutions on a more institutionalized basis in order to increase the pertinent expertise of its monitoring groups and Committees and to establish entrenched communication valves for stakeholders to draw attention to sensitive issues.

Another means of complementing the EP's monitoring power could be the introduction of direct links with the parliament of the treaty partner as has existed since 1999 with the EU–US Transatlantic Legislators' Dialogue which over time developed ever-broader agendas that mirrored the intergovernmental meetings (Jančić 2017, p. 203). Such links of an EP delegation with a foreign parliament could be established whenever trade negotiations are started, thus giving a rather institutionalized frame to parliamentary diplomacy, also allowing for directly advocating non-commercial negotiation objectives to the treaty partner. An inter-parliamentary dialogue taking place under such a frame might prove helpful for monitoring the executive, for influencing the substance of the trade agreement in favour of NTPOs, and as a forum for discussing issues in the later implementation stage.

The EP's Monitoring in the Implementation Stage with a View to NTPOs

State of Play, and Weaknesses

In contrast to the influential political and legal role of the EP at the mandating, negotiation and ratification stage, in the implementation stage of trade agreements it plays only a very restricted role, which of course also restrains its capacity to foster NTPOs in the implementation of a trade agreement. As implementation of EU legal acts is an executive task entrusted primarily to the Commission, the scant role of the EP basically conforms to its character as a parliament. Nevertheless, a parliament must have effective means for controlling the executive also with regard to the implementation of agreements. The right to information, however, does not apply in the implementation phase (with the exception of Council decisions under article 218 (9) TFEU). Thus, the EP has to use informal channels of information, including exchange with stakeholders, field trips of its delegations, in-house research such as European Implementation Assessment studies commissioned by INTA, and workshops (Puccio and Harte 2019, pp. 394–395). There are only very few formal monitoring mechanisms for the EP in the implementation stage of agreements. The Commission reports on the implementation of trade agreements; these annual reports are also sent to the EP (for the 2018 report, see European Commission 2019). MEPs can also attend the meetings of the Commission's Expert Group on the TSD chapters, enabling information gathering and sharing (Kerremans et al. 2019, p. 16). Furthermore, the EP has expanded the task of monitoring groups to include discussion about implementation (Puccio and Harte 2019, pp. 396, 400, 408).

One important instrument for implementing trade agreements is decision-making by treaty bodies whose decisions further elaborate on the agreement or even amend it. The EP's influence and control on this is extremely limited. The determination of the EU position in such treaty bodies, which the Commission has to represent is adopted by the Council, deciding on a draft by the Commission (article 218 (9) TFEU). The EP is not involved in the decision-making, but is only informed of the Council position by virtue of article 218 (10) of the TFEU, which might also include prior information on the Commission draft. The EP assigns itself a right to information on a draft Council decision under article 218 (9) of the TFEU. Rule 115 of the EP's Rules of Procedure provides for a right to have a debate and to issue recommendations once the Commission proposes such a draft. In contrast to internal implementing or delegated acts of the Commission, where the EP can veto a delegated act or withdraw the delegation (see article 290 (2) TFEU) or raise objections against a draft implementing act of the Commission (see article 291 (3) TFEU in conjunction with article 11 Comitology regulation 182/2011), the EP has no powers to veto or object to a Council decision under article 218 (9) TFEU, nor must the EP's resolutions be considered (in contrast to the EP's resolutions during the negotiation stage). The same lack of influence of the EP applies to the simplified procedure under article 218 (7) TFEU, which allows the Council to mandate the Commission to amend an agreement; the EP again is only informed before the Commission approves modifications (Framework Agreement 2010, Annex III, para. 9). Whereas MEPs take part as observers at international conferences and in decision-making bodies in multilateral international agreements, as part of the EU delegation (Framework Agreement 2010, para. 25 ff.), such right is not foreseen with regard to treaty bodies in bilateral agreements. Hence, these participatory guarantees do not apply to bilateral trade agreements (Puccio and Harte 2019, p. 396); in any case, these guarantees would not provide for any influence of the EP on the Council decision under article 218 (9)

TFEU or the decision-making of the treaty-bodies, nor any effective control over these.

In particular with regard to decision-making of treaty bodies, *ex ante* control appears important as decisions and rules agreed upon with a third party in treaty bodies, which also concern rather political issues of discretionary rulemaking, treaty amendment and decision-making in quite substantial affairs (Weiß 2018, p. 534 ff.), cannot be changed unilaterally; hence *ex post* control is insufficient as any stipulations formulated as a result thereof cannot be implemented. The EP hardly has any influence on decisions of treaty bodies, and the efficiency of the above-mentioned informal *ex post* control mechanisms is not ensured. Such lack of influence of the EP is worrying as the Parliament might be obliged to implement such decisions in case they require changes to or adoption of secondary EU law.[27] For, under article 216 (2) TFEU, the obligation to implement decisions of treaty bodies concerns the EP if they require amendments to secondary EU law.

Another common instrument of enforcing compliance with human rights commitments in trade or related cooperation agreements is the human rights conditionality, which enables the suspension of trade preferences or of the whole trade agreement and which is an important tool for sanctioning material failures of the treaty partner to comply with human rights or other essential commitments in trade agreements (which might also be used with regard to enforcing sustainability provisions as currently under discussion). The decision-making in this respect is again attributed to the Commission and the Council only, without involvement of the EP (first alternative of article 218 (9) TFEU). Of course, the EP can monitor the human rights situation in the treaty partner by carrying out consultations and can communicate its assessment in resolutions and call on the Commission to monitor the implementation of human rights clauses effectively and systematically, to consider and assess measures in response to serious breaches of human rights, and to provide it with regular reports on how partner countries respect human rights (Zamfir 2019, p. 11); the EU's practice, admittedly,

[27] In the case of CETA, for example, amendments of EU legislation could be necessary for the implementation of mutual recognition of professional qualifications agreements adopted in the framework of chapter 11 of CETA (for requirements for change of the EU Directive 2005/36 on the recognition of professional qualifications, see Office des professions du Québec 2018, p. 20), or for the implementation of committee decisions on the procedures for the mutual exchange of product warnings, based on article 21.7(5) of the CETA.

may be assessed as rather selective and inconsistent (de Witte 2011, pp. 127, 143). Such postulations from the EP may not prove effective as it has no power in the enforcement of treaty commitments by initiating dispute settlement procedures or suspending trade preferences. The decision-making is in the hands of the Commission and the Council. Thus, any enhancement of EP's monitoring over implementation of NTPO commitments might in the end prove ineffective as there is no follow-up mechanism which the EP could instigate on its own.

In conclusion, there is no effective *ex ante* control mechanism for the EP at the implementation stage, and only limited *ex post* control which the EP can exercise by resolutions and informal channels, to stir up debates also with regard to the implementation of NTPOs in the trade agreements. Of course, the EP is in a position to use its general accountability mechanisms (e.g. inquiries, article 230 (2) of the TFEU), or the *ultima ratio* of a motion of censure (article 17 (8) of the TEU i.c.w. article 234 of the TFEU) with a view to issues occurring in the implementation of trade agreements in order to add force to its positions, but has never done so, and might not ever do so because of the high political costs implied in the use of such mechanisms.

As a consequence of these monitoring deficits, on the one hand, and of the increased requirements for strengthening the democratic legitimacy of trade policy as another politicized and not merely technical area of EU competence, on the other, there is both room and need for improving and enhancing the EP's monitoring mechanism with regard to the implementation phase of trade agreements. The resulting increased politicization of trade policy will be reflected in particular in a better coordination between trade policy and the pursuit of NTPOs, especially as the use of the normal decision-making procedures with decisive participation of the Parliament has a positive impact – compared to other forms of policy formation in the EU – on the consideration and inclusion of human rights requirements (Dawson 2020, p. 73), and hence probably also on other non-commercial policy objectives, in the EU's policy formulation.

Enhancing the EP's Monitoring in the Implementation Stage

The Commission has recently been a proponent of strengthened EP monitoring mechanisms over the implementation of EU trade agreements. In its "Trade for All" communication it had announced a more effective trade policy by setting up an "enhanced partnership", inter alia with the EP, to implement trade agreements better (European Commission 2015, p. 15). Therein, the Commission also promised to expand measures beneficial for sustainable development, for fair and ethical trade and for the protection of human rights, including by ensuring effective implementation of related FTA commitments and the GSP preference scheme, and acknowledged the particular importance of the EP in the implementation of the TSD chapters of the trade agreements (European Commission 2015, p. 15).

Indeed, as one can conclude from the previous section, there are different areas in which the EP's monitoring rights and capacities may be enhanced, and which might particularly serve for better coherence between commercial trade policy aims and NTPOs. In what follows, some proposals to address the weaknesses identified above will be formulated.

With regard to treaty bodies' decision-making, the EP should be granted more influence *ex ante* by involving the EP in the decision-making of the Council under article 218 (9) TFEU (even to the degree of a consent requirement in instances where the rule-making function of the EP is interfered with) and by subjecting the Commission to a "comply or explain mechanism" with regard to EP resolutions adopted with regard to a Commission draft for a Council decision. Furthermore, MEPs, for example from the pertinent monitoring group, should generally be given observer status in decision-making treaty bodies, or, even more, should become part of the EU delegation in the treaty bodies. Moreover, the *ex post* control of the decisions should be increased in its effectiveness by establishing follow-up mechanisms that enable revisions. In this regard, the EP should be granted a right to oblige the Commission to initiate a suspension or repeal procedure for treaty body decisions (Weiß 2021, p. 224). Furthermore, the *ex post* control capacity of the EP could be strengthened by establishing a parliamentary committee that has certain rights with regard to treaty bodies. Some of the EU association agreements already provide for direct parliamentary links. In the association with Ukraine, a Parliamentary Association Committee is foreseen, which consists of members of the EP and the Ukrainian parliament; this inter-parliamentary body has a right to request information on the implementation of the agreement from the Association Council established in the association agreement, and on its decisions and recommendations; furthermore, the Parliamentary Committee can adopt recommendations directly addressed to the Association Council (articles 467 and 468 of the EU–Ukraine Association Agreement).

Similarly, the role of the EP in the monitoring of compliance with human rights and TSD commitments, both of which are of particular relevance for achieving NTPOs, should be strengthened. With regard to the human rights conditionality of trade agreements, stakeholders have already proposed remedies to improve the role of the EP in the application of human rights clauses with regard to decision-making on the suspension of trade preferences. The EP should be granted a right to oblige the Commission to initiate the suspension procedure (Zamfir 2019, p. 11). Such improvement should also apply once the enforcement of TSD chapters has been improved beyond the soft level currently provided in the EU agreements. But even under the current system of soft dispute settlement with regard to the TSD chapters, the monitoring capacities of the EP could be strengthened by inviting MEPs to participate in the EU Domestic Advisory Group meetings and in the transnational Civil Society Forums provided for in many EU trade agreements with regard to the implementation of TSD commitments. These platforms for deliberative discussions and consultation currently meet without participation from the EP (Mancini 2020, p. 6 ff.), even though they may be important forums for gaining information on implementation problems. Participating would foster the EP's function as a forum to communicate with civil society. The EP's participation could contribute to remedying the many weaknesses and shortcomings of the currently foreseen civil society dialogues (Marx et al. 2016, pp. 599–600) by making a key actor in trade politics aware of the actual processes and giving it a chance to hold the Commission accountable (even though merely by debates, resolutions and discussions in meetings with Commission staff) for how it deals with the input from civil society.

The EP's Powers in the Autonomous Trade Policy

In its legislative capacity, the EP is on a par with the Council when the ordinary legislative procedure applies. Autonomous trade policy is subject to the ordinary legislative procedure (article 297 (2) TFEU) so that any laws and regulations setting out the framework for executive action by the Commission in the area of trade policy need the consent of both the Council and the EP. Thus, the EP has an influential voice in determining the basic rules for autonomous trade policy, for example trade defence measures. This can be observed in the current trialogue between Council, Commission and EP on the proposal for amending the Trade Enforcement Regulation 654/2014, where the EP demands considerable amendments which, if adopted, enlarge the scope of application of the regulation and vest the EU with strong powers for unilateral countermeasures in case of material breaches of the EU's trade rights (Weiß and Furculita 2021). Thus the EP has the power to provide for the consideration of NTPOs in the adoption of trade policy instruments by the Commission (which is in charge of the implementation of the basic legislative instruments of trade policy due to article 291 (2) TFEU), if the basic legal instruments foresee rules to this effect. Hence, the co-legislator is capable of indicating, for example, which kind of interests the Commission has to consider in its determination of Union interest and how much weight such interest has in its discretionary decision-making. In the same way, the EP as co-legislator is in a position to make the granting of tariff preferences by the EU's Generalized System of Preferences, in particular the additional benefits of the GSP+ dependent on fulfilling non-commercial objectives of sustainable development and good governance by the beneficiary states.[28] In this respect, the EP was slightly stricter in formulating the criteria for benefits (Van den Putte et al. 2014, p. 7 ff.). Thus, the EP can use its legislative leverage to achieve better consistency of trade policy instruments with NTPOs.

The Commission enjoys considerable discretion in the implementation of the basic legislative acts of autonomous trade policy as these acts use rather indeterminate formulations and concepts (such as Union interest, injury to an EU industry, the notion of dumping) which give ample room for manoeuvre in the decision-making of the Commission, but which increase the need for its accountability. In implementing the basic legislative acts, the Commission usually adopts implementing acts in accordance with article 291(2) TFEU. The use of this legal instrument is foreseen in the legislative acts, such as in the trade defence legislation, the trade enforcement regulation or the GSP regulation. However, the EP only has meagre monitoring powers over the Commission's decision-making on implementing acts. As mentioned, article 11 of the so-called Comitology Regulation 182/2011[29] provides for the EP a right of scrutiny which is not very effective ("control without an effective consequence",

[28] For the rising importance of NTPOS in the GSP/GSP+ schemes see Borchert et al. (2020, p. 14 ff.).

[29] Regulation (EU) No. 182/2011 of the European Parliament and of the Council of 16 February 2011 laying down the rules and general principles concerning mechanisms for control by Member States of the Commission's exercise of implementing powers, OJ L 55, 28.2.2011, p. 18.

Dordi and Forganni 2013, p. 374). The EP can only indicate to the Commission that, in its view, a draft implementing act exceeds the implementing powers provided for in the basic act, but cannot interfere for strategic political considerations (Willems et al. 2019, p. 273). Furthermore, even if the EP uses its right of scrutiny, which happens only rarely, the Commission is under the duty merely to review the draft implementing act, taking account of the positions expressed, and to inform the EP whether it intends to maintain, amend or withdraw the draft implementing act. In accordance with article 291 (3) TFEU, the comitology procedures applicable to the decision-making of the Commission give powers of scrutiny to the Member States representatives in the pertinent committees (article 291 (3) TFEU in conjunction with articles 3–6 Regulation 182/2011), which allow them to influence the Commission's draft (Dordi and Forganni 2013, p. 371); the EP is not involved. The committees' powers are rather effective when the examination procedure applies because then the Commission's draft implementing measure can be blocked by a positive vote from the national representatives' majority. The examination procedure applies in cases such as the adoption of definitive anti-dumping measures, the adoption of enforcement measures, or the termination of anti-dumping investigations without measures. Hence, there is little accountability of the Commission to the EP and an imbalance in control powers between the Council and the EP. The lack of control by the EP is particularly deplorable as the Commission enjoys wide discretion in adopting trade measures (Dordi and Forganni 2013, p. 380 ff.). The reporting requirements for the Commission usually foreseen in the legislative acts do not provide for effective policy impact; they only work *ex post*, with a considerable delay.

One remedy could be to enhance the EP's right of scrutiny by allowing it to interfere for reasons of the political consequences of a draft implementing act. Another option would be to grant MEPs at least an observer status in the comitology committees, as demanded by the EP in the legislative procedure leading to Regulation 182/2011[30] (Willems et al. 2019, p. 276). Still another remedy would be to replace implementing acts by delegated acts under article 290 TFEU because the latter allow more intensive scrutiny by the EP as it may withdraw the delegation or block the adoption of the draft act by voicing objections (article 290 (2) TFEU).

[30] Ibid.

Such a shift could be justified by the fact that, in the case of trade-restrictive measures, the Commission takes decisions on matters of – at least sometimes[31] – considerable political importance and enjoys considerable discretion which needs to be monitored (see also Willems et al. 2019, p. 277).

Other implementing measures within the autonomous trade policy must be adopted by the Commission as delegated acts in the sense of article 290 TFEU, for example the list of the countries benefiting from the GSP scheme and the further GSP+ benefits.[32] As mentioned, in such cases, the EP enjoys stronger rights of scrutiny, which allows the EP to have a considerable impact on the decision-making about the granting, but also about the suspension, of GSP+ benefits.[33]

Conclusion

The EP is a meaningful actor in trade policy, but more so in its definition than in its implementation. This diminishes the position of the EP as a political counterweight to and monitoring instance over the Council and the Commission. Still, the EP can play a powerful role in shaping trade policy towards better coherence with NTPOs. There are different means the EP might use to strengthen this coherence: The EP may use its veto power more effectively to make the Commission negotiate stronger disciplines on NTPOs in EU FTA with regard to both substantive obligations and effective monitoring mechanisms and to rule on consequences for breach of the commitments. The EP should communicate its red lines to the Commission in the negotiation stage in order to ensure that such stronger disciplines will finally find their way into the treaty text, and the EP could do so by proposing detailed rules-based mandates. However, these attempts might face resistance from the other party. Therefore, the EP is well advised not to overstretch its influence on the negotiations as extensive exigencies regarding NTPOs may become a stumbling block for successful negotiations. Lower NTPO commitments that have suitable, though not the most effective, enforcement mechanisms are more

31 Admittedly, the adoption of anti-dumping or countervailing measures or safeguards may in many cases be a decision based on purely economic assessments. But in the context of a trade policy that has to serve NTPOs as well, and that moves in highly politicized trade relations (e.g. with regard to China), trade instruments no longer appear to be instruments of mere executive kind in any situation.

32 See Regulation (EU) No. 978/2012, articles 5 and 9.

33 See ibid., article 15(9).

beneficial to coherence of trade with non-trade objectives than having no commitments or no enforcement at all. The EP thus may also act wisely and search for other ways of impacting the negotiation result to the benefit of NTPOs. One avenue would be the establishment of institutions such as parliamentary committees or consultation and dialogue fora or advisory institutions, which might enhance the EP's position in the implementation stage after the entry into force of the agreement by providing for more transparency, also to the benefit of public participation. Another avenue would be direct inter-parliamentary links with the other party.

While the EP has a strong position in the negotiation stage, its monitoring powers are rather limited and hardly effective in the implementation stage. Thus, enhancement of EP's monitoring powers is particularly necessary here. The EP must be strengthened in its control over the decision-making of treaty bodies and the compliance of treaty partners with directly NTPO-related disciplines such as human rights commitments and TSD chapters. The EP should be involved in the pertinent fora and in the decision-making about suspension of concessions in response to grave human rights breaches. Additionally there are remedies for the hitherto limited role of the EP in the implementation of trade legislation. The efficiency of these suggestions, however, depends on the capacity of the EP to use enhanced monitoring mechanisms. Their mere existence will not improve coherence of trade policy with NTPOs.

References

Asteriti, A. 2017. "Art. 21 TEU and the EU's Common Commercial Policy," *European Yearbook of International Economic Law* (8): 111–137.

Bartels, L. 2014. "The European Parliament's Role in Relation to Human Rights in Trade and Investment Agreements," Study for Policy Department for External Relations, European Parliament, 13 February, www.europarl.europa.eu/RegData/etudes/etudes/join/2014/433751/EXPO-JOIN_ET(2014)433751_EN.pdf

Beke, L., D'Hollander, D., Hachez, N. and Pérez de las Heras, B. 2014. "Report on the Integration of Human Rights in EU Development and Trade Policies," www.europarl.europa.eu/cmsdata/86030/FP7%20report.pdf.

Bilal, S. and Hoekman, B. 2019. "Introduction: EU Trade and External Policy in Troubled Waters." In S. Bilal and B. Hoekman (Eds.), *Perspectives on the Soft Power of EU Trade Policy*. London: CEPR Press, pp. 9–15.

Borchert, I., Conconi, P., Di Ubaldo, M. and Herghelegiu, C. 2020. "The Pursuit of Non-Trade Policy Objectives in EU Trade Policy," *EUI Working Papers, RSCAS 2020/26*.

Committee on International Trade. 2011. "Minutes: Meeting of 12 July 2011, from 15.00 to 18.00, and 13 July 2011, from 9.00 to 12.30 and from 15.00 to 18.30 Brussels (INTA_PV(2011)0712_1)," www.europarl.europa.eu/meetdocs/2009_2014/documents/inta/pv/873/873646/873646en.pdf.

Committee on International Trade. 2014. "Minutes: Meeting of 3 September 2014, Brussels (INTA_PV(2014)09-03-1)," www.europarl.europa.eu/meetdocs/2014_2019/documents/envi/pv/1034/1034592/1034592en.pdf.

Coremans, E. and Meissner, K. L. 2018. "Putting Power into Practice: Administrative and Political Capacity Building in the European Parliament's Committee for International Trade," *Public Administration* 96(3): 561–577.

Cremona, M. 2017. "A Quiet Revolution – The Changing Nature of the EU's Common Commercial Policy." In M. Bungenberg, M. Krajewski, C. Tams, J. P. Terhechte and A. Ziegler (Eds.), *European Yearbook of International Economic Law*. Cham: Springer, pp. 3–21.

Cremona, M. 2018. "Shaping EU Trade Policy Post-Lisbon: Opinion 2/15 of 16 May 2017," *EUConst* 14(2): 231–259.

Da Conceição-Heldt, E. 2013. "Do Agents 'Run Amok'? A Comparison of Agency Slack in the EU and US Trade Policy in the Doha Round," *Journal of Comparative Policy Analysis* 15(1): 21–36.

Dawson, M. 2020. "Fundamental Rights in European Union Policy-making: The Effects and Advantages of Institutional Diversity," *Human Rights Law Review* 20(1): 50–73.

De Witte, B. 2011. "The EU and the International Legal Order: The Case of Human Rights." In M. Evans and P. Koutrakos (Eds.), *Beyond the Established Legal Orders: Policy Interconnections between the EU and the Rest of the World*. Oxford: Hart Publishing, pp. 127–148.

Dordi, C. and Forganni, A. 2013. "The Comitology Reform in the EU: Potential Effects on Trade Defence Instruments," *Journal of World Trade* 47(2): 359–390.

European Commission. 2015. *Trade for All. Towards a More Responsible Trade and Investment Policy. COM(2015) 497 final*. Brussels: European Commission.

European Commission. 2019. *Report from the Commission to the European Parliament, the Council, the European Economic and Social Committee and the Committee of the Regions on Implementation of Free Trade Agreements: 1 January 2018–31 December 2018 (COM(2019) 455 final)*. Brussels: European Commission.

European Parliament (EP). 2014. "European Parliament Resolution of 13 March 2014 on the Implementation of the Treaty of Lisbon with Respect to the European Parliament (2013/2130(INI))," 13 March, www.europarl.europa.eu/sides/getDoc.do?type=TA&reference=P7-TA-2014-0249&language=EN&ring=A7-2014-0120.

European Parliament (EP). 2017. "European Parliament Resolution of 26 October 2017 Containing Parliament's Recommendation to the Council on the

Proposed Negotiating Mandate for Trade Negotiations with New Zealand (2017/2193(INI)),” 26 October, https://eur-lex.europa.eu/legal-content/EN/TXT/?uri=CELEX%3A52017IP0420 www.europarl.europa.eu/doceo/document/TA-8-parliamentary2017-0420_EN.html.

European Parliament (EP). 2019. “European Parliament Resolution of 12 March 2019 Regarding the Voluntary Partnership Agreement between the EU and Viet Nam on Forest Law Enforcement, Governance and Trade (2018/0272M (NLE)),” 12 March, www.europarl.europa.eu/doceo/document/TA-8-2019-0141_EN.pdf.

Framework Agreement. 2010. “Framework Agreement on Relations between the European Parliament and the European Commission,” 20 November, https://eur-lex.europa.eu/LexUriServ/LexUriServ.do?uri=OJ:L:2010:304:0047:0062:EN:PDF.

Hoekman, B. 2018. “‘Behind-the-Border’ Regulatory Policies and Trade Agreements,” *East Asian Economic Review* 22(3): 243–273.

Hoffmeister, F. 1998. *Menschenrechts- und Demokratieklauseln in den vertraglichen Außenbeziehungen der Europäischen Gemeinschaft*. Berlin: Springer.

Jančić, D. 2017. “TTIP and Legislative-Executive Relations in EU Trade Policy,” *West European Politics* 40(1): 202–221.

Jaremba, U. 2020. “Non-Economic Values and Objectives in EU Trade Policy: Different Models of Externalization and Enforcement.” In W. Weiß and C. Furculita (Eds.), *Global Politics and EU Trade Policy: Facing the Challenges to a Multilateral Approach*. Berlin: Springer Nature, pp. 163–184.

Kerremans, B., Adriaensen, J., Colli, F. and Coremans, E. 2019. *Parliamentary Scrutiny of Trade Policies across the Western World*. Brussels: European Parliament, 25 March, www.europarl.europa.eu/RegData/etudes/STUD/2019/603477/EXPO_STU(2019)603477_EN.pdf.

Mancini, I. 2020. “Fundamental Rights in the Institutional Architecture of EU Trade Agreements,” *EUTIP Working Paper 04/2020*.

Marx, A., Lein, B. and Brando, N. 2016. “The Protection of Labour Rights in Trade Agreements. The Case of the EU–Colombia Agreement,” *Journal of World Trade* 50(4): 587–610.

Meissner, K. L. 2016. “Democratizing EU External Relations: The European Parliament’s Informal Role in SWIFT, ACTA and TTIP,” *European Foreign Affairs Review* 21(2): 269–288.

Meissner, K. L. and McKenzie, L. 2017. “Human Rights Conditionality in European Union Trade Negotiations: the Case of the EU–Singapore FTA,” *Journal of Common Market Studies* 55(4): 832–849.

Milner, H. and Moravcsik, A. 2009. *Power, Interdependence, and Nonstate Actors in World Politics*. Princeton, NJ: Princeton University Press.

Müller-Ibold, T. 2019. “Die externe Dimension der EU-Politiken.” In A. Hatje and P.-C. Müller-Graff (Eds.), *XXVIII. FIDE-Kongress vom 23. Mai bis 26. Mai*

2018 in Estoril: die deutschen Landesberichte, Europarecht Supplement 1/2019. Baden-Baden: Nomos, pp. 79–179.

Office des professions du Québec. 2018. "Content of CETA and Comments on the Draft Mutual Recognition Agreement (MRA) for the Architectural Profession, April 2018," www.opq.gouv.qc.ca/fileadmin/documents/Commissaire/CommProjARMCanEuArch2018_va.pdf.

Ott, A. 2016. "The European Parliament's Role in EU Treaty-Making," *Maastricht Journal of European and Comparative Law* 23(6): 1009–1039.

Passos, R. 2016. "The External Powers of the European Parliament." In P. Eeckhout and M. López-Escudero (Eds.), *The European Union's External Action in Times of Crisis.* Oxford: Hart Publishing, pp. 85–128.

Passos, R. 2017. "Some Issues Related to the Provisional Application of International Agreements and the Institutional Balance." In J. Czuczai and F. Naert (Eds.), *The EU as a Global Actor: Bridging Legal Theory and Practice.* Leiden: Brill Academic Publishers Nijhoff, pp. 380–393.

Petersmann, E.-U. 2017. "Democratic Legitimacy of the CETA and TTIP Agreements?" In T. Rensman (Ed.), *Mega-Regional Trade Agreements.* Cham: Springer International Publishing, pp. 37–59.

Puccio, L. and Harte, R. 2019. "The European Parliament's Role in Monitoring the Implementation of EU Trade Policy." In O. Costa (Ed.), *The European Parliament in Times of EU Crises.* Basingstoke: Palgrave, pp. 378–412.

Rosén, G. 2018. "The European Parliament." In S. Khorana and M. García (Eds.), *Handbook on the EU and International Trade.* Cheltenham: Edward Elgar, pp. 117–134.

Schütze, R. 2014. *Foreign Affairs and the EU Constitution: Selected Essays.* Cambridge: University of Cambridge Press.

Van den Putte, L., De Ville, F. and Orbie, J. 2014. "The European Parliament's New Role in Trade Policy: Turning Power into Impact," *CEPS Special Report No. 89 / May.*

Van der Loo, G. 2019. "National Parliaments and Mixed Agreements: Exploring the Legal Bumps in a Rocky Relationship." In J. Santos Vara and S. Rodríguez Sánchez-Tabernero (Eds.), *The Democratisation of EU International Relations through EU Law.* London: Routledge, pp. 210–256.

Van der Mei, A. P. 2016. "EU External Relations and Internal Inter-Institutional Conflicts: The Battlefield of Article 218 TFEU," *Maastricht Journal of European and Comparative Law* 23(6): 1051–1076.

Weiß, W. 2017. "Die entwicklungspolitische Dimension der EU Handelspolitik." In G. J. Felbermayr, D. Göler, C. Herrmann and A. Kalina (Eds.), *Multilateralismus und Regionalismus in der EU-Handelspolitik.* Baden-Baden: Nomos, pp. 301–338.

Weiß, W. 2018. "Delegation to Treaty Bodies in EU Agreements: Constitutional Constraints and Proposals for Strengthening the European Parliament," *European Constitutional Law Review* 14(3): 532–566.

Weiß, W. 2021. "The European Parliament's Role in the Operation of Trade Agreements: Parliamentary Control and Executive-Legislative Balance in External Action." In D. Fromage and A. Herranz-Surrallés (Eds.), *Executive-Legislative (Im)balance in the European Union*. Oxford: Hart Publishing, pp. 209–225.

Weiß, W. and Furculita, C. 2021. "The EU in Search for Stronger Enforcement Rules: Assessing the Proposed Amendments to Trade Enforcement Regulation 654/2014," *Journal of International Economic Law* 23(4): 865–884.

Wessel, R. A. and Takács, T. 2017. "Constitutional Aspects of the EU's Global Actorness: Increased Exclusivity in Trade and Investment and the Role of the European Parliament," *European Business Law Review* 28(2): 103–117.

Willems, A., Jinaru, A. and Moroni, A. 2019. "Accountability in Antidumping: The Silent Death of Lisbon," *Global Trade and Customs Journal* 14(6): 268–277.

Yildirim, A., Basedow, R., Fiorini, M. and Hoekman, B. 2021. "EU Trade and Non-Trade Objectives: New Survey Evidence on Policy Design and Effectiveness," *Journal of Common Market Studies* 59(3): 556–568.

Young, A. R. and Peterson, J. 2006. "The EU and the New Trade Politics," *Journal of European Public Policy* 13(6): 795–814.

Zamfir, I. 2019. "Human Rights in EU Trade Agreements: The Human Rights Clause and its Application," *EPRS Briefing PE 637.975*.

Conclusion

Even though there were linkages between European Union trade policy and "values" before 2009 (in particular with the institution of dialogues under the various association agreements concluded before 2009 or via the link between development policy and trade), linking non-trade policy objectives (NTPOs) and EU values to EU trade policy has become an increasingly prominent feature. The further politization of trade policy with greater power of the Parliament, which must give its consent to the conclusion of trade agreements since the Lisbon Treaty (Article 207 Treaty on the Functioning of the European Union, TFEU), and the rising citizen concerns on the impact of some trade agreements on NTPOs – as shown by the manifestations related to the Transatlantic Trade and Investment Partnership (TTIP) and EU–Canada Comprehensive Economic and Trade Agreement (CETA) – has created more political pressure to enhance these linkages. Finally, the realization that trade can be a useful tool for achieving NTPO objectives, for example in promoting policies in line with climate change objectives, has also called for the multiplication of these trade/NTPOs linkages in bilateral, regional and multilateral engagement with third countries (using soft power via dialogues and non-binding agreements) but also for the enhancement and proper enforcement of NTPO provisions in trade agreements (moving toward a stronger hard law approach in the future). The latter is notably the main objective of the most recent European Commission Communication published in June 2022 on the power of trade partnership as tools to foster green and just economic growth.

This approach and the political desire to enhance the inclusion of NTPOs in EU trade policy raises questions regarding the current nature and their current effectiveness of integrating these "values" into trade policy. How does the EU incorporate the so-called non-trade policy objectives into its trade and economic policy? What shapes EU stakeholder preferences over NTPOs? What is the impact of the EU's pursuit of non-trade provisions (NTPs) in its trade agreements with third countries? Do these provisions drive investment decisions? Do such linkages between trade and non-trade objectives lead to better performance indicators? Do EU Member States align their non-trade policy objectives with those of the EU institutions? Several chapters in this volume look at these questions.

The EU has been commonly portrayed as using its preferential trade agreements (PTAs) to pursue NTPOs such as environmental protection and the promotion of human rights in third countries. As Chapter 1 by **Lechner and Yildirim** shows, the European Union tends to set higher standards than other industrialized economies in its trade agreements and leads with respect to most NTPOs in PTAs over developing countries. The authors' data point to the fact that the EU has been maintaining a relatively higher commitment level to pursuing NTPOs, on average, than many of its other trade partners. In addition, empirical evidence suggests that promoting environmental protection and labor rights especially are pursued by the EU via PTAs, while direct mention of civil and political rights shows a decreasing trend.[1]

As the authors note, however, further research is needed to better understand the consequences of including NTPOs in preferential trade agreements. While scholars have shed light on the dynamics of including non-trade issues in trade agreements, as well as the institutional design choices on NTPOs in PTAs, our understanding of how – and if – these measures are implemented on the ground in third countries is very limited. One of the most significant issues facing policy-relevant academic research is to unpack the dynamics of implementation, since linkage strategies and the inclusion of NTPOs in trade agreements are essentially of no use without proper implementation.

What is the impact of the EU's efforts to promote non-trade issues?

The first question could be whether provisions safeguarding labor rights and standards, environmental protection and other economic and political rights in trade agreements could have an economic impact, for example affecting FDI flows. While potentially those multinational enterprises (MNEs) that have stronger corporate responsibility and social awareness policies will prefer stronger commitments on non-trade issues to reinforce their own global policies, international image and public relations stance, these provisions could also increase costs for MNEs.

[1] The likely reason why direct mentioning of civil and political rights shows a decreasing trend is because they are contained in other agreements – e.g., political cooperation agreements (PCAs) – that apply to the same trade partner.

These cost increases can stem from higher operational and compliance costs, which can both reduce the growth of established MNEs or even hinder entry into these countries. However, the empirical evidence presented in Chapter 4 by **Rojas-Ramagosa** shows no negative correlation between the inclusion of these non-trade issues in PTAs and bilateral FDI flows; rather, there is indication of a *positive* correlation related to the inclusion of civil and political rights provisions in PTAs. This can be the result of initial or changing institutional conditions in the country that facilitate and/or incentivize the inclusion of non-trade provisions in the trade agreement in the first place.

While there is no indication of a negative impact of NTPO provisions on FDI, another important question is whether such provisions do actually improve outcomes to achieve the relevant non-trade policy objectives. PTAs may further enhance the prospects of improving non-trade outcome indicators if they are complemented by flanking measures such as technical and financial assistance. However, the inclusion of NTPs in EU PTAs may also have detrimental effects insofar as it induces potential partner countries to refrain from participating in PTAs, reducing their ability to expand exports to the EU, and thus limiting the potential positive effects of trade on non-trade outcomes. Nevertheless, there is a lack of robust empirical evidence that trade–NTPO linkages "work" in the sense of leading to better non-trade outcomes as measured in a variety of non-trade indicators, as shown in Chapter 7 by **Ferrari et al**. Employing a synthetic control method, there is no indication of a causal link between PTA provisions in civil rights, environmental protection or labor rights, and corresponding outcomes in these areas. While there could be heterogeneous responses across EU trade partners to NTPs, as the country-specific analysis provides some indicative evidence of such heterogeneity. This latter suggests that analysis of the potential effects of NTPs in PTAs could reveal more by focusing on the country level as opposed to cross-country analysis of panel data. These results also suggests that from a policy perspective the possibility that other instruments are likely to be more effective in improving non-trade outcomes deserves more attention.

Chapter 6 by **Maduko, Pál, and Bruszt** helps address this gap by looking at how domestic factors may influence the capacity of the EU to promote NTPOs. The authors start by introducing an analytical framework that takes into account the interests and the capacity of non-EU stakeholders from the EU's trade partners – the third-country states and their exporters, as well as their labor organizations. They conduct a mixed-methods analysis and examine the extent to which domestic factors in the EU's developing partners – *in casu*, Moldova and Morocco – shape the ability of the EU to promote labor standards through trade.

Two important highlights can be drawn from their analysis. First, the authors clearly show the importance of *economic* factors – namely, the export destination and sectoral composition of exports – help determine the effectiveness of EU labor governance efforts in its own neighborhood. The authors point to a vicious cycle that tends to take place during which exports driven by cheap labor tend to go towards countries with lower labor standards – and primarily from sectors of lower technological complexity, requiring largely unskilled labor. A shift away from such sectors, such as textiles, to more technologically sophisticated sectors generally entails an improvement in working conditions and on EU labor governance efforts.

Second, the authors combine economic factors with political ones – namely the capacity, independence and strength of labor organizations as well as the strategies of states. The results indicate that the impact of external assistance to NGOs, state administration and unions might be relatively low on their own, but more attention can be paid to combining such governance efforts with market-based approaches – such as incentivizing exports to more advanced EU Member States with higher labor standards. In turn, changes in the composition of exports are more likely to accentuate the effectiveness of business associations and domestic businesses' capacity to improve workers' skills and conditions. From a broader perspective, the authors conclude that the EU's governance efforts through legal instruments is more likely to be effective when reinforced with market-based governance strategies.

Another reason for lack of evidence of positive outcomes could be that most of the NTPO provisions lack enforceability or have been poorly implemented. Enhancing monitoring and enforcement, as suggested in the last European Commission Communication, could be key.

Considering the importance of parliaments in the promotion of NTPOs, Chapter 9 by **Weiß** considers that, in order to improve performance and enforcement, the monitoring powers of the European Parliament (EP) in the implementation should be increased. The author shows the role and the positive contribution of the EP in promoting NTPOs in trade agreements. For that purpose, the EP has used its newly acquired power in the context of the conclusion of trade agreements; indeed, the Treaty of Lisbon essentially gave the EP a veto power on trade agreements (the Council must obtain the consent of the EP to conclude trade agreements in line with Article 207(3) and Article 218(6) TFEU). While the author finds an important role of the EP in the negotiation stage of trade agreements, its monitoring powers are rather limited and hardly effective in the implementation stage. Indeed, the chapter finds that there is only limited *ex post* control which the EP can exercise via the issuance of resolutions or via informal channels, to stir up debates about the implementation of NTPOs in the trade agreements. The author also briefly looks at the EP's monitoring role existing in the framework of trade legislation. He concludes that the EP should be more involved in the pertinent fora for the implementation of trade agreements and that it should be included in the decision-making regarding the suspension of concessions in response to grave human rights breaches. Additionally, the author considers that the EP's power ought to be enhanced in the framework of the implementation of trade legislation. Still, as he suggests, the efficiency of any instrument and mechanism to enhance the monitoring role of the EP will essentially depend on the willingness and capacity of the EP to use such enhanced monitoring mechanisms. Their mere existence will not improve coherence of trade policy with NTPOs.

Another country-level case study was conducted in Chapter 5 by **Pelkmans**, who look at promoting certain outcomes without any bilateral legal basis in the case of China. Here, there is no FTA and promoting values consists of a rather "soft" form of EU policy, usually "cooperation". Pelkmans argues that the EU has systematically pursued green policy cooperation with China (and via EU trade policy where suitable) with this cooperation deepening and widening over time. Whether this systematic effort by the EU has been effective in supporting a process of convergence, given contemporaneous efforts both in China and internationally, makes it impossible to verify causality, except in some specific instances where China requested specific support for immediate policy purposes (for example, car emission standards; operational support for the Emissions Trading System China-style; sustainable timber certification; early support of renewables technology). All that one can say is that the mutual preparedness, the high frequency of all kinds of interactions and the eagerness to go for joint funding point to a strong interest to work together and improve green policies. Pelkmans stresses that different types of non-trade instruments may be more effective in realizing NTPOs than trade policy/trade agreements. A greater willingness to "unbundle" and focus on identifying whether and when trade–NTPO linkages (conditionality) is likely to "work" could help to make trade policy more effective and do more to achieve NTPOs.

Trade–NTPO conditionality could be enhanced via using other instruments such as trade-related aid, technical assistance or other types of trade-related support. Under the guidance provided by the World Trade Organization (WTO) and its Trade for Aid policy framework, both the EU and its Member States have been allocating trade-related aid to many trade partners, both in and around Europe. While trade policy is an exclusive competence of the European Union, other trade-related policies are still shared with the Member States, which act in *parallel* to the EU. This is the case for development aid policies. One crucial question for NTPO conditionality to be more effective in using trade and development aid is whether there is coherence between the EU institutions and its Member States in pursuing non-trade policy objectives via their trade-related aid and development aid. For the moment, our understanding of the extent to which the EU Member States and EU institutions support similar goals and project the same values has been quite limited. **Holmes, Garrett and Rollo** in Chapter 2 explore this dynamic and demonstrate a high degree of similarity between EU institutions and Member States' development aid allocation – especially for the two largest members, France and Germany – but less so for the Netherlands and (no longer a member) the United Kingdom. Perhaps more importantly, the authors show that, regarding non-trade issues, aid from EU institutions tends to focus on sustainable development objectives with partners that have an Economic Partnership Agreement (EPA) with the EU, while Member States do not seem to prioritize such goals through aid. Similarly, trade-related aid flowing from the EU institutions focuses on closely integrated association countries with potential future accession to the EU – for example, Turkey – while Member States' allocation of aid does not show a similar pattern. The authors conclude that while the EU and its members are broadly pulling in the same direction, the Union would benefit from further developing complementarity among members and its institutions – a timely and important contribution considering the importance of the EU's global ambitions.

Stronger complementarity between other trade-related support and NTPOs could also be enhanced. Chapter 3 by **Dawar** looked at the example of Export Credit Agencies (ECAs) and their regulation. The author considers that greater transparency on public export financing is the *conditio sine qua non* for international efforts to develop a more inclusive and sustainable legal framework to prevent a race to the bottom in the provision of subsidies in the form of public export finance and to promote the Sustainable Development Goals (SDGs) through the work of ECAs. The contribution analyzes the rules on transparency of public export financing in the EU, its Member States and third countries. It also looks at the international governance rules present in the framework of the Organisation for Economic Co-operation and Development (OECD) and WTO and how they have been implemented in practice. The author shows that the efficacy of the current governance approach is increasingly questioned in the EU and beyond, in terms of providing a fair competitive market for ECA support, and in preventing a subsidy war and race to the bottom in the terms and conditions for official export financing. The uneven application and enforcement of these two sets of international rules (OECD and WTO) to different governments is contributing to the lack of a level playing field in the international trading system itself. Transparency requirements and a clearly defined policy space for legitimate government support instruments are needed to distinguish between those export subsidies that are vital to fulfill domestic policy objectives and those that governments use to support certain firms or domestic industries to give them an unfair advantage over international and other domestic competitors. For that reason, the author considers transparency and monitoring requirements for publicly funded export credit interventions to be in the countries' interest. These transparency and monitoring requirements could further be used to ensure more coherence between export credit interventions and the promotion of NTPOs.

Recent developments in EU trade policy show a picture in which the EU is giving priority to its "strategic autonomy", complementing its long-standing multilateral and bilateral approach to trade policy. The EU's adoption of investment screening mechanisms and reinforced trade defense instruments – such as the "anti-coercion instrument" – are clear examples of this trend. Finally, in the current global context, **Hoekman and Wilkinson** demonstrate in Chapter 8 that successful achievement of non-trade policy objectives could also be achieved, with the EU taking more of a leadership role through the Group of Twenty (G20). As the authors show, the G20 remains the primary platform bringing together the leaders of these countries on an annual basis, creating a near-unique platform to tackle issues involving global trade governance. Few would argue that G20 members are *all* on board to address trade grievances through multilateral cooperation – and not all members need to be on board either. In fact, the current plurilateral discussions under the auspices of the WTO have shown that a subset of countries may be enough to generate a critical mass.

Considering the challenges faced by the EU and many other advanced economies in the world, ranging from the adverse economic effects of the Russian invasion of Ukraine to the yet-to-be-resolved US–China trade conflict, sustaining cooperation in international trade governance has become increasingly difficult. As the authors show, such a challenge requires the EU to utilize opportunities involving arrangements within international organizations such as the WTO and the G20. A mix of plurilateral agreements, initiatives to reform the WTO, as well as a legal framework that ensures developing countries can better realize the benefits from the international trade system should be jointly considered. In short, the EU is more likely to realize its potential to promote non-trade policy objectives and pursue its values by taking multi-leveled governance options, involving key players from the G20 and creating a critical mass that will help remedy trade grievances and at the same time rejuvenate multilateral trade cooperation.

INDEX

www.ingramcontent.com/pod-product-compliance
Lightning Source LLC
LaVergne TN
LVHW011810200926
848484LV00005B/1137
* 9 7 8 1 0 0 9 3 0 8 1 5 1 *